IMPRINT

Being Alone With
ONESELF

CHARMIAN CLIFT

*Edited and introduced by
Nadia Wheatley*

W0007138

ANGUS
& ROBERTSON

An imprint of HarperCollins*Publishers*

This book is for Charmian Clift's readers,
who have remained so loyal over the years

AN ANGUS & ROBERTSON BOOK
An imprint of HarperCollinsPublishers

First published in Australia in 1991 by
CollinsAngus&Robertson Publishers Pty Limited
A division of HarperCollinsPublishers (Australia) Pty Limited
Unit 4, Eden Park, 31 Waterloo Road, North Ryde NSW 2113,
Australia

William Collins Publishers Ltd
31 View Road, Glenfield, Auckland 10, New Zealand

Angus & Robertson (UK)
77–85 Fulham Palace Road, London
W6 8JB, United Kingdom

Copyright © in individual essays Charmian Clift 1968–1969
in this collection Johnston Estate 1991
in Introduction, selection and arrangement Nadia Wheatley 1991

National Library of Australia
Cataloguing-in-Publication data:

Clift, Charmian, 1923–1969.
   Being alone with oneself.

   ISBN 0 207 16623 4.

   1. Australia - Social conditions - 1945–1965. 2. Australia
   - Social conditions - 1965–1965–1972. I. Wheatley, Nadia,
   1949-   . II. Title. III. Title: Sydney morning herald.

994.06

Cover illustration by Cressida Campbell
Typeset in 11/12 pt Varitimes by Midland Typesetters
Printed in Australia by Globe Press

5 4 3 2 1
95 94 93 92 91

CONTENTS

ACKNOWLEDGEMENTS

My deepest thanks go to Jason Johnston and the Johnston Estate, for permission to compile this material.

Acknowledgements and thanks are also due to the *Sydney Morning Herald*, the *Herald*, Melbourne, and *Pol*, in which the essays reprinted here were first published.

I am also very grateful to Margaret Vaile and John Douglas Pringle, Charmian Clift's editors at the *Sydney Morning Herald*, who wrote and talked to me about the Clift column.

Thanks also to my agent Barbara Mobbs, and to Tom Thompson and Nikki Christer from CollinsAngus&Robertson Publishers, who have overseen this project from the beginning.

I would also like to thank the librarians and library technicians at the State Library of New South Wales and at the National Library of Australia, who enabled me to include the facsimile illustrations.

Finally my gratitude is due to the Literature Board of the Australia Council, without whose financial assistance I would not have been able to work on this book.

N.W.

INTRODUCTION

Charmian Clift knew what she was doing. Although according to George Johnston she 'invariably referred to her writing as her "pieces", never by a term so high-falutin' as "essays" ',[1] a year after the start of the column Clift did privately tell her London agent that she was 'writing essays for the weekly presses'.

The problem, as far as Charmian Clift's critical reputation is concerned, is that she was writing essays at the wrong time and in the wrong place. In the mid 1960s, the essay was generally out of fashion; not only had it dwindled away somewhat after the deaths of the mid-war generation of British writers, but the New Journalism of the tough young Americans was making the form seem soft and dated. Even worse, as far as Clift was concerned, was the fact that essays have never really been part of the Australian literary tradition. For most of her compatriots, the essay was a foreign and dull genre, to be studied at school and then forgotten as quickly as possible.

Despite all this, Charmian Clift's column did immediately attract a great popular following. There has remained, however, a kind of critical question mark over her place as a writer, for there is no one in this country with whom she can be compared, and even the guidelines of her chosen genre are fairly unfamiliar.

As this volume brings together the last of Charmian Clift's unanthologised writing, it seems appropriate to run through the traditional theory of the essay, so that we are better able to place Charmian Clift amongst the classics.

1 George Johnston, Introduction to *The World of Charmian Clift*, Ure Smith, Sydney, 1970.

What, then, is the essay? What are its aims, its limitations, it freedoms? What does it do? How does it work?

The obvious starting point is Montaigne: 'I am myself the subject of my book.' The essay is above all the expression of an individual viewpoint. While the novel or drama projects characters to develop a narrative, the essay projects the personality of the writer to develop a mood and a point of view. Yet if the essay aims at expressing opinion, it is different again from the review or the 'in-depth' journalistic feature, for the essay makes no pretence of objectivity: it is the most blatantly subjective of prose forms, and bias is part of its definition.

The essayist is allowed moments of egotism and gentle moralising, but the writer's self-indulgence must be subdued to the indulgence of the reader. Virginia Woolf—who as well as writing essays produced some of the seminal theory about the form—declared:

> The principle which controls [the essay] is simply that it should give pleasure; the desire which impels us when we take it from the shelf is simply to receive pleasure. Everything in an essay must be subdued to that end. It should lay us under a spell with its first word, and we should only wake, refreshed, with its last. In the interval we may pass through the most various experiences of amusement, surprise, interest, indignation . . . but we must never be roused. The essay must lap us about and draw its curtain across the world . . .

But, Woolf warned, 'it must be a curtain that shuts us in, not out'.[2]

While the essay shares at least the common literary aim of communication, the form which this communication takes is peculiar—and personal—again, for the essay is above all a conversation, in which the writer addresses the reader directly and intimately.

Well, enough of generalisations and definitions. How does all this apply to Clift, and she to it?

As to Montaigne, Charmian Clift claimed ignorance of the *Essays*,

2 Virginia Woolf, 'The Modern Essay', *The Common Reader, First Series*, The Hogarth Press, London, 1925.

for her father had pushed them on her as a young child until she had sworn that '[she] would never read Montaigne as long as [she] lived'.[3] Despite her declared unfamiliarity with Montaigne's writing, Clift's vow did not exclude the reading of books *about* Montaigne, and her natural bent as a writer was anyway similar to his. While her novels[4] show that she is well able to project character, to plot a narrative, to pace action, her talents find better outlet in the two Greek travel books, *Mermaid Singing* and *Peel Me a Lotus*, where the writer herself is very much the subject.

If childhood memories caused Clift to 'gag' at Montaigne, Virginia Woolf's two-volume essay anthology, *The Common Reader*, was one of Clift's regular 'dipping' books, and we can be certain that she was aware of Woolf's views on the essay. Once again, however, the rule book wasn't necessary, for Clift was ever a writer who laid the reader under a spell.

At the same time, Charmian Clift drew upon a more modern essay tradition than the one that Woolf was describing in the early 1920s, for at times she decided that the pleasure of Australian newspaper readers was less pressing than the lack of pleasure experienced by starving children, napalmed Vietnamese, jailed conscientious objectors, disenfranchised Greeks, or dispossessed black Australians, and on these occasions she did set out to rouse her public. Though Clift's concern with the horrifying human results of political decision-making would have been anathema to Lamb or Beerbohm, it was in line with the way some of the mid-war writers such as George Orwell and E.M. Forster had used the essay to appeal to the collective social conscience.

While Clift sometimes tried to wake the reader from what she perceived as the noon-time drowsing of lotus land Australia, she never substituted tub-thumping for communication, or ear-bashing for conversation. As

3 'Read Any Good Books Lately?', *Trouble in Lotus Land* (hereafter *TILL*).

4 *High Valley* (in collaboration with George Johnston), *Walk to the Paradise Gardens*, *Honours Mimic* (all available in A&R Imprint).

to the primary importance of communication, Clift noted: 'I suppose all that any writer asks, apart from a labourer's wage, is the knowledge that he is in communication with responsive people.'[5]

If, then, the pleasurable (and occasionally rousing) communication of an individual viewpoint in a conversational fashion is the aim of the essay, there is still the question of how the thing works.

Though every essayist brings her (or traditionally his) own innovations to the genre, the basic form of the essay is as regulated as that of the Shakespearean sonnet. Usually the essay has an arresting opening, which succinctly sets up the idea or mood which is going to be explored. Now comes the comparatively long development, which can often—like a conversation—seem like a strange grab-bag of ideas, as personal anecdotes are jumbled against specific facts, quotations from literature against references to current events, and a full range of stylistic devices is employed to challenge and entertain the reader. And then suddenly, in the equivalent of the Shakespearean sonnet's last couplet, the thesis is proved or the mood summed up, and the conversational ball is fairly lobbed into the reader's court.

Of course the form of the essay, like that of the sonnet, has partly been determined by the thing's length—or lack of it. While the fiction writer herself decides whether her idea should be expressed in a short story or a trilogy, the essayist has to force the topic into a size that has usually been decided in advance by an editor. But if the essayist must always, as it were, say everything in fourteen lines, in Charmian Clift's case the specific place where she published forced a reduction of length from that of the sonnet to the haiku.

While the essay's form is generally bound by the enforced brevity of the genre, and while each specific essay is to a degree shaped by the space available in its particular publication outlet, a further restriction on the essayist is the fact that the nature of the available readership

5 'On Trouble in Lotus Land', *TILL*.

4

is to a large extent determined by the nature of the publication in which the thing is to appear. This in turn can influence the writer's style, tone, choice of examples, even the selection of topic. At the same time as the ideology—or market appeal—of the publication can shape the content of the essay, the physical shape of the publication can determine both how the essay will be written, and how the essay will be read.

Once again, Charmian Clift had to work under circumstances which were, objectively at least, far more difficult than those experienced by the traditional British essayist. While journals such as *Horizon* and *New Statesman and Nation* provided a leisured, liberal and highly literate audience for Orwell's socialism and Forster's humanism, Clift wrote for conservative newspapers that were pitched at the ordinary Australian commuter. And while the British magazines and journals allowed the essay to spread across the page, Clift's work was jigsawed up and down the column between a mass of illustrated advertisements.

If the circulation and format of the publication outlet can influence an essayist, so can its frequency. While most major essayists have written for monthly journals or quarterlies—and intermittently at that—Clift was producing essays once a week for a daily newspaper. This dramatically reduced the amount of available writing time, and also meant that Clift wrote in the full knowledge of the ephemeral shelf-life of her material: a journal hangs about the coffee table, available for re-reading and reflection, until the next issue is out, but by midday the morning tabloid is in the garbage bin.

Despite the fact that her given task was more difficult than that of most essayists, Charmian Clift either sidestepped the added restrictions, or made a virtue out of them. She used the brevity of her space and the frequency of publication to give an even greater urgency and concision to her expression, and to a great extent she refused to compromise her material. At the same time, the form was perfect for her, for if the essay must be a perfect fusion of personality, thought, and prose style, Charmian Clift had all the requirements.

As an essay is a conversation, it is something in which the reader takes part as well as the writer. So who was Charmian Clift addressing?

Despite the difference of a hemisphere and four decades, Clift's work was very much directed to Virginia Woolf's 'Common Reader', which was a concept that Woolf had in turn borrowed from Dr Johnson:

> I rejoice to concur with the common reader; for by the common sense of readers, uncorrupted by literary prejudices . . . , must be finally decided all claim to poetical honours.[6]

The common reader, Woolf explains, 'differs from the critic and the scholar', for 'he reads for his own pleasure'. This idea is very close to Robertson Davies' notion of the clerisy, which Clift enthusiastically passed on:

> 'The clerisy', [Davies] says, 'are those who read for pleasure, but not for idleness: who read for pastime but not to kill time: who love books but do not live by books.'[7]

Charmian Clift was herself this kind of reader, and she directed her work to ordinary readers who shared her joy in books and words. Yet if Clift expected that her reader would be a word-lover, she also expected (or at least hoped) that her reader would share her commitment, not to any political ideology, but to humankind. Though Clift declared that 'I don't think it is my business to educate or elevate or convert anybody',[8] she spoke to an audience who could think and feel and respond.

In a way, then, Charmian Clift was addressing a reader who had a lot in common with Charmian Clift, and indeed she firmly declared that she was writing to please herself.[9] This is, I think, part of the key to Clift's amazing appeal, for if the writer treated the reader as if she

6 From Dr Johnson's *Life of Grey*, Quoted by Virginia Woolf in the introduction to *The Common Reader*, *First Series*.

7 'The Magic Carpet of Learning'.

8 'On a Second Chance', *TILL*.

9 'What Are You Doing it For?'

6

were her equal and her intimate, this was of course true—because her reader was to some extent herself.

At the same time, however, Clift never forgot that she was conducting a dialogue. Indeed, she created in her readers the uncanny feeling that not only was she speaking immediately to each one of them as an individual but that they were each part of a very personal conversation with her:

> I had the strangest feeling that Charmian Clift was in fact a friend, someone I knew. When reading [her essays] I felt that they were accounts of things we could have talked about (given the chance) over a cup of tea in the kitchen.

That comment, made to me recently, sums up the response of thousands of Clift readers. The extraordinary thing is that while Clift's fans all felt she was chatting privately with them, these fans came from a wide variety of backgrounds.

The letters from women readers published in the *Sydney Morning Herald* after Charmian Clift's death [10] range right across the city, from the posh northern suburb of Wahroonga to lower middle-class Miranda in the south, and from the well-heeled harbourside suburb of Neutral Bay to working-class Blacktown in the outer west.

Such a spread, while showing Clift's popularity, is of course also indicative of the wide appeal of the *Sydney Morning Herald*'s women's pages, which had had fresh life breathed into them in the mid 1960s by their new editor, Margaret Vaile. Though Vaile believed that the role of these pages was to 'inform and entertain rather than to educate', and though she felt that 'subjects such as the pill and IVF were not things that the average woman wanted to read with her breakfast egg', Margaret Vaile was unswerving in her belief that 'we were a newspaper', and she was, in her own very individual way, a liberated woman, though not a Women's Libber. Thus two of her first actions were to get rid of the sewing hints and change her own title from Social Editress to

10 cf. facsimile, p. 214–215.

Women's Editor, and she was keen to include articles about women making news in their own right. She was also no snob. Though the paper's direction overall was establishment, Vaile opened up the social pages to include the weddings of ordinary subscribers as well as the functions of the elite.

While the *Sydney Morning Herald* Women's Section provided Clift with a large and varied female readership, the valedictory letter from Donald Weir of the exclusive eastern suburb of Double Bay is a reminder that the women's pages were (in Vaile's words) 'a must for many businessmen', for though the advertisements were directed at women the products were by and large designed, marketed and owned by men, and the women's pages gave an insight into women's interests.

If I have concentrated on the *Sydney Morning Herald* side of Charmian Clift's work, it is because this was more immediate to the writer, for she delivered her copy directly to Margaret Vaile and sometimes discussed her column with Vaile and the paper's Editor, John Douglas Pringle. However, any discussion of Clift's readership must of course also include that of the Melbourne *Herald*. This Melbourne audience was probably a bit different from the Sydney one, for although editorially conservative, the Melbourne paper was less 'establishment' than the *Sydney Morning Herald* and the Clift column in the Melbourne *Herald* was not always targeted at women. Through 1964, 1965 and the beginning of 1966, Clift appeared in the Saturday Weekend Magazine; this of course made her more accessible to male readers, and perhaps allowed for a more leisurely reading of the column. By October 1966 Clift had been moved to the Wednesday Women's Section, but in 1968 the column was appearing in the Friday paper, sometimes on the women's page and sometimes in amongst the ordinary news.

Broad though the potential readership of the two papers was, it was Clift herself who captured the attention and love of her particular audience. She also herself attracted at least two more groups of readers, who would not normally have been aficionados of what was still disparagingly termed 'women's journalism'.

8

As the valedictory letter from L. Paschalides for the Committee for the Restoration of Democracy in Greece reveals, Charmian Clift had enormous support in 'the progressive Greek community', for while the Australian press virtually ignored the Greek situation, Clift's opposition to the Junta rang loud and clear. If there was particular support from Australian Greeks, Clift was also popular among other ethnic minorities, because at a time when multiculturalism wasn't even a word, Clift not only supported the rights of non-Anglos (including Asians and Aborigines) but looked at Australia with a migrant's eye view.

As well as winning the affection of these outsiders, Clift also had her own following among young people—among both the radical demonstrators (or 'protestants') whose causes she so often espoused, and among ordinary teenagers, whose problems she understood.

Thus if, overall, Charmian Clift wrote to please herself, it was a self who could simultaneously reach all sorts of people. To some extent this was due to Clift's ability to listen, as well as talk. A great number of her essays have their starting point in conversations—with taxi drivers, local shopkeepers, neighbours, friends, and her children's friends. Even more importantly, the essays reflect the conversations that Clift's readers themselves had with her, by way of letters. There is no way of measuring the extent of the mail response, but it is clear that hundreds of people wrote to Clift.

Though Charmian Clift, as an essayist, can proudly take her place with the twentieth-century British masters of the genre, the unique nature of the communication that she had with her readers is her own special contribution to the form. Put at its simplest, this unique quality is the way Clift opened up the dialogue to allow her readers not only to influence her thoughts, but to have their say in her column.

This innovatory extension of the dialogue was to some extent occasioned by the nature of the essayist's publication outlet. Though, as I have stated, the cramped column format, the weekly deadline, and the ephemeral nature of a daily newspaper exerted a certain pressure, there were compensations. Firstly, the fact that a piece was published

9

a few days after its writing meant that Clift could use current events, and the short time between the appearance of one piece and the next meant that Clift could refer back to an earlier opinion or incident with the reasonable expectation that the reader would know what she was talking about. Thus for example a week after her optimistic look at the future in 'Towards the Millennium', she could change her mind and ask 'Towards What Millennium?'.[11] And a description of ordering new furniture for her flat could be followed, seven weeks later, by an account of how she was still 'Waiting for Things to Turn Up'; three months after this, she could complain that already the four new beds had broken.[12]

Secondly, the very fact that Clift appeared in a newspaper, and was that not-very-exalted figure, a woman columnist, demystified her work, and made both the writing and the writer herself seem more accessible. This meant, on the one hand, that she could use heightened language or obscure allusions without frightening the reader off, for the overt tackiness of the format—the newsprint, the ads for wigs and wrinkle cream—provided a reassuring context. At the same time, readers felt free to write to her about their opinions of her opinions, or indeed about their personal problems, in the way that they might get in touch with, say, Dorothy Dix or John Laws—and in a way that readers of British quarterlies would not get in touch with Aldous Huxley.

As Charmian Clift, then, brought the conversational side of the essay to its peak, let's briefly look at how the dialogue worked.

From the Clift half, to begin with, there was a greater sharing of the writer's domestic life than is common in the essay. From week to week, the Clift reader met familiar characters (Clift's husband, her children, some of her friends, her cat Jeoffrey, and of course the columnist herself) who lived and acted against a background of everyday family life and

11 'Towards the Millennium', *The World of Charmian Clift* (hereafter *WCC*); 'Towards What Millennium?' *TILL*.

12 'Getting with the Forward Lookers', 'On Waiting for Things to Turn Up', 'On Not Getting What You Pay For', *TILL*.

current political events. While this revelation of the 'show behind the show'[13] worked towards a feeling of intimacy, Clift also increased the intimacy by involving—or seeming to involve—the reader in the sense of the writing of the column.

Of course, the essayist has always to some extent fractured the form in order to remind the reader that she is reading a piece of writing. For example Samuel Butler, after conducting the reader through Cheapside, abruptly concludes by saying that he had been told not to see more in Cheapside than he could get into twelve pages of the *Universal Review*, and Beerbohm ends 'Speed' (which was originally a radio broadcast) by suddenly wishing his audience Good Night. Similarly— but more frequently—Charmian Clift draws the reader into her world by reminding the reader of the arbitrariness of the act of creation. Thus in her account of 'A Death in the Family'[14] the sense of immediacy and grief is furthered by the 'hands on' opening:

> I was writing about something different entirely when the telephone rang
> and I learned that my only brother is dead.

And in 'Democracy Laid Low' the opening warning that 'this column almost didn't get written because I am sick' allows the writer to write about the Greek situation while claiming that she is too ill to write 'a follow-up on a piece' that she had written about the Junta a couple of weeks previously.

This sort of device is also often used in Clift's conclusions. While her essay on time leads to the idea that it is time to finish, 'The Stuff of Dreams' ends with a dream that Clift's 'employers arrived unexpectedly and asked where my copy was' and 'On Being Unable to Write an Article' works up to the realisation that 'I should be ... writing this article'.[15]

13 'A Room of Your Own', *WCC*.

14 cf. *Images in Aspic*.

15 'On Tick and Tock',' 'The Stuff of Dreams', *WCC*; 'On Being Unable to Write an Article', *TILL*.

If in a sense the Clift column functioned as a kind of serial story, the audience, through their letters, were also part of the drama. So what did the readers' side of the conversation mean to the essayist?

Though the answering of the great number of letters that she received made her feel like Sisyphus rolling an enormous paper ball uphill,[16] Clift herself was in no doubt that her mail represented the other half of the dialogue:

> Sometimes a communication lands up on my desk that sings for me so sweet and clear, person to person as it were, that I turn giddy all over with enchantment . . .
>
> It's like an exciting conversation. I say this. You say, yes but. And ideally we should be off . . . [17]

Apart from bringing sheer pleasure to the writer, the letters were 'very important' to Clift because they 'gave [her] an indication of the thoughts and opinions and angers and philosophies of a very wide range of people.'[18] At the same time, the correspondence provided the writer with a kind of people-meter that showed her how her views—and the expression of them—were being received.

Clift in turn used the positive responses to give added authority to her argument; she also played fair (in her biased essayist's fashion) and allowed contradictory voices to chime in from time to time. In 'Democracy Laid Low' for example, she notes that while her recent piece on the Junta had caused no outcry from Australian Greeks, it had brought 'attacks, rebukes, castigations and instructions' from Australian-born Australians—which of course she deflects. And in 'The Hungry Ones' she supports her argument for the greater toleration and help which she feels we should extend to the Have-nots by quoting an illiterate, ill-informed and thoroughly nasty correspondent who believes the opposite.

16 'On Not Answering Letters'.
17 'Feeling Slightly Tilted?' *WCC*; 'On Not Answering Letters'.
18 'The Hungry Ones'.

12

As well as providing enjoyment and market research, the letters provided copy—which can tend to be a problem for anyone churning out a weekly column. For example, in 'Feeling Slightly Tilted?' Terry the postman brings a letter from 'a disciple of that admirably lunatic sixteenth century Danish astronomer Tycho Brahe', which causes the essayist to spin off into her own admirably lunatic circles, and in 'Notes from Underground' the arrival of a bundle of student news-sheets provides the material. Similarly—and here we see how the dialectic of essay-response-essay added to the serial nature of the column—the 'Requiem for a Spinster'[19] brought letters about Miss Young which gave the writer a gentle opening into a forthright piece she wanted to do about the treatment of Aboriginal people.[20]

Finally, and on a practical level, the letters could provide solutions, such as the combination of advice and money that rolled in after Clift wrote about a widow who was tangled up in the bureaucracy of the Means Test.[21]

In 'What Are You Doing it For?' Charmian Clift noted that 'A whole human life of struggle, bravery, defeat, triumph, hope, despair, might be remembered, finally, for one drunken escapade'. Sadly—and unfairly— it sometimes seems that the incident of Clift's life that many people are most interested in is her death.

While I don't intend to discuss here either the details or the whole background, I would like to note the enormous pressure that the writing of the column itself exerted on Charmian Clift.

As I pointed out in the introduction to *Trouble in Lotus Land*, Charmian Clift was a painstakingly slow writer, whose method did not fit comfortably with the way she had, each week, to think up a topic, and then often research it, make notes, plan the structure, and draft it and

19 cf. *WCC*.

20 'On Black and White Balls'.

21 'A Home of Your Own', 'In Response to Letters'.

13

draft it and draft it again before the *Sydney Morning Herald* car arrived on Saturday afternoon to collect the finished copy. In 'On Being Unable to Write an Article', [22] written thirteen months after the start of the column, Clift herself described the strain:

> This week, as every week, I have come smack bang up against crisis. Annihilation even. Because I know myself to be completely incapable of writing an article. This is the most terrible feeling, of panic and desolation, of terror, of the most awful loss. I have compared notes with other writers about this chronic recurring paralysis of the talent and find that it is common. Everyone gets it. I suppose that ought to help, but in the grip of the paralysis it doesn't seem to be of any consolation at all.

Of course, while most writers do suffer this 'recurring paralysis', few have it recur absolutely every week. And if, after a year at the column, the crisis was so wearing, one can only imagine how it felt when weekly annihilation had been going on for more than four and a half years. (Indeed, in the last nine or ten months there was a monthly *Pol* deadline as well.)

That Clift did meet the deadline each week requires verification, for in his biography of George Johnston, Garry Kinnane states, with particular reference to the 1968-69 period:

> She frequently phoned her editor excusing her failure to get it done because of 'pneumonia' or 'flu'. Sometimes she did have such ailments, but that was often itself a consequence of prolonged drinking bouts, insufficient sleep and poor diet. [23]

In fact, Charmian Clift was never less than professional about her column. As to time off, she had two weeks' holiday in September 1965, after eleven months straight on the column. In March-April 1966 she had five consecutive weeks off, officially because of her own illness,

22 cf. *TILL*.

23 Garry Kinnane, *George Johnston—A Biography*, Nelson Publishers, Melbourne, 1986, p.278. The editor referred to here is John Douglas Pringle.

14

but perhaps also in preparation for the return home of her invalid husband, who was discharged in late April after eight months in hospital. Then at Christmas that year she had one more week free of the column. In 1967 Clift had three weeks' holiday in May–June and another week off at the beginning of August. In the twenty-three months that elapsed between this August week and her death in July 1969, Charmian Clift had three weeks' annual holiday in June 1968 and again in May 1969, and not a single extra week off—despite the fact that she was coping with a very sick husband, three children, and the housework.

Though this in itself would be enough to fill the life of any normal writer and woman, it should be realised that Charmian Clift had other professional commitments. Through 1964–65 she wrote the script for the twelve-part television series *My Brother Jack*, and she later wrote extended treatments for at least four other feature and documentary films and series, as well as helping in the shoot of an ABC documentary about Sidney Nolan. She was also a frequent guest on radio talk programmes, made appearances at fêtes and vintage car shows, and addressed public meetings ranging from school speech days and architects' dinners to anti-Vietnam and anti-Junta rallies. More importantly—and more harrowingly—she was trying throughout this period to write her own big autobiographical novel, *The End of the Morning*.

If the regular production of the column was so difficult, why did Clift do it? Well, partly because, despite the strain, she loved writing in the essay form, and she loved the sense of being in personal communication with her readers. At the same time, however, the driving force was economic. For most of this period George Johnston, who was struggling with the writing of *Clean Straw for Nothing* as well as with his illness, was not generating much immediate income. Though there were periodic royalties from *My Brother Jack*, it was Clift's column income that provided the family's day-to-day support, and she simply could not afford to have a long break from the weekly deadline.

While the column exerted a direct physical and emotional pressure

15

on Charmian Clift, it also created a form of personal dislocation.

As Virginia Woolf noted in relation to Montaigne:

> To tell the truth about oneself, to discover oneself near at hand, is not
> easy ... For beyond the difficulty of communicating oneself, there is the
> supreme difficulty of being oneself.[24]

In 'The Modern Essay', Woolf went on to make a vital distinction between the public self and private self of the essayist, declaring 'Never to be yourself and yet always—that is the problem'.

While Charmian Clift both in life and in the column appeared to be very open and gregarious, she was in fact a private writer and an extremely private person. Thus the problem of never being herself and yet always being herself produced a form of role-playing, in which the fictional and non-fictional characters overlapped and sometimes became confused. A few years ago Clift's elder son, Martin Johnston, explained how the public and private sides rubbed up against each other in his parents' work:

> I think that with any writer ... public and private sides tend to get
> inextricably confused. A novelist, and particularly as overtly
> autobiographical a novelist as my father eventually became, is performing
> a paradoxical trick-cyclist act in the first place by making public at least
> one side of what is the fairly private side of his life, telling the world—
> publicly—that it *is* private.

After explaining that 'David Meredith does not map, point by point, onto George Johnston, or vice versa' but that Meredith is 'a selective George Johnston, if you want', Martin Johnston went on to describe how this sort of fictional selective process worked for Clift:

> My mother's situation was slightly different of course because most of
> her writing after we came back to Australia was in the column, was not
> fiction at all—except of course it was. Any columnist of her kind adopts
> the persona of friend talking to friends—'This is the real Charmian Clift

24 Virginia Woolf, 'Montaigne', *The Common Reader, First Series.*

16

having a chat to you over the back garden fence', and what not. In fact it's nothing of the sort. Again it's a very artful, fictionalised, literary construct. So in a way public and private for her, in her aspect as an author, are just as confused as they are with George Johnston and David Meredith. Except she never went so far as to *call* the persona she adopted in her column, well, Cressida Morley, shall we say.

If Charmian Clift the columnist was to some extent a fictional character, she was not always easy for the non-fictional Charmian Clift to live with—and indeed to live up to—and in a sense she impinged on Clift's privacy.

In the title essay of this volume, 'On Being Alone with Oneself', we see, I think, the writer's 'trick-cyclist act' at its paradoxical extreme: Charmian Clift the person—the wife and mother—is 'for the first time in exactly half [her] life . . . quite quite alone, as [she] had so often longed to be'. While she proceeds to explore herself alone—watching herself, listening to herself—she is of course not alone at all, for she is simultaneously Charmian Clift the columnist, sharing her aloneness with thousands of anonymous strangers.

Little wonder that, when the clatter and involvement of family life returns, she feels 'that there was some marvellous opportunity in all that silence [.] That I missed.' Little wonder, too, if the physical and emotional demands of the column, together with various personal pressures, caused her eventually to retreat into her own privacy.

While Charmian Clift had a great gift for living, she was able to share her gift so unselfishly with her readers that she went beyond the essayist's brief of giving pleasure, and gave encouragement to life itself. For example, the recent publication of an article about the release of *Trouble in Lotus Land* brought me a letter from a woman who in the 1960s had been a housebound mother with two small children, and who had 'put [her] career in a cardboard box'. She noted that she had 'lived and loved every word Clift wrote in the Melbourne *Herald*' and that Clift had given her 'such hope and courage':

What she did was enlighten me to the other Woman's World ... Her encouragement to me was mainly through her helping me to realise that although I was the victim of an extremely poor education system with the added inheritance of poor parents, I could still 'have a go', which of course I did.

Twelve years later, Clift's encouragement bore fruit, and this reader returned to the workforce, where she is 'still employed in a most satisfying and well-paid job'.

Though such an individual achievement may seem to some to be a small thing, I believe that this response is symptomatic of the amazing legacy that Charmian Clift bequeathed to her readers. Through her positive approach to everyday life, through her loving and humorous exploration of the familiar details of a housewife's world, she helped other women to feel less isolated and humdrum. At the same time, she shared in the pains and perplexities of those other outsiders, migrants and young people, and by her passionate questioning of the war machine and the system she expressed the worries and beliefs of the silent protestants. Finally, through the beauty of her prose style and her mastery of the essay form she brought literature onto the breakfast table of thousands of very different Australians.

In the light of all this, it doesn't really matter that Charmian Clift is left out of the critical histories of Australian writing. If, as Dr Johnson says, it is the common reader who finally decides the distribution of poetical honours, the reputation of Charmian Clift is in excellent hands.

Nadia Wheatley
1991

A NOTE ON THE EDITING
OF *TROUBLE IN LOTUS LAND* AND
BEING ALONE WITH ONESELF

As Charmian Clift's column was written from week to week, there are at times inconsistencies in her punctuation (e.g. hyphenation, capitalisation) which would not have been noticed by the reader of an individual essay, but which would be distracting in a collection. I have therefore standardised some of the minor points, but have retained Clift's idiosyncratic punctuation style overall.

In regard to the great majority of the essays in these two volumes, I have been working directly from Charmian Clift's typescripts (held in the National Library of Australia). However, in the case of nine essays in the first anthology and one essay in this,[1] I have had to rely on the *Sydney Morning Herald* version. Though Clift's essays were not sub-edited in the normal sense of the word, the column format did cause paragraphs to be chopped into short units, often of only one sentence. I have, therefore, in these ten cases, sometimes joined up some of the short newspaper paragraphs.

One of the striking features of Charmian Clift's work is the way in which the writer would refer to current political events. These topical allusions have therefore been retained, with the exception of two short references (in 'On a Choice for the Maja' and 'Report from a Migrant, Three Years After'). End-notes have been provided, where possible, to give the context.

---

1 These essays are: 'The Creeping Towers', 'What Price Rubies?', 'Getting with the Forward Lookers', 'Feverless Festivals', 'A is for the Atom Age', 'On Being Unable to Write an Article', 'Saturnalias, Resolutions and Other Christmas Wishes', 'On Being Middle-aged', 'The Joy of a Good Old Cuppa', and 'Anyone for Fish and Chips'.

Here, as in *Trouble in Lotus Land*, I have included some facsimiles of the newspaper pages, to give a sense of the context of Clift's essays as they were originally received, and I have reproduced a few pages of Charmian Clift's essay notes, so that readers can see the kind of work that went on behind the scenes. I have also included a chronological listing of the essays, so that reference may be made to the companion anthologies.

N.W.

A RIFT IN MY LUTE

Well, we got this whole stack of LPs in a job lot, of which we are quite ashamed in a way, although since we've confessed them we find that quite a lot of our friends have got the job lot too, and now everybody feels much better about it. It might even be an In thing to do. Or In-ish, anyway. In any case it was cheap. I rather wish they didn't say so blatantly 'The World's Most Famous Concertos' and 'A Treasury of Concert Favourites' and 'Piano Masterpieces', but I suppose we can always nick the actual records out without anyone seeing the sleeves.

Anyway, in 1968, we're having a beaut old razzamatazz with all nine of old growly Ludwig, which reminds me that there are a whole new batch of jokes current, of which you are given the answer and have to find the question. 9W is the answer of this one. And the question is: 'Mr Wagner, do you spell your name with a V?' I have heard some others, but I don't think they are printable in these pages.

And talking of Mr Wagner, we got a couple of Ring things in with our job lot, and I have been fascinated to play them, just to see if they are as truly awful as I have always thought. I had lunch with Anna Russell a little while ago and we had the most marvellous time comparing our pet hates from the great pen of 9W. Mine is the Rhine Maidens, although the Valkyries run them close second. Whoop Whoop Whoop. Shriek Shriek Shriek. I was brought up on the beastly women shrieking and whooping, a small child, defenceless, and all I could ever do in retaliation was whip out into the kitchen with my brother and shriek coincidental Rabelaisian obscenities (my father was insistent upon Rabelais as well as Wagner as essential for the education of the young: Laurence Sterne was on the list too, and Gibbon: sometimes it amazes me that I ever grew up even halfway sane).

Anyway, all these little extra dibs and dabs are nice for the nostalgia, like 'The Hall of the Mountain Kings' and the 'William Tell Overture' and 'Gayeneh' and Chopin's 'Polonaise' with memories of Cornel Wilde pounding away with blood spattering the ivory and Merle Oberon of immaculate profile saying distantly 'Paint on, Mr ———.' (Who on earth *was* painting her?)

Well, having this beaut job lot of lovely records started me off on thinking what we were playing a decade ago, and the decade before that, and the decade before that, and so on back (this is really terrible).

In 1958 we were playing Nana Mouskouri, I think, and Mikis Theodorakis, who was just coming up then, and Hadzithakis, and Ella Fitzgerald, and Oscar Brown Junior, whom we had just discovered, and Edith Piaf over and over and over, and 'My Fair Lady' which we had just discovered too and served marvellously well for encouraging music to pump to, since at that time we had a hand pump for our peculiar Greek plumbing arrangements. Looking back on it 1958 seems to have been a lightish time musically, but we were a bit gone with the Greek Folk and Trad and Classic, Athenian cantatas, Melina Mercouri, Aliki Vouyiouklaki, and the bouzouki as a way of life. There was a great big butch girl who wore her stockings rolled under her knees and belted out Greek pop and we were mad about. A bit of Brahms sneaked in now and then and some *eine kleine nacht*; perhaps we had some small guilt about our origins and didn't dare to quite go overboard for the savage and strange.

1948, on the other hand, was a serious year. We were earnest about Schönberg, Stravinsky, Handel, Brahms, Benjamin Britten, and we had about sixteen tons of 78s in great whopping albums which took up most of the cupboard space in our little flat, and I think we wore rapt expressions when listening to our favourites, but we still liked 'The Hall of the Mountain Kings' because it was a family joke, and we were still newly enough married to care tremendously about family jokes. I think that was the first year I thought of the little flat as 'home' instead of the house I had grown up in. I was pregnant again that year too, and deliciously, sleepily animal, and was given to terribly romantic music, études and sonatas. Lots of strings I liked, and harps even, and Borodin and Mussorgsky. And I still had a sneaky partiality for Tchaikovsky's 'Pathétique', and all ballet, which made me weep buckets. As I remember it we hadn't quite grown into Mozart, although we pretended we had.

In 1938 it wasn't we, but only me, and I was a very small girl very defiantly rebelling about Wagner and mad about Bach. We had this funny old clumsy gramophone which my father had made from bits and pieces and this and that, and he used to send my brother and me down to the beach to pick aloe thorns for needles. They were the most beautiful tender rose pink against the silvery bloom of the fleshy leaves, and my father used to pare them down very carefully and fit them to the gramophone head and crank the old thing up and oh Lord how it thundered and bellowed and hollered and shrieked. Caruso and Melba and de Reszke and Galli-Curci and Toti del Monte and Gigli and Schumann-Heink and Chaliapin and Dame Clara Butt changing gears all the way through 'Land of Hope and Glory'. It was a festival, festa, festal deluge of sound. We were battered and bashed and drowned in it and flopped about like stranded mullet, panting. And just when I was feeling absolute exaltation the terrible tyrant would submit me to the whole album of the Wagnerian Festival of 1928, which was his pride and joy and had every awful thing in it that that man ever wrote.

Well, 1928 I don't remember much, except that I was going 'in Jackie Lang's boat'—whatever that meant—and that we had musical Sundays at my grandparents, with operatic favourites and Stanley Holloway doing 'Sam Sam Pick up Thy Musket' and the young Yehudi Menuhin being brilliant, and my grandmother had an album in which she pasted pictures of all her musical favourites, cut into ovals and decorated with leaves and flowers. It was said in the family that 'she used to sing in opera', but they were all such awful liars that I strongly suspect she was really only in the chorus of an amateur Gilbert and Sullivan company in the provinces. Still, they were nice Sundays, and nice music, and I am grateful for them, even for 'Sam Sam Pick up Thy Musket'.

So now after all those decades I have this beautiful job lot of records of which I am slightly ashamed, but still I'll manage to nick them out without anybody really seeing the sleeves, and when nobody is around I'll play Big Bill Broonzy and Lightning Hopkins and Mississippi John Hurt and my old mate Jack Elliot and Odetta and the Fugs, and I have a faint idea that 1968 might be a lightish year for music.

CONCERNING THE
HIPPOPOTAMUS

In all the spate of words that have been poured out on the election of Senator Gorton to the leadership of his party and the leadership of his country there was one sentence in one report that may have been missed by some of you or overlooked as irrelevant by others, so I would like to bring it to your attention.

I quote: 'Senator Gorton's tie was dotted with tiny pink hippopotamuses.' (I had always thought the plural of hippopotamus to be hippopotami, but I could be wrong about that as about so many other things.)

Now why, I wonder, did Senator Gorton choose the Horse of the River, a ponderous and non-committal beast, as his totemic emblem? What influence, if any, did this have on the ballot? And does this indicate a move towards heraldry in the ranks of the government as well as a move towards highly educated politicians?

I have looked very closely at all the news pictures of the other candidates but cannot make out what emblems they wore on their ties, if any. The ties just look like ordinary stripy affairs, but it's very difficult to tell from a greyish news picture. For all I know Mr Hasluck may have had a wee gryphon or some such device printed on his, and Mr Bury the lyre of Apollo, which would have been very appropriate to a Cambridge man, and would certainly have rallied the artistic push.

If one thinks about it, though, even stripy ties are not always ordinary. I had an Australian friend in London who bought a stripy tie that pleased him exceedingly and wore it on every possible occasion (I think it was the only one he had anyway, his wife having thrown out the old greasy gravy-stained one he had before). Much to his surprise he found that there were some English who were very disturbed—clubbish chaps who informed him that he was wearing the tie of the Coldstream Guards, the understandable mistake of an ignorant colonial, but . . .

My friend said in some puzzlement that he didn't mind at all. He hadn't bought the tie because it belonged to the Coldstream Guards but because he liked the stripe. He said he still liked the stripe. I don't think he ever did understand why they were so cross about it.

And while I am thinking of England, it is interesting that we now have an Oxford man at the helm, and that a Cambridge man was one of his contenders for the prize, and I am reminded of the first boat race I ever saw and that was the year Oxford sank. It was the most spectacular event, especially for a newcomer to England, and the most impressive thing about it to me was that the Oxford crew were still indefatigably rowing on in perfect unison when they were actually up to their necks in muddy water. Zuleika Dobson would have adored it. There were totems and emblems in plenty that day, but I suppose there were no hippopotamuses (i?) about in the Thames. Although it occurs to me that if this dramatic riparian event had taken place in the last few weeks one might suspect that there *had* been a hippo in the Thames, a Cambridge one, and therefore pale blue.

Which brings me to colour. I can see that Senator Gorton might not choose pale blue for his tiny hippopotamuses, this being Cambridge's colour (although it is also the colour of his own old school tie and cap), but why on earth would he choose pink? Whoever heard of a pink hippopotamus? Pink elephants yes, but pink hippos no. Pink is the traditional motif colour of inebriation, and is it possible to imagine an inebriated hippo? White would be more understandable as being the sacred colour of animals, although white elephant has also a nasty connotation, and should perhaps be avoided as an emblem. But who could quarrel with a white hippopotamus, or even a procession of them? Particularly if they were small. (Thinking of white as a colour for emblems

26

it occurs to me that it might be fairly simple to find an emblem for the tie of Sir William Yeo, who could easily settle for a small sacred cow.)

Well, even if I can't understand the significance of an amphibious African pachydermatous ungulate mammal as the chosen device of our new Australian leader (Sir Robert Menzies' thistle is different, I feel) I do approve of the apparent move towards heraldry. It will make the House so much more colourful. Besides all the loyal lions and unicorns and such, and the obvious kangaroo and emu devices, there are endearing creatures like the wombat, and the charming native companion, which surely somebody would like to adopt as his own. (Mr McEwen perhaps?) And of course the phoenix for Mr Whitlam. Then there are the dove and the hawk, birds of great significance in these days. The possibilities are unlimited. There are so many birds and animals hallowed by heraldic tradition—goats and two-headed eagles and bantam cockerels and greyhounds, and indeed practically the whole animal and avian kingdom—and all could be depicted variously as rampant, statant, passant, guardant, or whatever, to indicate firmly the political stances and positions of their wearers. (There were instances in the nineteenth century of railway engines being used as devices, and in the twentieth even a cogwheel, but I don't think that sort of thing should be encouraged.)

Nor do I see any reason whatever why the wearing of emblems should be confined to ties, which, in any case, are a most ludicrous article of clothing and should properly be abandoned. What are they for? What purpose do they serve? If any man took a pair of scissors and cut through his collar and tie and counted the number of layers of cloth he is choking himself with he would throw the damn thing away and never wear another ever again. Anyway, if this heraldry business really catches on ties will have to go in favour of ruffs and ruffles and collars of Chantilly lace, which might be actually just as choky but would lend to their wearers such an air of dignity and gallantry that they might consider it worthwhile being choked a bit for the sake of their

27

new public images. In any case I don't think a collar and tie would look too good with a tabard, and politicians would need a garment something like a tabard on which to display their devices to the best possible advantage.

Then it might be a good idea also for them to transfer their mottoes from their office desks and walls (if they have mottoes on their office walls these days, like a couple of lines from Kipling's 'If', and *Think*, and *Do It Now*, and that one about 'I had no shoes and I complained . . . ' etc.) and have these embroidered on their tabards, thus reviving an interest in the pleasant art of fine embroidery, and giving employment to wayward girls in institutions, who are practically the only girls, I do believe, who learn the craft thoroughly these days.

Anyway, I really meant to write this article about the hippopotamus, that ponderous pachyderm, and looking up references I came upon these interesting lines from T. S. Eliot, which may or may not throw some light on the matter of Senator Gorton's tie with emblem.

'The broad-backed hippopotamus
Rests on his belly in the mud;
Although he seems so firm to us
He is merely flesh and blood.'

ON ENGLAND,
MY ENGLAND

Well, Australia Day is coming up, and Coral Sea Week is going down, and Britain has declared herself to be a tiny island only, and perversely I, who have always been anti-Empire, feel a twinge. There must be something in the blood after all.

My father was English, my paternal grandparents were English, my great-grandfather served in the Indian Army, and all his ten sons excepting for my grandfather Will served in the army too. All ten were over six feet tall, and every one was in a different regiment, and just once they all had leave together and marched into the village church each in his different uniform and it must have been a fine sight. Grandfather Will was bitten on the head by a sacred monkey when he was a baby, which seems to have exempted him, or perhaps my grandmother Emma, a frail blonde creature of implacable will, caught him while he was still a youth only teetering on the brink of enlistment, as it were, and firmly dragged him back to the safety of a nice commercial office, where she could keep her eye on him.

One grows up on this sort of family thing, stories and legends, and what is true and what is false I haven't the faintest idea. Did my great-grandfather, dying in cold England, really set his beard alight to keep his chest warm? Among his plunder from the Zulu Wars was there really King Pempe's stool? My grandfather Will used to tell such things, and he was a truthful man, but then he was old too, and memory is a tricky thing, forever discarding, rejecting, or embroidering what is retained, making transformations, building up the small and ordinary into the grand and exceptional. Anyway, certain it was in the matter of Empire, that my grandmother Emma was absolutely pro and my father absolutely anti, and they fought it out every Saturday afternoon on the verandah under the staghorns and the maidenhair where my grandfather, upon his arrival in Australia on his retirement from his nice commercial office, had hung his bowler hat upside down on chains and grown a fern in it as a symbol of his new freedom. My grandmother Emma spoke of England as 'home', quoted Kipling on Empire, and furiously drowned out my father with her huge contralto turned on full belt in 'Land of Hope and Glory'. My father spoke of 'that dismal little island' and quoted Norman Douglas as saying that 'living in England was like living in the heart of a lettuce'. My grandfather Will played 'The Boys of the Old Brigade' on the wind-up gramophone and held his peace.

I concluded that my father was a Roundhead and my grandparents were Cavaliers. A renegade also, my father. But how that renegade feverishly paced the house through the Battle of Britain and the debacle of Dunkirk, and how he trotted out all his martial ancestors and the family stories of their exploits on the outposts of Empire as irrefutable proof that the English could not be beaten.

I first saw England in the early months of 1951, with late winter still gripping it harsh and the aftermath of war still glumly apparent. We queued for everything, even Welfare State codliver oil and orange juice for the children, and people looked dank and shabby and terribly meek, and I wondered how it was that these same meek people, meekly queueing, could have been capable of such heroism so very recently. I had an inkling of what it was about twice, once when I was trapped in a lift in Selfridges, and once when I drove to Stratford in a blizzard. On each occasion the reticent English sharing the moment of drama became positively exhilarated. In the lift they made jokes, were solicitous of old ladies and small children, and actually seemed to enjoy the experience. On the icy road to Stratford, with the cars waltzing behind a snowplough or caught in drifts by the side of the road, they waved and laughed and stopped to help each other and me too and I have never met such courtesy on the roads before or since. That was the year of the Festival of Britain too, and there was a lot of pageantry one way and another, and England was going to be great again.

And then when summer came we explored the English countryside, and came to know the pleasures of drifting in a punt among the swans at Bray on a Sunday afternoon, and watching a village cricket match, walking in Burnham Beeches, picnicking in apple orchards and castle keeps, discovering pubs that forever would be 'our' pubs, and it might have been like living in the heart of a lettuce, but I understood my grandmother's deep love of it, just as I understood my father's deep anger with the social system he had fled a world away from, and my grandfather's unquenchable delight in the bravery of uniform and drum. I wished very much that they were not all dead, all three of them, so that I might have written to tell them so.

All the same, after a driving holiday in Europe, I felt a bit uneasy about England. If the aftermath of war was evident there it was so much more terribly so in France and anguished Germany, with the crosses in the fields to remind you all the time, and so many mutilated young men still wearing army greatcoats, but in Germany the fields were ploughed right up to the very edge of the roads, and you were conscious of the intensity of the effort towards reconstruction. As one of my friends said later, talking of the doughty Lion of Empire: 'You're not tryin', lion.'

But then we had the death of a King and the coronation of a Queen, and there was lots and lots of splendid pageantry, and many people said that the new Elizabethan age had come and England was going to be great again. I enjoyed all the pageantry, being Cavalier enough to respond with as much delight as my grandfather to all the bravery of uniforms and drums and flags, but the Empire seemed to be dwindling away, and I didn't see how England was going to be great again unless she got on with it at a faster clip. The Welfare State was in full swing and everybody took it for granted now, and there was no more rationing of anything, and the countryside would make you weep

31

for beauty sometimes, and people didn't look meek any more, only fretful, and they seemed to complain a lot.

We left England at the end of 1954 and didn't go back until the winter of 1960–61, and in the meantime the Angry Young Men had lisped out their anger and been absorbed into the Establishment, and London was beginning to be really swinging and the shops were filled with every wonderful thing in the world, and in the country village where we were living the wives of gentlemen farmers served champagne cocktails and the gentlemen farmers lived handsomely somehow on their losses and kept their shooting woods well-stocked, and National Health had become, I thought, shockingly unwieldy and expensive. I didn't want to live in England any more.

I've never been back since that winter, nor wanted to much, particularly now, what with the Thames rising and London sinking and foot-and-mouth raging, although I think it would be interesting to see the flower people sleeping in Trafalgar Square in the summer, and the girls marching about in jackboots, and nobody meek at all any more, but apparently declining and falling with some panache and a derisive thumb to the nose.

Still, Germany is doing well. And so is Japan, who might be able to take over the east-of-Suez role and even produce a Japanese Kipling, which is an interesting thought, or some lines like these:

'And what good came of it at last?'
Quoth little Peterkin.
'Why that I cannot tell', said he,
'But 'twas a famous victory.'

THE VOICES OF GREECE

I have hesitated about writing anything on the Greek situation, mostly because I felt I didn't entirely understand it, and I have been afraid to write to friends there for elucidation since I might very well compromise them by doing so.

The voice of Melina Mercouri, stripped of property and citizenship, rings clear as a morning bell. 'I was born Greek, I will die Greek; Patakos was born Fascist, he will die Fascist.' One would not expect less than that from her. 'When I am 'appy,' she said once, 'I explose. And when I am angry, I explose.' One imagines her to be very angry indeed, and that she will go on explosing. Melina's is the authentic Greek voice of resistance, the voice of Marathon and Salamis, of the pass at Thermopylae, of the Byzantine Constantine Palaeologus, of the klephts harrying the Turks from their mountain lairs through all the hundreds of years of Turkish overlordship, of the heroes of the War of Independence, of Metaxas' famous 'No!' to the Italians, of the underground fighters who waged unremitting war on their German masters. This is the voice of people of the Dodecanese Islands, who, during their occupation by the Italians, painted their houses blue and white, the colours of the Greek flag.

Melina is, of course, a wealthy and famous woman, living in America, and it is perhaps easier to hurl defiance if you are not going to be seized for it and beaten up and hurled yourself into some terrible prison camp. All the same I do believe the note would be just as clear and just as authentic if she were inside Greece, as the note of conservative Eleni Vlachos was clear and authentic in refusing, in spite of all persuasion and all threats, to publish her newspapers under censorship. What the composer Mikis Theodorakis said in defiance we don't know, because he was nabbed pretty early and we haven't heard anything of him for a long time, excepting that when he was due for trial he did not appear and it was said he was in a coma, having most curiously developed diabetes a couple of days before. I would guess he was in a coma, all right, but for very different reasons. One of the letters smuggled out of the prison island of Yioura to London last year states that prisoners were arriving in such terrible condition from security headquarters that the military doctor said: 'But for God's sake! Were they beaten up by cannibals?'

But torture has never broken Greek spirit before. For 3000 years they have been starved, beaten, burnt, roasted on spits, they've had their tongues cut out and their ears cut off, they've been blinded, enslaved, and for 3000 years they have cried, 'Freedom or death!'

And this is what I can't understand about the present situation. How can it be that they are so completely intimidated, or appear to be so intimidated, as to accept this monstrous regime that has wiped out every constitutional liberty, and imprisoned every liberal, every humanist, every intellectual of even moderate persuasion, every trade union leader, professors and poets and lawyers and the mayors of municipalities, the aged and the sick, pregnant women and the mothers of large families, under the most appalling circumstances and with no right of appeal. Even an ordinary Greek gaol is nothing short of frightful. (I know a European woman who spent three months in gaol in Athens and she said sometimes she thought she was playing Moll Flanders. She had a lot more grey in her hair when she came out, although, on the other hand, she came out speaking fluent Greek: she always did learn everything the hard way.) The prison islands are notorious.

It is bewildering enough that the United States and Britain, as avowed enemies of fascism, should accept the Junta with no more than a 'tut! tut!' of disapproval, more bewildering that Australia appears to approve of it so heartily that we deny a visa to anyone who is likely to speak out against it. But it is most bewildering that the Greeks in Greece seem to have taken it so tamely. I say 'seem to have' because the resistance could be underground, as it has been so many times before, and if it is it could erupt violently and bloodily. I've known a lot of those resistance fighters of the German occupation, including a few who were caught—one girl had her baby kicked out of her by the Germans, another was under sentence of death after being forced to watch her mother executed—and the one thing they had in common was an insatiable appetite for heroism. I wonder very much what they are doing at this minute. I've gone through the names in the smuggled Yioura letters, but of course they aren't complete lists, and although many names among them are names I know well—like the poet Yannis Ritsos, the Biennale prizewinner Vaso Katraki, the actor Karousos, the marvellous liberal journalist Papadimitriou—I haven't found the names of any personal friends, so I hope desperately that security hasn't caught up with them yet, or they've gone to ground. I can't imagine them keeping their mouths meekly shut under tyranny of any sort.

In fact I can't imagine any Greek keeping his mouth meekly shut. Every man is a politician and an orator. The most impassioned speeches I ever heard on the Cyprus issue came from Tzimmy the pedlar. And once, before an election, I watched two labourers unloading asbestos from a caique. They were engaged in political argument, and put their sacks down on the quay while they got on with it. A crowd gathered, and each protagonist appealed to the bystanders, until at last they turned their backs on each other completely, the better to harangue the audience. As they were both very resonant orators each began moving away in opposite directions so as not to be drowned out by the other, until finally one, with attendant audience, was at one end of the waterfront, and the other, with his audience, was at the other end of the waterfront, and the neglected sacks of asbestos lay in the middle. I have also seen an electioneering politician thrown into the sea, and another hurled back into the steamer from which he was trying to land. How can spirit like that turn tame overnight?

It has been suggested to me that resistance is easy, indeed inevitable, when you have nothing left to lose. But in the last ten years or so there has been emerging in Greece a definite middle class, who for the first time have a great deal to lose. Jobs, prestige, property, possessions, children's education, investments—things which might weight the scales against conviction. I watched through ten years just one island's development out of absolute poverty into relative prosperity and the change in manners and attitudes that the change in economics brought about. It wouldn't be simple for those people to risk their very new security. The voice of caution might suggest that it would be prudent to wait and see how things turn out and keep mum in the meantime. It is exactly the sort of prudence on the part of decent middle class people that allowed the Nazis to take over Germany.

Well, as I said at the beginning, there is much about the situation that I don't understand, but oh Lord!, I know where my emotions lie. With Melina the Greek, and all the Greeks like Melina, outside Greece or inside Greece, and whether I can hear their voices or not. They'll all ring out loud and clear one day soon. After all, they always have.

WHAT ARE YOU DOING IT FOR?

One day last week, by reason of a bit of bad timing, I was forced to come home from the city in peak hour, which is a pretty hideous ordeal if you're not used to it. Although, at that, it might be an even more hideous ordeal if you are used to it. Actually, does anybody ever get used to it?

So I sat in my taxi, caught in the nose to bumper stream, with lane beyond lane beyond lane also packed nose to bumper, like a series of monstrous metal caterpillars sluggishly crawling, and I looked at the querulous and fretful and angry and impatient faces, and I thought of all the thousands and thousands of people who had to go through that every afternoon and every morning too, and of the further thousands and thousands hanging on straps in trains and buses, jostled and pushed by irritable strangers, irritable and harassed themselves, suffering discomfort, indignity, and downright rudeness in order to get to or get away from jobs in which most of them would have no passionate interest or sense of dedication or burning belief, and I thought that they would spend five days of every week like that, for fifty weeks of every year, and I wanted to ask them:

'But what are you doing it *for*?'

And I know that although ambition comes into this, and status, and the acquisition of more possessions, and 'getting on', the basic answer is survival. Survival, of course, on the best possible terms, and with the maximum of immediate comforts.

I shouldn't think that many people have a distinct purpose in life beyond that—always excepting the dedicated few, the visionaries and the dreamers—unless a further purpose is to give their children a better education and greater opportunities than they had themselves (and then upbraid them for not being grateful enough, or for having it too easy).

But beyond the immediate goal of education we are not much inclined to labour for our children, or even plan for them in the sense that older races plan for descendants yet unborn, planting the trees and the vineyards, acquiring the property, arranging the alliances that will be most beneficial to those who come after.

I have been told that the salt mines in western China are actually subterranean reservoirs of brine, which is pumped up through bamboo drills to the surface where the brine is evaporated into salt. There was a time when a Chinese man would spend his whole life putting down a new drill, and his son would do the same thing after him, to the end that the original miner's grandchild would benefit. What happens under Chairman Mao I don't know, but I do know that most of us are incapable of even the concept of two generations working entirely for the third. Or even one generation working entirely for the next, as happens still in peasant economies, where survival could be dependent upon such a fixed pattern of past proof.

There was a family I knew well in Greece, two brothers and their wives and assorted children, who had pulled themselves up from the illiterate peasantry to become small-time grocers. They never employed anybody, the wives worked as hard as the husbands, they denied themselves every comfort that cost money, they were frugal to stinginess, but they sent their children to school, and they brought their nephews and nieces over from the mainland tomato patch and sent them to school too, or provided the girls with dowries and arranged marriages for them, and so, in one generation, raised the social level of the whole family to solid bourgeois. Their grandchildren will no doubt speak four languages and aspire to art and letters and despise their grandparents' uncouth ways, and whether this is a good thing or a bad thing I don't know, but it was impressive to watch such utter determination in action.

I think the same thing still happens with some migrant families here in Australia. They will work all day and all night too, or take two jobs or three, and work weekends and never take a holiday, sleep a whole family to a room and live off scraps, so that their children will inherit the Promised Land on terms of equality with—if not superiority to—the indigenous inhabitants, who are inclined to wonder whatever happened.

On the other hand, talking of Europeans, a Czech art dealer, himself very successful, told me that Middle Europeans, persecuted for so long, work only for food and wine. The very best food and wine. His theory is that they have suffered so much and lost so much in the way of possessions and material things, they have started again from scratch so many times, that they have lost faith in the efficacy of possessions as a means to security and have come to believe that the good things of life are the only things worth having, things that can be consumed and enjoyed here and now. Thus they don't own houses. They rent them. And they would rather, he said (I thought rather gloomily), buy good delicatessen than a good painting. He is himself, naturally, a gourmet.

And while we are on the subject of paintings, there is a quaint notion still current that painters and poets and sculptors and novelists and folk of that kidney do have a higher and loftier purpose than survival and immediate comfort. They are working—shhh! please—for posterity.

I admit that most of them work under an imperative—nobody would be such a fool as to engage himself in such arduous labour for so little reward otherwise—but I think the posterity bit is poppycock.

The real drive and purpose of Shakespeare's life appears to have been to establish himself as a landed gentleman in Stratford, with his very own coat of arms. And this he achieved by dint of a lot of writing and a lot of sycophancy to the great and influential, and one imagines that he was very happy about ambition fulfilled. But of course his line died out and there was nobody left to inherit the coat of arms, and posterity, in any case, judged him quite differently.

Balzac too, who wrote like a tormented fury, wrote only when the clamour of his creditors, to whom we should all be eternally grateful, drove him back to his desk and his pen. His stated ambition was to marry a very rich woman and be kept in luxury. He was a dreadful social climber at heart. And Dostoyevsky wrote for the gambling tables, which were his great obsession.

It is the most pretentious nonsense to believe that the work you do will live after you. It might, but then again it might not, and history will be the judge of that, not you. What most of us leave to posterity are only a few memories of ourselves, really, and possibly a few enemies. A whole human life of struggle, bravery, defeat, triumph, hope, despair, might be remembered, finally, for one drunken escapade.

So what are you doing it for? If you are doing it for fame, that is a transient business. If you are doing it for posterity, she's a fickle jade. If you are doing it for money, you can't take it with you, and it will be little consolation to have engraved on your tombstone—like the Connecticut con men of the last century—'He Amassed Wealth'.

My greatest admiration and respect goes to the few who do it—whatever it is—for the betterment of other human beings, now and in the future, but few of us are capable of that sort of dedication or even have the talent for it. So I suppose survival and immediate comfort will continue to motivate us in our labours, and self-interest will prevail.

You are perfectly entitled now to ask me what I am doing it for, and I promise to answer you honestly. I am doing it to please myself.

TOMORROW IS ANOTHER DAY

There was a time once when I did not see a newspaper for ten months. And when I did see a newspaper again no time seemed to have elapsed at all.

There was 'Foreign Office Sensation' and 'Princess Margaret Surprise' just as usual, and as usual some Middle East clashes, and the usual black potentates and dignitaries being dignified by visits to 10 Downing Street and Buckingham Palace. Lady Docker and her gold-plated Daimler were still news, and so were the comparative bust measurements of Lollobrigida and Diana Dors. It might have been the day after I had seen my last newspaper instead of ten months.

When the Suez crisis (I mean the Anthony Eden one) was shaking the world I didn't know anything about it until it was all over and I discovered, to my astonishment, that I and my family had been on an evacuation list.

There is a certain bliss in such ignorance, of course, but nowadays I read my newspapers as assiduously as anybody else. More assiduously than most, probably, since I have to write about something or other every week and need to know what is going on in the world.

And it seems to me, from my reading of newspapers, that more things are going on faster than they ever used to—going so fast, in fact, that we seem to be in the future before we've decently acclimatised ourselves to the present. I find it all most confusing.

I mean before we've conquered the common cold we are transplanting hearts, before we have solved the problem of old-fashioned schools, overcrowded classrooms, undertrained teachers, and antiquated methods of learning we are being chatted up about computerised education. While we still commit victimised young girls to Dickensian institutions of correction, equate morality with the reproductive organs, argue about working wives, insist on men wearing collars and ties, wrestle with smelly garbage bins, or—if we live in the outer suburbs—wait for sewerage to be installed, we are reading in our newspapers of the possibility of giant reflectors on the moon to abolish night altogether. The traffic tangles become more hopeless in the cities, drought and fire lay waste to the country, water runs out, and a scientist gravely warns us, through the columns of our newspapers, of the dangers implicit in space debris.

Before we are even in tomorrow we are stepping backwards into a brutality of thinking and action that belongs, more properly, to the Dark Ages. The hordes of Genghis Khan never inflicted more callous suffering on women and children than we are doing. We have become so accustomed to brutality that we don't even notice it any more. Skip the horror pictures and turn to the stocks and shares or the social notes, and maybe take in the day's 'kill' on the way. Actually I wonder that the daily 'kill' isn't reported as the 'bag', like gentlemen grouse-shooting on the moors, or early settlers dedicated to the extermination of the Aborigine.

Guns, I read in my newspaper, are crushing Hue's art treasures and toppling her ancient temples and palaces, and if I turn on my television I can watch it happening. And try not to weep. What bloody-minded barbarians we have become, for all our specious morality.

The Russians are gaining in the race for missiles, and Mrs Mary Whitehouse, of the British National Viewers and Listeners Association, is anxious, I learn, to extend the influence of her 'clean-up-television' organisation to Australia. Get Alf Garnett by all means, because it is disturbing to have one's own bigotry and prejudice reflected quite so clearly, or to be reminded that the monarchy, sex, religion, politics, racial prejudice, and the grosser natural functions are subjects that ordinary people do discuss and quarrel about, sometimes irreverently and mostly ignorantly. Besides, occupying ourselves with the opinions of Alf Garnett will prevent us from worrying about other things.

Like the swing of the German soldiery to neo-Nazism. Or what is happening in Greece. Is that what tomorrow is going to be like?

Or all that space debris which Sir Bernard Lovell is so concerned about, and which, he says, could trigger a war if mistakenly identified, as it was once in 1962 during the Cuban crisis. He says also, and with terrifying conviction, that in all the successful and attempted space launchings in the last ten years the military aspect has far outweighed the civil and the purely scientific. That is not what we have been given to understand previously, but it is there in my newspaper, and makes the prospect of tomorrow even darker.

So does the report of Professor Porter, of Harvard University, talking to a conference in Canberra on the ability of scientists to manipulate human genes, and therefore the very nature of man. Reassurance came from a Swedish scientist, who said that such manipulation need not necessarily result in evil, although it would be dangerous knowledge in the wrong hands. But how is such knowledge and power to be kept in the right hands? And whose hands are the right hands anyway? We of the civilised west are doing some terribly immoral things these days on the grounds that anything is moral as long as it is our side that is doing it. Are we likely to be more moral tomorrow, with more and more power to play with?

Day after day after day I read in my newspaper of the increasing disparity between the Haves and the Have-nots of the world. Two-thirds of the world's population are suffering from under-nutrition or malnutrition or both. Since there are going to be more people tomorrow than there are today it follows that there will be more hungry ones. Unless the Haves share out more evenly, and there is as yet not the slightest indication that they have any such intention.

Assiduous reading of the daily newspapers could lead one into the profoundest pessimism, or the profoundest anger. Or sheer hysteria. I was probably a lot better off when I didn't read any newspapers at all, and only knew about the events of the world from the travellers passing through, and confidently anticipated that tomorrow wouldn't really be all that different from today, or if it was different there was a chance that it might be better.

I suppose there is still a chance that it might be better, but only, I suspect, if we do something about making today better first. And my reading of my newspapers convinces me that today isn't really much, at least, not much for most people in the world, and not likely to improve by reflectors on the moon or the manipulation of human genes or a speeding up of the missile race or new hearts for old or any other promised or predicted wonders.

Nor will Mrs Whitehouse's purity campaign clean up bigotry and prejudice, today or tomorrow either, or prevent ordinary people from arguing and quarrelling about such matters as the monarchy and politics and racism and sex. Or even the nature of God. One could even blasphemously suspect, from a culling of newspaper reports of the events of today and the predictions for tomorrow, that something funny is happening to God on the way to the twenty-first century.

And now, having added my quota of gloom to somebody else's daily reading, I will put my newspapers in the incinerator and my fears for tomorrow in the back of my mind, and tackle, as best I can, the problems and pleasures of today. There doesn't seem to be much else one can do.

DON'T FENCE ME IN

The house next door has changed hands, and the new owner most obligingly agreed with me that it would be in our common interest to pull down the dividing fence, thus giving us both a clear passage between our houses, and getting rid of an eyesore at the same time.

I have never seen anything aesthetically pleasing in slumped, decayed, gappy grey palings, and of slumped, decayed, gappy grey palings this particular fence was the daddy of them all, blood relation to decrepit cow bails and country outhouses, but lacking such picturesqueness or any claim to function. It had gone too far to sustain even the weight of a ritual choko vine, with which I once considered disguising the hideousness. So now it is under the house, waiting to be sawed into lengths to feed winter fires, and I have room to plant some more trees. Yip!

I have never understood the Australian mania for fences, any more than I understand the Australian passion for front lawns, watered and mowed and clipped and groomed but never used for living. People do their oudoor living at the back of their houses mostly, the barbecue slap by the rotary hoist, or in classier areas a patio with cressets, perhaps because the front lawn isn't private enough for an uninhibited rort, even with a fence, or perhaps because it is considered unseemly to tread on such hallowed ground. Then why have a front lawn at all? Or a fence either?

Last year I did a lot of flying over this vast brown land, and one of the most peculiar of all the peculiar things I saw was fences. I understand that there is a functional purpose in fencing properties to keep sheep and cattle within a given area (although how about all those rabbit-proof fences that the rabbits happily burrowed under?), but why on earth, in the middle of thousands

45

of acres or even miles of your own domain, would you consider it desirable or necessary to picket your house with a stockade of palings? Wild beasts? Savage natives? No, I don't understand it. Unless it is there, not to keep anything out, but to keep the lawn in. Because the lawns exist in the middle of nowhere too. Tawny, tufted, half bald, withered, struggling, but indubitably existent, like little postage stamps of suburbia stuck down on the primeval earth, signifying something but what I don't know, unless it be respectability. And since I'm not terribly up on respectability I haven't a hope of understanding such a motive.

But someone (I can't remember who) told me a little while ago of a man who loved the bushland so deeply and passionately that he saved all his working life to buy himself a block of land so remote, so wild, so lost and strange that you practically needed a time machine as well as a chart and compass to find your way to it. And on this block of land he built a neat red-brick, bow-fronted bungalow. And put an equally neat picket fence around it. Boggles the mind. My mind, anyway.

Of course it might be a hangover from our English ancestry, 'landscape plotted and pieced', but there they do it so much more prettily, stone walls and hedges of dog-rose and flowering may and hawthorn, like those stone walls the convicts built in my own home country of Illawarra, walls that still meander over the gentle hills, grown with briar and blackberry and mosses and lichens, purposeless now but pleasing to the eye.

My mother, who nurtured an unrequited passion for privacy, used to wish with a fervent hopelessness for a ten foot wall around our little weatherboard cottage, probably to foil her neighbours' patronising glances at the gruel-coloured mess she made of the weekly washing, or perhaps so that she could get to the sentry-box at the end of the yard without having to tack uneasily through a series of deceptive manoeuvres that took her from the clothesline to the woodheap to the vegetable beds to the plot of cannas before—with one wide, wild, shying glance up the hill—she could make a dash for her objective. Later I did achieve the ten foot wall and the privacy she longed for, and very nice and very private

46

it was too and if I could afford it I would reproduce it here in Australian suburbia and make courtyards and fountains and ponds for my selfish pleasure and be damned to the neighbours and the neatness of the street.

But all that has nothing whatever to do with pickets and palings, which don't do a thing for privacy, and are exceedingly ugly to boot. Yes, I know they keep dogs and small children within bounds, but I suggest that toddling children, for whom wandering might be dangerous, are usually under their mothers' surveillance anyway, and not entirely let loose even in their own backyards.

While the destruction of the old paling fence was in progress I was gripped by an evangelical fervour, and standing on our back deck and contemplating the tired and slouching geometry of grey paling fences crossing and criss-crossing all the way up and down the block I thought how splendid it would be if everybody pulled their fences down too, and then all our back doors would be open to one great park. Because, between us all, we do occupy a very great deal of land. If you've ever looked down at suburbia from an aircraft you will have observed just how much land is occupied by the average suburban block and just how pointlessly it is cut up into useless front lawns and fenced backyards when it might be used, collectively, for the recreation and pleasure of everybody. And if you are going to protest that such a scheme would be inviting prowlers and burglars, whenever did a slumped paling fence keep them out? Even I can scale a normal paling fence with comparative ease.

I don't see either that individuality need be sacrificed. Every householder could still plant as he pleased, although it would be even better if we had a communal reafforestation scheme under the guidance of a professional nursery gardener. We could even, communally, build a swimming pool. Every block in this area shares enough land for there to be a pool to every block. Collectively, every block could afford it, and collectively afford its upkeep too.

Well, maybe I'm being carried away by my own vision splendid. But I don't see why not. American housing estates do without fences and householders still manage to be private. There are even some Sydney suburbs where fences are the exception rather than the rule, and these are the suburbs where more people grow more trees than anywhere else and very pleasant they are to look at too.

My husband has just reminded me that the richer the household the higher the fence as a rule, and it was an old friend of his who, every Sunday morning, used to fling himself upon the high wrought gates of a neighbouring mansion where the gentry were wont to entertain out of doors, and hang there spread-eagled, crying 'Master! Master! The peasants are starving! The peasants need bread!'

And this in turn reminds me of the Carl Sandburg poem about the fence of a millionaire, through which nothing could enter, he said, but the wind and the rain and death.

And now I will be accused of being gloomy again, and I'm not at all really, only delighted to have pulled down one of my fences, and mad to pull down the rest, and happy to welcome whatever comes in.

THE HUNGRY ONES

In the course of writing this column I get a very great deal of mail. Some of it is cranky, some of it is chiding, some of it is patronising, but most of it is extremely interesting and rewarding, and I am truly sorry that I can't answer all of it or even half of it. These letters are very important to me, not entirely out of gratification, but because they give me an indication of the thoughts and opinions and angers and philosophies of a very wide range of Australian people.

And what is evident is that a very wide range of Australian people are as baffled, uneasy, and profoundly perturbed as I am about the probable future of the human race. Not just the Australian race. The human race.

Among my mail too there is always a bewildering variety of periodicals and pamphlets offering a bewildering variety of cures for the ills of the human race, everything from drastic surgery to faith-healing. And of these I would like to talk about two which have impressed me deeply and which I would most earnestly recommend to those of you who are troubled as I am troubled. (I would most earnestly recommend them to the cranks and the complacent too, but I think I would be wasting my time.)

The first is a copy of the second Evatt Memorial Lecture, given by George Ivan Smith, the senior Australian official of the United Nations Secretariat, at Melbourne on 23 January this year. You could, I am sure, get a copy from the United Nations Information Centre.

The second is a publication called 'Hunger', written by Professor Keith Buchanan, Professor of Geography at Victoria University, Wellington, New Zealand, and published by *Outlook*, an independent socialist review which is published bimonthly and is obtainable on bookstalls.

Both of these documents concern themselves with what is concerning so many of us—the global problem of the Haves and Have-nots of the human race—and both of them have clarified for me my own muddy, clouded, and terribly troubled thoughts on the subject, which might be put something like this: yes indeed I do like being a Have, and want to go on being a Have, but I wish every other human being in the world could be a Have too, so I can go on being one with a clear conscience.

From your letters I conclude that a great many of you feel the same way.

I, and you too, I am sure, have often been hungry. Ravenously, beautifully, healthily hungry, and being hungry has been a most agreeable sensation, winning approval from our parents in childhood and our family doctors in adulthood, who have patted us on our heads for our cleverness in having hearty appetites.

Here is a paragraph from 'Hunger':

'One does not really die of inanition after having eaten nothing for four weeks. One dies from diseases that are sometimes dirty, sometimes decent—of tuberculosis, of cholera, of influenza, of rat-bites—after having lived for one, five, maybe thirty-five years on millet, on maize, on manioc, on black beans and bacon, and after having picked up on the way one of the deficiency diseases in which chronic hunger disguises itself and which make man feeble-minded, feeble-bodied, blind, impotent, and easy prey to microbes and parasites.'

That, of course, is the way half, or even two-thirds, of the peoples in the world feel hunger and nobody pats them on their heads for it. In fact the Haves of the affluent world, the other world, upbraid them and rebuke them, and lecture them on the criminal folly of their procreative recklessness in producing more mouths to feed. They ought not and must not go on reproducing themselves so lavishly, and if they insist on doing so the Haves are quite entitled to wash their hands of them, or go even further and restrain by force any attempt by the furious and frustrated Have-nots to claim their share of the earth's abundance.

50

(Here I must interpolate. The post has just arrived and in it is a letter for me, signed 'A Stranger in His Own Country'. It is about the desirability of fences, and reads in part: 'It was the worst day's work the Australian Govt. ever done was to let the sliprails down. And now I read that a stupid b—— in Canberra is trying to let in a Horde of Asiatics and Spaniards ... The Greek wog will eat anything he'd even eat —— [I don't think these pages would print that word] ... I say keep the fences up and keep the scrubbers out. If your fences are down the mongrel Adriatic mediterranean —— [that word again] get in and then you only mongrelise the Pure Bred British stock from whence we sprung ... the aggressive ignorant illiterate half-educated Alien Wog B—— is taking over ... the Dirty Greek Wog would even give you B.O. that's the only thing they would give ... Australian boys fight [in Vietnam] & Wog B—— stays behind and makes a lot of babies.' Etc. Etc. Etc. As I said, my mail is very interesting.)

Makes a lot of babies. I must admit that I too have been something mesmerised (both Professor Buchanan and George Ivan Smith used that word) by the exploding population of the earth, and have found it very difficult to see beyond the terrifying multiplication of human mouths howling for their daily bread. Yet a high density population does not necessarily equate with hunger. England has a high density population. So does Japan. So does tiny Holland. (So, for that matter, does Kings Cross.) Nor is the earth anywhere near the stage when it will be necessary to put up a House Full sign. The problem lies in the capacity of the earth to feed the human beings on it, and Professor Buchanan suggests that it is not the earth that is niggardly, but civilised man.

The earth is still being used only partially. It would be possible, with present scientific skills and agricultural techniques, to add millions and millions of acres of cultivable land to the world's potential larder, with improved irrigation to grow two or three crops a year in monsoonal Asia instead of single crops, with improved seed and fertilisers to double or treble crops in other areas. Israel, whose carrying capacity of people was officially estimated by the British at 600 000, now supports five times that number, by virtue of massive input of money and sophisticated scientific techniques.

'It is just not possible,' Professor Buchanan says, 'to estimate the effect of the diversion into peacetime uses of the scientific manpower being prostituted by each great power in the perfecting of weapons of destruction or of the $133 billion being spent by the world on military hardware and personnel.' A world which can litter heaven with the remains of its satellites can afford to put a meal into every hungry mouth.

And George Ivan Smith says: 'I believe that we have to now widen the dimension so that in our thinking, specifically in our schooling, and also in our economic planning, we operate within the framework of the world unit. The aim has to be the development of man himself, irrespective of his race or place on earth.'

'I feel challenged,' he says. 'I feel that we have the possibility of the new earth. And it does not matter how brilliant we are technically, how superbly we boost our production, how well and how quickly we develop our *own* standards of life in Western countries. This could be a pyrrhic victory unless at the same time we have the matching purpose, the matching skill, the matching vision and imagination to do the same in the field of human rights and human development the world over.

'Because the dogmas of the quiet past are inadequate to the stormy present and we, too, should disenthrall ourselves.'

GURU TO YOU TOO

Well well. So they're all back from the magic mountains after a crash course in very public meditation, and Mia is reported to be not so serene after all, and Ringo, who seems to be an honest fellow, says that the Maharishi's set-up is the biggest Butlin's in the world, and one wonders what on earth any of them really got out of it. Apart from the Maharishi, that is, who obviously got a bit more burnish on his already quite luminous charisma and adeal of extremely valuable publicity.

Meditation is, of course, not a particularly recent discovery, and has always been fashionable with the eccentric few. The mystics and quasi-mystics, from Nostradamus through Rasputin and Krishnamurti and Madame Blavatsky right on to Henry Miller, have always had an enthusiastic, and sometimes fanatic, following. But there's never been such a run on the transcendental as there is presently. Meditation is a must—not only for the great, and near-great, the merely rich, the cranks and faddists—but also for quite ordinary people who live in ordinary houses in ordinary streets and occupy themselves with ordinary things like earning a living and cooking the dinner and supervising the kids' homework and planning garden beds and annual holidays and worrying about their tax assessments and all that. Nowadays the swamis have swarmed the suburbs and any housewife with a kink that way may contort her obligatory leotards into any number of extraordinary positions and burn incense too and thrillingly invoke Krishna and engage in all sorts of novel exercises of the body and the mind to the end of apprehending the ineffable, which is now, apparently, more apprehensible than it used to be, or, at least, is being spread around further.

Oh, jewel in the lotus! One can imagine these nice ordinary

thoroughly materialistic people meditating, but what do they meditate *on*? I'm sure that big brass like the Beatles and Mia have equally big things on their minds, things that might be worth rumination, like royalties and contracts and publicity and managers and agents and where the next million is coming from and whether their meditation gear is really becoming and their profiles tilted to the right angles and their expressions properly contemplative, but most of us lot are reduced, by reason of our more limited circumstances, to pettier considerations. I suspect that it is quite different to stand on your head, even in leotards, and invoke Krishna with the adequate amount of ecstasy while wondering at the same time whether you've left the iron switched on or if you'll have time to nip in to the butcher between class and the time school gets out and you have to pick up the kids: actually I think I would feel silly.

I've talked with my husband quite a lot about mysticism and gurus and tulkus and swamis and all, since he has been to the places where such people are bred most prolifically, like India and Tibet and the Himalayas and Persia and the Zen monasteries in Japan and the Brown Derby in Hollywood, and he's stayed in really remote lamaseries and chatted up a Living Buddha and watched an Indian holy man be buried alive and cemented down and dug up a week later none the worse although a bit dirtier, and what he says is that you can't get within cooee of a really devout and dedicated mystic because the ones who are in it for real and not just for a living have made themselves so remote and inaccessible that they have become more rumour than actual. He says that as he understands it the essence of the matter is renunciation of the material and physical, and absolute solitude. He says that real mystics are not, in any way, evangelical. In fact they are thoroughly self-centred and selfish and so concerned with their own individual absorption into the ultimate that they haven't the time or the need to gather up disciples.

I confess to being out of my depth on this subject, never having met a mystic in the flesh (or out of the flesh, which they are supposed to be), although I was quite potty about *The Razor's*

Edge in my youth, and I once knew an American boy named Steve who always wore black gloves and was such a passionate meditator (with incense and all the trimmings) that he forgot to eat and finally became quite transparent and disappeared: what was peculiar was that our eighteenth century map of Tartary disappeared with him. I would not have thought it a reliable guide in his spiritual wanderings.

I am probably out of my depth too because I have an outrageous liking for life. To be in order not to be is not to me a viable proposition. As far as I know I am. And if I have an embodied soul it is probably embodied for some good reason. Our poor human bodies have been so maligned and abused and despised and disregarded in our quest for sanctity that one wonders why, if the seekers of spirituality are right, we were afflicted with such encumbrances in the first place. We would have been saved so many misadventures if we had been born angels from the beginning and had never been burdened with those desires and appetites that cause us so much trouble and are resisted only with pain and peril.

I can't believe that the human body is an irrelevance or somehow inferior to the human spirit, and I am quite happy to accept the human condition on the terms I was born into it. Anyway I wouldn't want to transcend it until I've explored it thoroughly the way it is and one lifetime doesn't seem to be long enough even for that.

Transcending the human condition means, I think, escaping it, and why ever would one want to do that, unless one's human condition was indeed so utterly miserable that oblivion would seem preferable in comparison. I know that it is true for some unfortunates on earth, but I would doubt if it were true for the Beatles and Mia or even the faddists and followers of fashion who are pursuing The Ultimate Reality with such ardour and zeal. I wonder what would happen if they applied an equivalent amount of ardour and zeal to the business of being alive, here, now, in the flesh as well as the spirit.

Arthur Koestler, who has explored these spiritual matters quite earnestly (if mordantly—some of his comments on the physical control of the body are funny enough to make you split) has come to the conclusion that man is mad and is in the process of opting out of existence. He says also that man's highest capacity is self-transcendence, or unselfishness. And I wonder if that's what holiness really is. Unselfishness and sweetness of spirit and kindness. And to achieve unselfishness and sweetness of spirit and kindliness is it necessary to deny our physical selves or pretend they do not exist? That is like saying it would have been better if the world had never existed, or existed without consciousness, and that seems like spitting in the eye of God.

As for meditation, I doubt if it is really necessary to be a private anchorite on a pillar or a public one in the Maharishi's spiritual Butlin's camp, or even to attend suburban classes to get with Krishna.

I know a gentle and kind old man who grows flowers and goes fishing from the end of a jetty every weekend, and he meditates quite a lot on the way things are and the way they might be. He says it is good to watch things growing and living and moving and breathing. It gives you faith in life, he says, and you need faith in life as you get towards the end of it. You wouldn't want to think it had all been for nothing.

MORE ON THE LONELY ONES

My divorced bachelor friend, of whom I wrote a couple of weeks ago, has unwittingly stirred up more response than he ever dreamed of.

Or that I ever dreamed of, either. There are letters not only from the lonely divorced, but from lonely young widows, lonely not-so-young widows, lonely widowers, and lonely pensioners. And all of them feel that to be alone is to be a social pariah. Not one of them is alone from choice, but every one of them has experienced this strange caste-change upon entering into a solitary state. Last week, respectably attached to the other half of a pair, you were socially acceptable. Even desirable. This week, amputated of your social Siamese twin, you have become an embarrassment. Almost a freak.

Curiouser and curiouser.

'What can you expect,' writes one of my correspondents, 'of a society which treats its old people as lepers and any pensioner as having lower status?'

She pleads the case of the older widow, left without what my grandmother used to call 'means', willing and eager to supplement her income but prevented by law from doing so. She does not want to be the 'Poor Mrs So-and-so' that society has decided is her only role. She believes that she, and other widows like her, have a future where they might fulfil earlier ambitions—education, travel, training of some kind to hold down a job other than domestic chores for another housewife.

'What really hurts most,' she writes, 'is the lack of compassion in our affluent society,' and describes going for advice and help to the section manager in one of the departments concerned with housing. The moment she said she had come to discuss her financial position she was told curtly that he 'didn't want to hear about my problems: he had enough of his own.'

She loves books and music, and one imagines from her letter that she is a lady with intellectual resources, but she is also human, and feminine to boot, and presently feeling utterly deprived of any sort of recreation or sheer frivolity. Theatres are expensive. Dining out is expensive. And in any case what woman really relishes dining out and going to a theatre alone, even if she can afford it?

Another letter from a young widow endorses this. She says friends are prodigal in their love and sympathy in the first weeks of bereavement, but when the bereaved makes a great brave effort to carry on with the business of living the love and sympathy changes into a comfortable 'Oh, she's marvellous; doesn't need anybody' sort of attitude, and after a while the widow finds that it is just as well she made the brave effort to carry on alone, because alone is what she is going to be. The love and sympathy, turned on at the conventional time, is now turned off, as if nobody had the imagination, or could be bothered to make the effort, to adapt attitudes to circumstances or to accept other human beings as being whole even when inconveniently unstuck from the socially undemanding twosome.

The young widow, thus relegated to limbo, has to make do with morning coffee sessions, ladies' luncheons, P&C meetings, and the attentions of the husbands of her best friends who take to dropping in while their own wives and children are on holiday, all in the spirit of the kindliest concern, naturally, and more than willing to alleviate her loneliness for the period of their own partner's absence.

This particular young widow, now verging, she says, on the middle-aged widow, has gone through every stage of bewilderment, outrage, anger, resentment, wounded vanity, hurt pride, and bitter loneliness, and has been strong enough and enduring enough (maybe stubborn enough) to come out of it with her individuality finely forged and tempered and pretty well unbreakable. But one imagines that she sometimes quirks an ironic eyebrow at social mores, and deliberates very carefully before she issues an invitation or accepts one.

What *is* the matter with us in our inadequate social patterning? Does it all go back to the fact that we have no strong family system, which makes for a strong social system? We have Senior Citizens but never a domestic inglenook for our old folks. No spare bedroom for widowed aunty. No place at the family board for country kin seeking a place in town. We do not willingly take in those of our blood who are sick in body or sick in spirit. We haven't got the room and we haven't got the time and it's all we can do to look out for ourselves. If we feel justified in adopting this attitude towards our own families there seems to be no reason why we should be more considerate towards our inconveniently lonely friends. If we think about it at all we reassure ourselves that people are better off standing on their own two feet anyway.

I have an idea that people need other people, of both sexes and all age groups. Our rigid system of isolating sections of the community into neatly labelled cells—Senior Citizens, Mums and Dads, Young Marrieds, Teenagers, Tots—is so inflexible that there are only the sketchiest lines of communication left open between the existing cells, and none at all for those members of the community who just don't happen to qualify for one of the labels. Unless they set up a cell of their own, that is, and label it Unwanted.

There was an article I read once, but I can't remember where, written by an Indian woman who had gone to live as a child in her maternal grandmother's compound in the provinces. And this compound was a marvellous, busy, brawling, seething organisation of grandparents and parents and uncles and aunts and cousins of every degree, old and young, married and unmarried, and everybody was individual, with individual concerns and ambitions, and everybody was also family, with his place and his duties.

The grandmother used to question the child about England, where the little girl had just come from school, and about the social pattern there. The old matriarch found it quite impossible to believe, for instance, that some aged English ladies lived alone in hotels, and only visited their children and grandchildren on appointed days. 'It is the saddest thing I have ever heard,' she said. And the little girl responded dutifully with, 'Yes, grandmamma, it is very sad for the old people.' 'I wasn't thinking about the old people,' said grandmamma. 'I was thinking about the young ones. How will they ever learn to grow old?'

I was thinking how far that concept of living is from our neat, arid social boxes. I was thinking that in such a warm, companionable, useful, flexible association of human beings nobody could ever possibly be lonely, or neglected, or unwanted. Not even a widow, young or not so young. But while I was thinking that I remembered that it isn't really so very long ago that Indian widows were expected to go up on their husbands' funeral pyres.

Which might have been kinder all round than the treatment meted out to them by our sophisticated society. The divorced and the aged and the lost and the lonely could go up too, and then the rest of us could have our nice cosy dinner parties for six or eight neatly matched couples without ever having to go to the bother of considering our guests as individual people.

ON PLUGGING POETRY

One of the nicest book launchings I have ever been to took place a couple of Sundays ago, on a richly blue Indian summer afternoon in a garden with many very old dark trees—huge ones, camphor laurels and the like—and a cat stalking through the shrubberies, dignified and disdainful.

Book launchings in general are apt to be boring or boozy or both, and you see all the people you saw at the last one and will see at the next one, and you hear a few bits of gossip, and very often you wonder whether anybody besides the author, whose reputation is at stake, and possibly the publisher, whose profits are at stake, gives a damn anyway.

But at this launching, most refreshingly, practically all of the faces were new. And I mean new in more senses than one, because they were so young that their owners had scarcely had time to grow into them yet—indeed some of them were so young it would be difficult to predict what their completed faces might eventually be. There were boys and girls both, and the boys wore degrees of gear and the girls wore their hair shining and their minis with degrees of confidence, and they were grouped about on the lawn under the old dark trees in bright clumps and ragged borders, arranged with such delectable carelessness that you might have thought a really first-class landscape gardener had been brought in especially for the job.

There were also oldies. Triumphantly grinning official oldies getting set to make speeches on the verandah behind the sweetly wrought iron columns and the table piled with congratulatory telegrams. Parental and avuncular oldies, trying to look properly deprecatory and recklessly risking the rheum and worse by sitting on the dampish lawn. Unattached oldies, like me, who had come

61

because they were interested, or to gawp, or just because they had been invited, and were finding themselves being caught up.

There was something very catching up about the whole occasion. After all, those boys and girls modestly shining away in the Sunday garden were poets. Australian poets. And today they were published Australian poets. Poets properly and officially launched in an anthology of their own: *Verse by Young Australians*.

Personally I have never seen so many poets, nor such engaging ones, all together at the same time.

And the officials up on the verandah were entitled to grin triumphantly. They had brought it off against pretty long odds and might justly feel pleased with themselves.

It began in 1965, when the Australian Council for Child Advancement held a poetry competition throughout Australia in memory of Dame Mary Gilmore. The competitors ranged from eight to eighteen, and the verses that poured in from all over the country were so overwhelming in number and so exciting in content that a couple of the more zany visionaries of the council (I use the word 'zany' advisedly, since I know them and know that they would be the first to agree) decided that the best of them should be published in book form, for the encouragement of young writers everywhere, for the further honour of Dame Mary Gilmore, and as an anniversary tribute to Henry Lawson, whose hundredth anniversary would fall in 1967, two years away. They had another motive too. They wanted to do it for the sheer pleasure of the thing itself. And a better motive I can't imagine.

The vicissitudes of these outrageously idealistic innocents abroad in the world of commercial publishing through the next couple of years rival the adventures of Don Quixote and Sancho Panza. It took so very long for them to get it into their heads that publishers, these days, are likely to equate the ideal with the ideal profit, and there was no smell of profit about this venture. Poetry is always dubious merchandise, unless it has a brand name so luminous or so fashionable that it is unthinkable that anybody who aspires to be anybody would dare to be missing that particular slim vol on the bookshelves. And how dubious, as merchandise,

62

were the amateur poems of several hundred ordinary Australian schoolchildren? Even in honour of Henry Lawson, or on the remote chance of prodigy turning up among them. Henry Lawson might be deemed to have honour enough, and there is never any need to gamble on prodigies because they're sure to turn up later if they're the real thing, when their talents have matured and are evidently marketable.

You would have thought that disillusion and discouragement would have finished off those starry-eyed believers in youth and poetry and a cultural heritage and all that stuff. But of course it didn't, or there would never have been a book at all, or a book launching on a lovely Sunday afternoon in a lovely Sunday garden with a group of students from the Independent Theatre Drama School to delight us (in the proper sense of the word) with readings from the anthology, readings that combined movement with words with grace with youth with gravity with understanding in a way that made some of us oldies—and me for one—choky a bit and blinky-eyed. How good it is that kids write poetry. And how right it is that they should be encouraged to do so. And to read poetry. And to say poetry.

I have been told by a friend that in London now poetry readings are greater drawcards for youth than theatres or cinemas or art exhibitions. I know that in Canada my friend Leonard Cohen reads his poems to packed thousands. And we all know about Yevtushenko.

Talking about the London phenomenon with my friend I asked him why he thought this was so. And he said: 'Poets are the only people that the young can believe in any more. They are the only people left with souls.'

I don't suppose for a moment that all the young Australians represented in this anthology will become full-time practising poets. I don't think it matters. Perhaps one or two of them will travel that lonely stony heartbreaking high road. But all of them, I believe, will understand something of that road even though they have not the equipment, finally, nor the courage, to take it.

63

I expect I should congratulate the publishers, Rigby Limited, for taking a flier on such a splendid and heart-warming venture. Excepting that I don't think they took a flier in any sense, since I understand they did not accept the book for publication until the Council for Child Advancement could guarantee the sale of enough copies to cover the costs, and I know something about the desperate moneymaking ventures that went on to cover that guarantee.

So I will congratulate the Council for Child Advancement, and I will congratulate the young poets, and I will save my congratulations to the publishers for the day when I see them advertising this anthology and pushing this anthology and making it such a success that we may expect, confidently, that there will be another volume: *More Verse by Young Australians*, and even: *Still More Verse by Young Australians*, until this becomes an annual event in the publishing world.

In the meantime you could all help by buying a copy of this first *Verse by Young Australians*. If only for your own delight.

LONG LIVE DEMOCRACY!

'A democracy,' wrote Aristotle, 'is a state where the freemen and the poor, being in the majority, are invested with the power of the state . . .

'For if liberty and equality, as some persons suppose, are chiefly to be found in a democracy, it must be so by every department of government being alike open to all; but as the people are the majority, and what they vote is law, it follows that such a state must be a democracy.'

I was bound to be nosing around after definitions (and I found this one in volume 7 of the *Encyclopaedia Brittanica*, Daisy-Educational) because a couple of Sundays ago I could have been discovered, rather surprisingly, on the stage of a scungy suburban cinema shouting 'Long Live Democracy!' to some hundreds of people, with absolute fervour, and what's more in Greek. Greek is a much more suitable language than English for fervour.

Now this is not the sort of thing I normally do, but it was a rather emotional evening one way and another, and a lot of other people were letting off steam too. One Australian poet recited Cavafy's 'Waiting for the Barbarians' in English, another Australian poet said 'Aghia Sophia' in Greek, a Greek group sang Australian bush ballads, another group danced Zorba, a very well-known folk singer belted out 'Freedom', another belted out Cuban folk, the lights dazzled, the mike went on the blink, a slide of Melina Mercouri flashed on the screen brought cheers, and one of King Constantine hisses and some cries of 'Pig!' There was bouzouki music (amplified to torture pitch), and sweetly harmonised songs sung cantata-style and unaccompanied. There were also speeches.

It was a grand evening and we all enjoyed ourselves hugely and made a bit of money for the funds of the Committee for the Restoration of Democracy in Greece, although whether our efforts will really contribute anything to restoring democracy in that unhappy country is something else entirely.

There are some who believe that only the outside pressure of world opinion can oust from their seats of power Europe's first military dictators since the war. And certainly the Scandinavian and Benelux countries have already protested vigorously against the supposedly temporary tolerance extended to the colonels by America and Britain. But cynically one feels that the tolerance is more long-term than temporary, and what disapproval has been expressed was never more than token anyway.

Last Saturday was the first anniversary of the colonels' putsch. The tanks rolled in and constitutional government rolled out and no democrat could raise a finger or a voice to stop it. To many Australian Greeks it was a day of mourning, falling as it did on their Easter Saturday, with Christ not yet risen and feasting not yet in order. It was a sad day. Fascism had been tolerated for a whole year, and many felt that the longer it was tolerated the more tolerable it would become to the western world. Even token disapproval would very likely diminish with time, and it would even be possible that the colonels could be transformed into respected ornaments of the 'free world'. Such things have happened before.

To simple-minded people like me it seems that such things ought not to happen. Nations which declare themselves pledged to safeguard the principles of democracy, individual liberty and the rule of the law, should, in my view, honour their pledges. Or declare openly for fascism if that's what they intend to support anyway. They might even have some arguments in favour of fascism that would be worth considering. Like Hitler built good autobahns, and Mussolini drained the Pontine Marshes. And the colonels have cleared up the festering corruption of Greek bureaucracy.

But is that enough? And is it even true? Why should one believe that the representatives of the new regime are somehow more resistant to bribery than those of the old? And did nepotism really die with democracy? Some reports coming out (I am presently reading one from Gordian Troeller and Claude Deffarge, two reporters from *Der Stern*, the mass-circulation West German weekly) suggest that the promised economic revival is a figment of propaganda. Many factories, they say, have in fact had to shut down night and holiday shifts, and there has been a big jump in unemployment. Also, prices have gone up.

Other reports, it is true, would have us believe that it is all for the best in the long run. I can't accept that any regime whose power rests on soldiers, police, stool pigeons, informers, intimidation and torture is for the best. Anywhere.

Troeller and Deffarge report that at the beginning of the last school term 6000 children were rejected from enrolling at their schools because their parents had left-wing pasts. Civil servants don't get jobs without signing loyalty oaths, or keep them if their relatives are politically active. Pressure is applied to anyone who visits a 'left-wing' doctor for treatment or consults a suspected lawyer. Those who hold the Greek flag in too much honour to display it compulsorily on holy days and colonels' days end up in gaol.

To me all this reeks with an old, familiar, and extremely nasty smell. And I think it is too high a price for a proud people to pay for a bureaucratic clean-up. If the clean-up has, in fact, taken place. Even too high a price for the west to pay for a conservative, client state. At least I think that prolonged toleration of fascism is too high a price to pay, but then, as I said, I am rather simple-minded.

In a new book by Stephen Rousseas and others, *The Death of a Democracy: Greece and the American Conscience*, Rousseas quotes six Italian economists, who say, in part: 'How is it possible for any army which is part of NATO to suppress that very freedom it is supposed to defend, without as much as losing its good standing within the structure of NATO? We have always believed that NATO was designed to defend us from tyranny, but episodes such as this cannot fail to erode our trust in NATO and the United States.' Ah well. Perhaps the six Italian economists are simple-minded too.

I think though, about condoning fascism, or condoning intimidation, or condoning torture, or condoning any infringement of the civil liberties of people capable of governing themselves constitutionally, for whatever the reason the toleration is extended, that it is rather like the story of Saint Denis, who walked three leagues with his head under his arm. A great lady, puzzled by this feat, asked her priest how it was possible for the saint, headless, to walk so far. And the priest said: 'Madame, it is, after all, only the first step that counts.'

And the German people, once, walked all the way to the gas ovens.

And I say, 'Long Live Democracy!' in any damn language I can get my tongue round.

THE VOICE OF THE PEOPLE

Probably the people, who are politely called the-man-in-the-street these days instead of hoi polloi or the great unwashed as they used to be, have never had more opportunities to use their individual voices since the days of the assemblies of citizens on the slopes of the Pnyx.

This, of course, is very proper and desirable in a democratic country, and we should be grateful to mass communications for making it possible for the widest variety of individual citizens to have their say on the current and controversial issues affecting them.

And have their say they do. There can be no doubt that it is the authentic voice of the people we hear on radio two-way sessions, in television snap opinion polls, and, through print, in our newspaper columns. What the young people think, what the old people think, what the workers think and the ladies who wash whitest and brightest, as well as union bosses, shire councillors, politicians, model girls, managers of palatial clubs, sports enthusiasts, and other such distinguished folk.

But what do the people think? This, to me, is the heart of the mystery, because I've never yet been able to find out. The people, as people, often seem quite pleased to have their opinion sought, and indeed the radio ringer-uppers volunteer theirs with almost indecent alacrity. And politicians, union bosses, shire councillors and others in authority smile frank and manly smiles to match their frank and manly voices, so you can tell how open and honest they are when answering questions. But how often, in fact, do you hear anybody say anything that has a real meaning, or produce a sentence that embodies a real idea?

I wonder why this is so, since it appears to be a national trait.

I mean, you see television programmes from America where student opinion, say, is canvassed, and the kids tell you what they think clearly and articulately, and you can say to yourself: 'Ah, so that's what that kid thinks about that issue,' or: 'You little punk,' or even: 'That one ought to have his head read.' But you're never in any doubt about the nature of the opinion.

Perhaps that is a wrong example to choose, since, in fairness, our own student body is, in fact, more generally articulate than any other section of the community, although the Governor-General had a few words to say himself on this matter at Sydney University recently, and expressed himself most articulately on the deplorable lack of articulate expression in society—even educated society.

I suppose I really should leave politicians out of this too, because they may very well have their own good reasons for saying absolutely nothing in absolute gobbledegook. Their real opinions, one imagines, are so impenetrably shrouded in secrecy that they probably need a set of pass keys or magic spells to even get at them themselves. And this would be necessary, I should think, if a politician is to keep up the frank and manly smile and the frank and manly words that mean absolutely nothing but which must be true because he just heard himself say them.

Perhaps there is a national conspiracy to keep all real opinion well battened down in the dark places where it can't pop up and frighten the complacent citizenry. Certainly there is a national language for public utterance that bears no resemblance to the language people use between themselves. It is a very soothing and reassuring language and well suited to disguise any meaning that might just creep through. People do not go from one place to another: they proceed. Instead of thinking things they muffle them up in their estimation, whatever that may be. Poker machines turn into facilities. Matters are not ended but brought to completion, or rather, it is confidently expected that they will be brought to completion in the not too far distant future. Could you imagine anybody saying in public anything as simple as: 'I am poor and live in a slum.'? No. No. He might be poor and

70

live in a slum, but publicly he is an underprivileged member of the community residing in a substandard dwelling.

I thought a hundred examples of this kind would trip off my typewriter keys. Heaven knows I've listened to enough. But obviously I don't really know the public language, because the words elude me, and I think they elude me because it is so difficult to get at the meaning of them that I must just blank out. And I suspect that that is what I am intended to do, in case I should stumble over an actual opinion.

It is possible, of course, that I am really a complete outsider, and the people understand the voice of the people perfectly well. I am reminded that one day in the saloon bar of 'The Antelope' in London, I listened in fascination to two chappish sort of chaps, with thousand-hour moustaches and brawny speckled tweeds, conduct a woofling conversation in which no sentence was ever completed and no single idea expressed. But at the end of half an hour they were in perfect accord and had apparently come to an entirely satisfactory agreement on the sale of a second-hand car. At least that's what I think it was about; I did overhear every word, after all.

Perhaps something like that operates here, and if I study the public language diligently enough I may be able to understand what people are saying. I have managed to cotton on to the language of the commercials. The words don't mean anything either, but the message comes through quite clearly: whatever product is being advertised is not only the best but indispensable to anyone who is not to be pilloried as a complete hick, moron, or downright imbecile.

But I think that is rather different from the-man-in-the-street committing himself publicly to an opinion. Because it would be a truly dreadful thing if he committed himself to the wrong one. He would be exposed as un-typical, un-average, actually un-Australian, and certainly unworthy of the benefits of this most golden of all golden lands, young and glorious, where decency prevails and mateship flourishes and there is a fair go for the underdog and an even fairer go for the upperdog and the upper

71

the dog gets the fairer the go, which is probably as it should be in a properly egalitarian society.

Yes, perhaps it is wise to keep one's opinions to oneself. Safer, anyway. At least until one is sure one's opinions are not running counter to the opinions of one's peers. By expressing, publicly, a belief or a conviction or an idea that is original one might find oneself in the unhappy position of being expected to lead rather than follow, and wouldn't that upset the even tenor of the great way of life and really muck up the weekends.

My elder son was in the habit of approaching me each morning with an imaginary microphone and mordantly saying: 'Please make an opinion, Miss Clift,' and by golly I did, out of devilment and to keep in practice. But I shan't any more. I'm practising saying nothing now. This article is my first real exercise, and if any hint of any real opinion of mine has crept through it's only because I'm not very good at it yet. I will improve. And eventually I too will be able to speak with the authentic voice of the people.

THE THINGS I
CANNOT CHANGE

His name is Bailey. He is the father of nine children and there is a tenth due any day. He is a Canadian, and in his youth he was a seaman cook and he travelled a lot, North America and South America and England and the ports of the Mediterranean. He liked the life and presently is a bit nostalgic for it.

And fair enough too. Because he's caught. He married his girl and she has borne him nine children and is big with the tenth, and all those children have to be fed and clothed. They all live in an upstairs apartment that you couldn't call a slum exactly. The walls are peeling but all the requisite furniture is there and the television and the refrigerator and the cooker and all the children sleep in beds, doubling up most of them, and have coats and shoes to wear to school. The baby is bathed in the washing-up sink and the kids wash their faces and hands there before meals and Bailey himself scrubs up there every morning and even manages to shampoo his hair. It could be much worse. There are lots of people who don't have running water at all.

This is a film I am writing about, called *The Things I Cannot Change*, and it is made by the National Film Board of Canada in collaboration with the Special Planning Secretariat of the Privy Council Office, directed by Tanya Ballantyne, and due to be released at the fifteenth Sydney Film Festival this month. My information is that it will be released about the same time in Melbourne, and I hope like mad that this is so.

And I hope this like mad because it is the sort of film we could make here if we were brave enough, and the sort of film I can't imagine us making here. Not officially, anyway. Because officially we don't admit to poverty, and if we made such a film unofficially, for a television channel, say, I suspect it would turn out sensational. The poverty the Baileys live with and in isn't sensational at all. The film isn't sensational. You, the audience, just move in and live with them for an hour (which covers an actual period of three weeks), and have your heart torn to shreds by ordinary human struggle and hope and resignation and despair, and somehow, at the end of an hour, you leave the Baileys with the conviction of human courage and dignity and love. Because with all the poverty, and all the distress, the ten children are beautiful and healthy and loved and alive, and you couldn't wish one of them not to be, not even to erase one of the pain lines on the face of their patient, enduring, classic, eternal mother. She is forty years old and simply is.

I don't know what her problem was about contraception, but her husband says that if he had seventy-five dollars he would ask to be sterilised. And yet he loves his children passionately, and in a sort of way you feel that they are, finally, the measure of his accomplishment.

He has a little text on the wall that says something like this: 'God grant me the courage to accept the things I cannot change, to change the things I can, and the wisdom to know the difference.' That's not right exactly, but the meaning is.

He doesn't work as a cook any more, but he often cooks for the family, and you see him delicately and precisely and professionally cutting vegetables into the stew-pot on one of his many days without work. They get stale bread from a Catholic welfare organisation, and he says sure he accepts handouts but he isn't going to hock the television or the refrigerator or the furniture because he bought those and worked for those and paid for those. He is a docker these days, only these days there aren't enough days when there is work for him. But he always hopes. You see him down there in the morning pick-up, waiting.

He is just cocky enough, has just enough bravado, just enough stubbornness, just enough assertiveness, to keep him going, but when he is involved in a fight with a man who owes him six dollars, and when he is pleading with the police not to arrest him, he cries, and I swear that you will cry too, with the dreadful humiliation of human dignity, with the fear of separation from the family that is his only *raison d'être*. And with loss. Utter loss.

Living camera isn't new, and it has been used with powerful effect before. But I have never seen such a total intrusion into a private world before. That fight could not possibly have been staged, or that fear acted. And when the tenth baby is born it is born before your eyes and to see it opening its own eyes for the first time is a miracle.

Now, how this was done I haven't the faintest idea. But I do think it would be marvellous if we were doing it too, although I can't imagine that we ever would. Not straight and honest like that. I think we are still too jealous of the precious image of land-of-sunshine-hope-and-joy-with-opportunities-for-every-girl-and-boy, and all that.

I have a book by me that was produced by the Commonwealth Government of Australia in 1962. It is called *Australian Profile* and it has a ducky slip cover and I think it is one great glossy sell from beginning to end. If I were a migrant and I had been hooked on this book I would be shaking with wrath to find the reality so different from the shiny come-on.

And yet Canada attracts more migrants than we do, and apparently feels she can afford the luxury of complete honesty about the way some of her citizens live. There must be thousands of Baileys in Australia as well as Canada, thousands in England too, and thousands in America. I was thinking of *Cathy Come Home* but I don't think the comparison is fair because *Cathy* was manufactured and *The Things I Cannot Change* is for real.

I do hope you can see this film because it is inspiring in a simple human way that we might be forgetting about. There weren't ten kids in my family but only three, and yet I recognised the Baileys and the Baileys' way of life, where the daily bread is the real importance of the day, and to eat is an act of grace and you scrub and wash for it under the kitchen tap. (I don't know about the Baileys, but we only bathed once a week when the laundry copper was heated up and syphoned off.) And if we didn't say grace at that family meal it was only because we were all heathens. We felt it. Grace, I mean.

It was probably wrong, or careless, of the Canadian Baileys to make ten children. And yet who could deny them, as a man and a woman, this beautiful produce, or the physical love and comfort of each other. What else do a man and a woman have, finally, apart form the Holden, I mean, and the architect-designed suburban house that *Australian Profile* assures me is typical, and maybe a cocktail bar in Spanish leather, and charge accounts at the biggest department stores, and the club in the evenings.

I think, as a country, we go on with a lot of childish cover-up nonsense about our great way of life. It's silly really, because actual people living actual lives are so much more interesting. In the Baileys' case, inspiring even. Anyway, see the film if you can, and let's all hope that one day we can make one even half as good ourselves.

DEMOCRACY LAID LOW

This column almost didn't get written because I am sick. And not, alas, romantically sick, although I have taken to the sofa and piled myself around and about with all the most brilliant and beautiful Cretan and Macedonian rugs and cushions I own, and installed my kitten Jeoffrey since I don't have a 'my dog Flush'.

But what is the use of trying to play Elizabeth Barrett when your hair is clinging to your face in sweaty rats' tails and your skin is as clammy as wet dough and your mouth is dried out and peeling with fever and you feel so bruised and aching that even the kitten's little weight is much too much: besides, the kitten wants to play and you don't? And anyway who would relish the entertainment of distinguished literary gentlemen (even if any were likely to call) with a streaming nose and a mucky bubbling chest and the embarrassing suspicion that you might not, in any case, actually smell very good?

So in this condition my head isn't clear enough or my resolution strong enough to tackle the subject I had in mind. I had intended, this week, to write a follow-up on a piece I did a couple of weeks ago on the question of the restoration of democracy in Greece. Or, rather, I wanted to write about the response to that piece, which to my mind was quite curious.

Now it would not have surprised me at all if whole numbers of Australian Greeks had written to attack me, rebuke me, castigate me, or even instruct me—poor ignorant woman that I am—on the complicated machinery of the Greek political system and the desirability of the present regime. In fact I half expected something like that.

But what happened was that the only attacks, rebukes,

castigations and instructions came from Australians. Australian Australians I mean, born and bred in democracy, schooled in democracy, sworn to uphold the principles of democracy, individual liberty, constitutional government, freedom of speech and the right of dissent until death do them part from such notions. Sworn, in fact, to choose death rather than part from such notions.

Curiouser and curiouser. What on earth can they mean? Do they mean, these irate democrats who rebuke me, that democracy is the prerogative of the affluent and complacent and much too good for poor foreigners? Or do they mean they are afraid their affluence and complacence might stand in jeopardy unless buttressed against communism by fascism? Or are they really saying that they thoroughly approve of fascism anyway? Anywhere? Here, for instance?

But I feel much too sick to nut it out so I will save it for another time, although I loved the outraged letter from the gentlemen who asked me if I belonged to any organisation for the restoration of democracy in Russia. No sir, I don't, knowing the complete futility of attempting to restore what never was, but I don't belong to any organisation for the restoration of serfdom either, so you can be easy about my Slavic activities.

Anyway, presently my activities are confined to a little desultory reading and watching the goggle-box as well as I can through the peculiar still-life arrangements that have accumulated on the kitchen table since my sickness.

(I must explain here that in sickness I am cunning, and install myself in a public part of the house, partly so that I won't miss out on anything interesting—which I can't bear—partly so that I can still supervise activities to a certain extent, and partly so that I am under everybody's noses and they can't forget about me or how sick I am and how necessary it is to pay me little attentions. There are disadvantages to this policy, of course, because some of the things I don't miss out on I would gladly not know about, and being sick I am at the mercy of anyone and everyone who feels like exerting a little authority over my helplessness. Why do people think that because you are sick you must also of necessity be either infantile or imbecile?)

However, I was watching this television programme out of bleary eyes that have grown piggy and dim (I know, because I took one look in the mirror and burst into tears and made them piggier than ever), and it was all about present scientific investigations into the workings of the human brain, and weighty prognostications as to the possible future application of the discoveries being made. The prognostications were horrific.

For instance it was suggested, on the basis of these discoveries, that in future the faculty of memory could be so greatly enlarged and enhanced that schools would be literally unnecessary. You would take a learning pill instead. It was also suggested that the success or competitive drive could be so stimulated that any fairly bright child, by a course of drug treatment, could be success-oriented and examination-oriented to an extent that would satisfy the most ruthlessly ambitious parents (who, I suppose, would be responsible for ordering the drug treatment). It was suggested that a quarrelling or nagging spouse could be made docile and tractable to order (whose order?). It was suggested that the instinct of aggression could be manipulated at will. Ah, but whose will? Who would have the choosing of the meek and the violent? How many Frankensteins are these bland scientific gentlemen blandly creating? And what will happen if they get loose?

The only experiment that to me was not fraught with the utmost peril was one in which man is practising the control of his own brain rhythms. I haven't read anything on brain rhythms since W. Grey Walter's *Living Brain* was published in 1953, but I was a bit hooked on the subject for a while, and it was fascinating to see on the box this girl student actually turning on alpha rhythms on request. Alpha, as I understand it, is the rhythm that scans for pattern, and we all fall into types according to its activity— visual types, non-visual types, and the big bulk of in-betweeners. What they didn't say was whether alpha is the only one they can control yet. And I was thinking that it would be marvellous if, instead of being controlled by somebody else, we could each control our very own selves. Literal self-control, and the dignity of being able to handle one's anxieties and fears and frustrations all by oneself in one's very own head, instead of shrieking for help from the nearest psychiatrist.

Or maybe that is fraught with peril too.

Anyway, it's all a long way off, and the clever scientific gentlemen have a lot of experimenting still to do before we become supermen or zombies either.

In the meantime, and quite personally, I wonder, when they are all so clever and can do such marvellous things, why they can't take a few minutes off one day to whip up some little old preventive drug for common ordinary miserable stinking aching sweating smelly influenza?

THE BORROWERS

When my children were much younger they had an enchanting series of books by Mary Norton about some little people called the Borrowers.

Like all the best children's books these chronicles of the Borrowers were really much too good for children and I came to believe unquestioningly in the existence of Arrietty and Homily and Pod and Hendreary and the other wee people who inhabit nooks and crannies in very old houses and furnish their apartments with such serviceable items as they can borrow—thimbles and cotton reels and snuffboxes and matchboxes too, and paper fasteners and thumb tacks and hairpins, and all those other small homely articles that are constantly disappearing in any establishment.

Wherever I have lived there have always been Borrowers living too, otherwise there is no accounting for the quantity of little useful things that vanish.

I have never minded for a moment (or not for more than a moment anyway) about these little acquisitive people. But there is another race of Borrowers, of normal adult size, disarmingly friendly in appearance, quite winning in their ways, apparently trustworthy, and these are the sort that bother me. Because they get off with books and records, and the books and records never come back. At least the same books and records don't come back, although sometimes one is landed with quite different ones, borrowed, I suppose, from somebody else entirely, while one's own precious possessions are being lent out further along the line.

I do not want two copies of Elizabeth Jane Howard's *The Sea Change* or an extra volume of Pausanius, but I do want my own

Will Durant, and my nice edition of *Madame Bovary*, and the Edith Piaf record and the Nana Mouskouri special and the only copy of the American edition of my own novel and my cook books and George Johnston says he wants, and rather desperately, the only copy he has left of *Journey Through Tomorrow*, which is long out of print and the only record he has of his Asian journeyings. Oh, and I want the Tom Lehrer record too.

I know that the simple solution to the problem of the Borrowers is never to lend. I can't understand why it is so difficult to stick to such a simple resolution, but all the incorrigible lenders I know are weak-minded about it. One could say, of course, that one wants to share one's pleasures and enjoyments, but I suspect that the process is actually more complicated than that. And just as there has to be a Susannah for the elders, and a murderee for every murderer, so there have to be lenders for borrowers. A fatal attraction exists.

I admit to having done a fair bit of borrowing myself in my time. I have borrowed money, and clothes, and cups of sugar and flour and half-pints of milk and just a couple of spoons of tea, and books and records too, and sewing patterns, and once, shamefully, I borrowed a saucepan from a little peasant lady who had a large family and presumably needed all her saucepans, and I kept that saucepan for ten months instead of simply buying one for myself. I was so guilty that I flinched every time I passed the lady's house, and I took to avoiding her in the market place, but I hung on to her battered old saucepan as if my life depended on it: for some reason it was the most desirable utensil in the world and I doubt if I could have cooked two boiled eggs in anything else.

The lady must have been a born lender herself because she seemed terribly surprised when I finally gave her saucepan back, and oddly enough once I had given it back and bought a new one I never missed the old and to this day have no idea what exactly was the fatal fascination of such an undistinguished piece of kitchen equipment.

I am only telling this story to show that I am anything but

a Simon Pure in the borrowing business, and could even show little Arrietty a couple of points on the borrowing of useful articles for housekeeping.

But books are different, especially when they are out of print, and records are different too, especially when they are rare, and I think both borrowers and lenders should adopt a more scrupulous attitude, or make a new set of rules.

The trouble is that when you live in a sizeable family, where every single individual member is a lender by nature, it is very difficult to keep track of all the books on all the shelves and all the records in all the sleeves. Did one only lend it out upstairs, or did one of that lot upstairs lend it out of the house? It is missing, but who has it? And when did it go?

Now when I was a little girl every single book on our bookshelves had its appointed place on the shelves, every single record stayed in its album. My parents did not lend. Neither did they borrow, not even the odd cup of sugar or a few fishhooks or a screwdriver or a half loaf of bread until the baker called.

So I do not know from where I inherited this reckless instinct or compulsion to press on the merest acquaintances possessions which are actually precious to me, nor why I should pass it on to my own children in an even more reckless form. Maybe I had some ancestor who was glad-handed to the point of sheer dottiness. In fact there are tales about my great-grandfather, who was said to have given away all the furniture, even to the grand piano, and to have lent all his money out on no security whatever, and to have died in a bare house by setting his beard alight to keep his chest warm.

I have no intention of going as far as that, although indeed I have leant out furniture more than once, mostly because I had no place to put it, and rugs if they didn't happen to suit my colour scheme, and paintings I wanted to have a rest from, and money when I had it, and clothes if somebody else really needed them or wanted them. (Money's different too: I think actually you have to give that never expecting to get it back: or lend it to people you don't like so that you'll be rid of them for good and all.)

But please please whoever has those records and those books will you return them, even to confirmed lenders like us who probably deserve to be stripped of every valuable or sentimental volume and disc we own. Or did own.

I swear for the hundredth time that I am going to buy a big exercise book and rule it out in columns and label it 'The Borrowers' and be meticulous from now on about entering names and dates and titles.

And whoever brought back *The Dove of Ishtar* can take it back to whatever other crazy lender lent it. We would like *Journey Through Tomorrow* instead.

A MATTER OF CONSCIENCE

The case of conscientious objector Simon Townsend, brought to public attention while indignation still seethes in at least some democratic breasts over the attempt to turn ordinary citizens into pimps, is making a great many people sit down (or sit up) and have a good old think about this matter of conscience.

Conscience, as I understand it, is the moral faculty of recognising one's own thoughts and actions as right or wrong, and far from making cowards of us all the possession of this faculty seems to make some people very brave indeed. At least I think it is brave for one single individual to defy the whole panoply and majesty and authority of the law, provided he is defying it out of deeply held conviction, I mean, and not from exhibitionism or ratbaggery.

I have been acquainted personally with quite a number of young men of draft age, and have listened in on a great many conversations of which the theme was 'To Register or Not to Register'. I say 'listened in' deliberately, because their case was not my case, and I did serve in the Australian Army myself for exactly 1110 days and look back on that period as one of the best times of my life, and in any case I didn't think then (and don't now) that any adult not liable to call-up was (or is) competent to advise or instruct prospective draftees. Quite literally it is their lives that are at stake.

Anyway, of the young men I have listened in on, some favoured dodging, some favoured public defiance, some were of the 'oh what the hell they'll get you anyway' school, and as the time approached for them to decide upon their actions I was very sad and worried for them, such kids as they seemed then to be facing such a harsh moral test. Because although they were all eligible for student deferment I thought that one or two of the more earnest of them might feel themselves to be morally obliged to make their protest anyway, and I didn't want to see them in trouble.

No, I'm not pimping, because what actually happened was that every one of them finally registered, some sheepishly, some shame-facedly, some angrily, and I believe that every one of them got their deferments, and I for one was glad it had worked out like that. Legally, I mean, and without drama or complications.

But it was about that time, or soon after, that an American friend sent me an article torn out of an *Esquire* magazine, and on the article he had pinned a little scrawled note that said: 'This thing hit me so hard that I pulled back in fear of going over-emotional. But for these aged, tired spirits it was a welcome tonic-relief from the waves of the unwashed.'

The article was about a young man called Tommy Rodd, who had just been locked up in the federal reformatory in Petersburg, Virginia, for a term of four years. He was a pacifist like other young pacifists, a demonstrator like other young demonstrators, he refused to register for the draft, he was convicted and paroled, he violated his parole by demonstrating again, and so he was put away for four long years of his very young life. He was nineteen years old and he said his conduct was decided by the law of God and his conscience.

Now the friend who sent me this story is a highly sophisticated and civilised gent of middle age, urbane and somewhat cynical. What he calls 'the waves of the unwashed' do not impress him, so it seemed quite odd for him to be getting emotional about a young demonstrator.

Only when I had read the article did I begin to see that aristocratic young Tommy Rodd, born to the very best upper-middle-class advantages of the Great American Society, handsome, educated, a little spoilt even, might be one of those rare shining people with the so deceptively gentle strength that is required to follow the path of conscience without a single deviation in easier paths or an uneasy pause for reflection and reconsideration about where the path is obviously leading, and to do this quietly, calmly, firmly, politely, and without a trace of bravado or shrill defiance.

What Tommy Rodd said, in effect, was that although he knew the government had made some provision for people like him who could not conscientiously learn how to kill, in that it was prepared to classify them as conscientious objectors and send them to serve for two years in various types of constructive civilian work, he could not accept this. He said that if he registered for the draft he was giving the government the right to determine whether he should learn to kill or not. He thought that the government did not have that right, and that by registering and applying to be a conscientious objector he was applying for a permit not to murder. No one, he said, should need a permit to love.

Tommy Rodd is, evidently, a complete conscientious objector. That is, he does not object only to the Vietnamese war, but to all wars. His conscience dictates to him not 'Thou shalt not kill Vietnamese', but simply 'Thou shalt not kill'. With devastating sincerity, in a world exploding with violence, he demands for himself the right of non-violence. In a world suppurating with hatred, he demands to be allowed to love.

He has been called crackpot, nut, yellowbelly, Vietnik, exhibitionist, and all the other choice epithets reserved by the outraged many for those stubborn few who will go so far as to force society to do violence to them rather than disobey their own fundamental beliefs in non-violence.

He calls himself a 'civil disobedient', a term coined by Henry David Thoreau, and says it means that a person so respects the institution of the law, and the laws of his country, that he openly, willingly, submits himself to prosecution while that law exists. 'For no law,' he says, 'can be proved unconstitutional until a person breaks it.'

Anyway, I was thinking of Tommy Rodd again while I was watching on the television screen young Simon Townsend being manhandled into a paddy-wagon en route for a cell at Ingleburn, the place where I did my rooky training.

'Spectator sports' somebody said grimly, and I thought, yes, there are some pretty devastating sports on that screen these days for us spectators whose consciences rest easy because we are not required to be on the playing field.

Let me say here, now, that I am not personally a conscientious objector. And if I have to face it I don't think I am really a pacifist either. But oh Lord how they haunt me, these people of true conscience. How dare they be so brave, in this world, to preach non-violence? And love of all things. Love! Young Tommy Rodd and young Simon Townsend, tracking firmly in the footsteps of Gandhi, and Martin Luther King. And I do believe, quite a long time ago, that Jesus Christ had something to say on the subject too.

THE HABITUAL WAY

I thought I would write about habits this week because all of mine seem to have been somehow smashed up overnight and if this is fate at least it is my own fate and I must learn to sit down and live with it.

I like habits, bad ones particularly, because habits make days into rituals, and it is easier to live a day by ritual than to play each one off the cuff. In theory I love the unexpected and the unprecedented, but in practice I think I would rather put the kettle on at the usual time.

Anyway, when you get to my time of life you get to a state of what is called 'set in your ways', and to have your ways unset suddenly is odd and unnerving. I mean if you have always got up at six-thirty and squeezed the orange juice and stirred the porridge it is fairly scary to find you can stay in bed if you want to. In fact you don't want to. You would rather stir the porridge. Only because that is your habit. And you feel secure in it. I do think I understand about people who retire with an illuminated address and a cuckoo cock and promptly drop dead. Because being lazy or self-indulgent is not their habit, and their poor constitutions just can't stand it.

I began writing this because my husband is incarcerated in a hospital, my eldest child has left home to pig it alone (I must add quickly with my cheers and blessings), my second has just come back from the local church all dewy with wedding plans and the bells of Saint Paul's (recorded) and choristers at ten cents a head and whatever extra extras are offering, including floodlighting I do believe, and I am left with my youngest and the pair of us rattling around like the last two peas in the pod and all my habits smashed.

Now some very curious things happen once you start smashing up habits. It has been one of my habits, for instance, to deplore opera and make mock of it, and of all operas to be deplored Wagner has always been to me the most deplorable. I grew up on Rhine maidens shrieking and Valkyries whooping and Siegfried hoop-laa-ing about his wretched sword until at the age of ten I swore that I would never again in all my life listen to such beastly noises. (I must confess that I did listen to Anna Russell and fell about and howled with laughter, but then she was making mock too, so it seemed nicely conspiratorial.)

Anyway, such is the smashing of habit that I might have been discovered (actually I was, by people who expressed some surprise) twice in one week at the opera, and one of the operas was Wagner. Beastly Wagner whom I repudiated at the age of ten. Shriek, whoop and hoop-laa and all. And what was awful was that I enjoyed it. Enjoyed it so much in fact that I could be very critical.

Tannhäuser is discovered in the lap of Venus (as I was discovered shamefully at the opera watching Tannhäuser being discovered in the lap of Venus), and Venus was very gilded and deep-bosomed. I don't know why I think that is wrong. Habit again, probably. I have got into the habit of Botticelli and Cranach, and my Venuses are little and light and not very gilt, and of course I did once know a small girl actually named Aphrodite, and she was little and light and black as pitch and she had straight jetty hair all tangled and eyes like ripe olives and an unpleasant habit of stoning new-born kittens to death and of course she will be grown up now with a smile like heaven and she is my idea of Venus. Not gilt. Not gilt at all.

But in spite of Venus I revelled in all that beastly music. I re-wrote the plot, naturally, and got rid of Elizabeth, who does muck it up rather, I think. I would prefer more rousing choruses, and pilgrims tottering, and musical contests. But I'm not grizzling really. Having smashed my habit of hating Wagner I'm getting out to buy me a nice LP so I can have pleasant breakfast sessions with the gentleman and sort of make up for all the years that I mocked and reviled him.

Or maybe I will make it lunchtime sessions with Wagner, because I need another lunchtime habit to replace the smashed one of sitting around with my husband every midday and lapping up beer. That has been going on for more years than I can count, and I don't say that it was a good habit exactly, but it was a fun habit, and a habit of talk and ideas, and I do miss it most dreadfully, especially as I find that I don't like beer at all, awful bloating stuff, and it does seem very odd to be liking Wagner instead. Oh dear.

The habits I can't smash, I find, are my worst ones. And indeed I often wonder why vice is so much more interesting than virtue. I am sure that if someone could find a way of making virtue as interesting as vice we would all turn good overnight. If the good Lord had intended me for a saint why is it my revolting habit to reach for a cigarette first thing in the morning instead of a tomato juice? I mean, I like tomato juice too, but after the cigarette.

Why do I prevaricate, procrastinate, habitually promise myself remarkable deeds of self-improvement which I know I am quite incapable of performing? Or perhaps I am? Once you start smashing habits anything can happen. I might make a habit of frivolity, for instance, instead of endurance, I might make a habit of good works, or long walks, or collecting stamps, or just lolling around with a hibiscus behind my ear listening to Mr Wagner, or birdwatching, or having roast beef for breakfast and porridge for supper, changing the sheets on Mondays instead of Wednesdays, keeping a diary of my Secret Thoughts (because of course I don't tell everything in these columns), eating oysters for lunch every day (with champagne, which I've always hated but which I might get to love, like Wagner, who has rather rocked me about habits). Anyway, the possibilities of new habits are endless.

The nicest habit that I ever knew anybody to have was one of my grandfather's, who, having been poor and careful all his life, found on his retirement that there was enough to live on fairly comfortably, so he kept his trouser pockets filled with small coins which he had a habit of jingling: I expect they made the sweetest music to him. And whenever he saw a small child in the street he had a habit of inviting the small child to have an ice-cream, always with a cherry or a strawberry on top, according to the season. My father always said that he had never known as a boy what a very nice father he had. And I think it was the changing of habits that did it.

So perhaps there is some hope of me becoming a nice old lady. But oh dear I do wish my kids were all at home and I was drinking beastly bloating beer with my husband every midday and I still hated Wagner the way I used to and was forced to squeeze the orange juice and stir the porridge at six-thirty every morning, but then, as I said, the possibilities of new habits are endless, and I might dream up some really wild ones. If I do they will go into my diary of Secret Thoughts, and not, I promise you, into this column. Although you might, of course, dream up some new ones of your own and let me know. We could even swop. And make, I do believe, a new social scene in this lovely land of Oz.

ON LITTLE NODDY,
CHRISTOPHER ROBIN,
GARGANTUA,
DON QUIXOTE,
AND ALL THAT LOT

Since this is Children's Book Week I suppose I ought to write about children's books.

But there are so many experts in this field that I'm not sure of it, particularly as I never did have any children's books myself. I mean, not really what you would call children's books. My papa, as I see in retrospect, modelled himself on Mr Shandy, and had firm ideas on the education of his young.

Thus we had Gibbon and Carlyle and Plutarch thrust upon us at a very early age. We had Cervantes and Montaigne (or Mr Shandy's opinions of Cervantes and Montaigne). We were well into Rabelais before we had fairly got started on *Tanglewood Tales* or *Wind in the Willows*. We had Balzac's *Contes Drolatiques* instead of fairy stories and the adventures of Gargantua instead of the adventures of Tarzan.

Now I am not at all sure (again in retrospect) that this was entirely a good idea. My elder sister seemed to be proof against bawdry, but my brother and I, possibly being bawdy children by nature, had intense pleasure out of Rabelais and picked up quite a lot of be-fouling and be- (never mind, I know these pages won't stand that), and I do believe now that we had such joy out of all that be-fouling because those were the only bits we actually could understand.

Cervantes was something different. We did love and understand Don Quixote, and we called our rocking horse Rosinante. He was the funniest rocking horse ever, being hand-carved by our father, who had great manual skills but not, I think, much aesthetic sense. But we loved him dearly and galloped away over the paspalum with which our backyard was filled and tilted at windmills and had high and splendid adventures. Kids do understand about brave-hearted fools: they are so foolish themselves and so long to be brave.

The first book I remember reading (I mean after *Henny Penny* and *Chicken-Licken*) was *A Yankee at the Court of King Arthur*, and I was seven years old and sitting on the woodblock behind the laundry and the sun was beating on the tin behind my back and there was that smell of hot tin and the smell of wood-chips and the smell of white stock that grew along the paling fence, heavy and hot and sweet beyond telling, and I still remember how Mark Twain got through to a small girl, and I howled with laughter and tears streamed down my face and I suddenly knew what a wonderful thing it was to be able to read and what incomparable treasure there might be in the world of books. World beyond world beyond world.

Thank Heaven I've never lost that, although I remember at the age of about thirteen I had a violent reaction against all that culture and took to reading romantic novels. The more trollopy the better. As Peter Sellers has so pleasantly put it: 'His hot breath was on her neck as he ripped the thin silk ... ' I thought it was great. I think I took up poetry at about the same time.

As a matter of fact I still have a passion for bad novels. My family laugh at me, but fortunately they keep me supplied. I think they think it is a charming eccentricity: Mum is a dope but let's keep her dopey, or maybe she'll ask for a silver-topped cane or a monocle or amber beads and an emerald ring: give her Ayn Rand and keep her happy.

Naturally, after my peculiar upbringing, I did all the right things by my own children. They got *Henny-Penny* and *Chicken-Licken* and graduated to *Wind in the Willows* and Alice and Christopher Robin, Pooh Bear, Little Golden Books, *The Sword in the Stone*, little history books, encyclopaedias, and all the proper reading matter for small children.

However, I'm not too sure about that either. The little history books for children were disastrous. I can remember one child (I won't say which or I might be massacred right here in my own kitchen) getting all het-up about Hadrian's wall and the splendid battles that were going on. And he (aged five) and all in battle array, decided he was a Pict and his poor little sister (aged four) could be a North Jute. I don't think she wanted to be a North Jute. I don't even think she knew what a North Jute was. But a North Jute she had to be. So you've got to be careful about history.

I think poetry is great stuff for kids. Heroic stuff. We've sat over the kitchen table sobbing happily over Don John of Austria and 'dim drums throbbing' and the Fight of the One and the Fifty-three, and I've always felt that slop might be slop but rhythms and words are very important, and so is heroism to kids, and so is real romanticism. You can get cynical later. You can even take to Harold Robbins. But a bit of 'Tirra lirra by the river' first is a good thing. Rather like getting something into your stomach before you go on a binge.

I don't have any rules about books for children. I admit that I avoid Little Noddy, but that is a matter of personal taste. If mine had wanted to read Little Noddy there was nothing to stop them. And some children's books are so gorgeous that they pass into family language. There was one, I remember, about a little railway engine, and the line that has passed into our language is: 'Stay on the rails no matter what.' (There is a splendid moral there.) There was another one about five little firemen who rushed to a little house which was in flames and said: 'Grab what you love most and rush out of the house.' And father grabbed his pipe, mother grabbed her feather pillow, one child grabbed the rabbit, another grabbed a bunch of wildflowers, and the fifth little fireman grabbed the jolly fat cook who was stuck in a window. Yes I know it's silly, but in difficulty we all say to each other now: 'Grab what you love most and rush out of the house.'

There is some controversy about whether it is wise to buy encyclopaedias for children. You know, sinking hundreds of dollars into expensive reference material and then sitting back and saying: 'Well I don't have to worry any more about that. Little Freddie or Mary or Jonathon or Martha has all the reference material he or she needs and we needn't worry about school projects any more.'

Now, just personally (and of course all this is strictly personal) I believe in sinking loot into encyclopaedias. They are so much fun for the parents. I do believe that parents ought to be taken into account when you are dealing with children's books.

For instance, one of mine took up science fiction at a quite early age, and if he hadn't I might never have become acquainted with Ray Bradbury and Isaac Asimov, and I would have been far the poorer. If I hadn't paid off an *Encyclopaedia Brittanica* for a child I would never have had such marvellous reference material for myself.

What I say about kids and kids' reading is 'Go To'. There is, I suppose, a stage between *Henny-Penny* and *Lolita* where you might keep an eye on it. But I don't think they ever take more than they are capable of absorbing, and if they want to read Clarendon or Marco Polo or Proust or anything else I believe they should be allowed to.

I don't really think even Rabelais actually did me any harm. I knew all the dirty words anyway.

HERE THERE BE CROCODILES

Between the time I write this and the time it is published I cannot tell what will have happened in the Gulf of Carpentaria, but obviously anything could, so today I feel compelled to set down something about it, if only because last year I was there for a while, and for a while was quite blazingly obsessed by prawns and prawn-fishers and prawn-trawlers and the mad frontier encampment of Karumba where this new (and old as the trades of the sea) industry is based.

After all, I had never been in a frontier encampment before.

It occurs to me suddenly that I was so very intense about it all that I probably tried to gobble up too much in too short a time, because I haven't been able to eat a prawn since. But at that time I thought wistfully enough that if I were a free-swimming prawn myself I would apply for a job in Craig Mostyn's processing plant and live in a little caravan on the sandbank by the evil river and sneakily fill notebook after notebook and get me the best material for an Australian novel or film or play that any writer could dream of.

And now, of course, the drama has become even more exciting than I dreamed of then. I think it had to. I think my writer's instincts were perfectly sound.

When I first saw Karumba, flying low in over the salt pans in an old DC-3, which was loaded with supplies for the encampment, my foolish, romantic, still childishly adventurous heart (oh, who would dare take mine for a transplant?) stung me with that sting of absolute recognition. Here is a place, it said, where anything could happen.

Here, it said, there be crocodiles.

The Gulf is all that remains of the Great Inland Sea, and through it have sailed the ships of Torres, looking for the Great South Land (which somehow or other he missed entirely: I've never quite understood that), the ships of Tasman, of Jansz, of Carstensz, Cook, and fabulous Flinders who charted it in the *Investigator* in 1802 and charted it so well that his charting remained official until a very few years ago. And that grim stern efficient seaman Bligh on his epic journey to Timor. And then back and still further back to the Malays, who, centuries and centuries ago, explored it for the aphrodisiac sea-cucumber, bêche-de-mer.

The Gulf country is sinister country, flat country, grey country, saltpans and dried mud, and the great grey greasy rivers sluggishly coiling through it (sorry about that but one cannot help but think of the Limpopo, and think too of mad Ludwig Leichhardt, and poor Burke and Wills). They are such broad heavy uninviting rivers, lined with mangrove, that witch tree of the arboreal world, spread claws in the mud and heavy grey-green head aureoled with mosquitoes. (Oh, whoever punted on the limpid Thames at Bray, lolling on purple cushions, feeding the swans, and the picnic hamper neatly settled at one's feet? I did, so I know, but in the Gulf country I couldn't believe it. Hawks in the sky here, and gulls, and sometimes a sea-eagle.)

Wild pig country. Crocodile country.

The settlement of Karumba lies at the mouth of the Norman River, just so heavy, just so sluggish, just so greasy, just so lined with mangrove, and with a sort of skin on it, under which the jellyfish pulse. Not a place, you would think, where human beings would choose to settle.

And yet they've settled. A strange settlement it is too, half shantytown and half luxury because of what is called The Lodge, which was once a refuelling base for Qantas and then a Catalina base during the war, and has been tricked out now with dining room and bar, dormitory bungalow, swimming pool, paths of crushed shells, and exotic plants struggling away gamely enough. Tourists can stay there, and sometimes do—hunters after wild pig and crocodile, sporting fishermen after barramundi and groper and salmon crabs (sometimes they get sharks in the nets instead:

we got seven sharks at the mouth of the river: they had chopped the other fish about dreadfully and I was scared, but the men shot them) and sometimes just people passing through on their way to somewhere else: they looked incredulous, I thought.

And down from The Lodge is the caravan park on the sandbank where the families of the prawn-fishers—those of them game enough to brave the Gulf—live, and further down the packing and freezing plant of Craig Mostyn, who was game enough to brave the Gulf too, and stick it out, and believe it was possible to start an industry.

And, of course, on the river the trawlers are anchored. Such little boats as they are, averaging only between forty-three and fifty feet, working boats, weathered boats—the way I like boats to look. And the boats are, you might say, the heart of the matter.

I can still remember the names of those pioneer boats, the first to give the Gulf a try, and to me their names are like a brave litany. *Cindy, Kotuku, Audrey June, Rama, Toowoon Bay, Sea Marie, Santa Maria, Ulitarra, Sea Fever, Clan Nellie, Sea Tang, Vixen Star, Troubador, Silhouette.* Perhaps the names have changed now, and I know that many more have been added to the list, but I know too that there would be the same sort of boats and the same sort of men. Very tough men, with tattoos on their hands and their forearms and beards grown or half grown and fists like plates of meat and calloused palms, and not, I think, a breed to be tangled with lightly.

Anyway, these tough men, with gravely amused patience, taught me a lot about prawns. The difference between a king and a tiger and a banana and a school prawn. So that I know certainly that now it is the season for bananas, and this is bonanza season.

Twice a month in the Gulf there are double tides, and this is when the banana prawns rise to the surface. They are river creatures, but go to the sea for the phosphorus which fertilises their eggs. The love life of a prawn would astound you. I had it straight from the CSIRO man who was working there (just for once the scientists were in first) and he astounded me to the point of blushing as I haven't since I was thirteen.

When the bananas are running (March to end of July is the season) they come up in mud boils—which is why Craig Mostyn uses a spotter plane—and all the trawlers home in on the boils and cast their nets. Such little boats as they are they can net two and a half to three thousand pounds of prawns in one shot. They sometimes do net as many as five thousand pounds in a shot, but in the past this has turned out to be an embarrassment of riches if the gear hasn't been strong enough to haul the catch in. Masts and stays have been snapped, and once we waited all night for *Cindy* to limp up the river, crippled but triumphant. I'll never forget that. I felt like standing up and cheering.

A boat—I mean one of these little ones—can haul 26,000 pounds of prawns in the five-month season. Last year there was one (and I'm furious not to remember which) that hauled 96,000 pounds, working two or three days every fortnight at the double tides.

No wonder the Russians horned in.

As a matter of fact we used to sit round in The Lodge at night among the turtle carapaces and the stuffed crocodiles and the plastic flowers, with the breeze blowing off the evil river but the heat so heavy we were all swimming in our own sweat and our clothes sticking to our skins, and we used to speculate on what might happen when the glad news of the prawn bonanza got around the world. At that time there was a Japanese mother-ship with her own processing plant and her own fleet of trawlers working out from Weipa, further up the Gulf, and everybody thought that it wouldn't be long before the fishing fleets of the world homed in.

It is, after all, a very big Gulf, and a very big bonanza.

Well, as I said at the beginning, I cannot make prognostications about what will happen between the time I write this and the time it is published.

But I have unloaded prawns, up to my hocks in slushy ice water, I have sorted prawns, I have eaten prawns until I was ready to throw up. I have mended a prawning net and I have shovelled ice into baskets to preserve the future catch. I have victualled a prawning boat. And most importantly I have met a lot of prawning men, courteous men, amused men, real pioneer men, but oh Lord! tough.

And there in the steamy Gulf I thought then, and I think now, I would not care to tangle in anger. One had a funny feeling that all this was inside the law but only just. And one did not ask questions about identities or past histories.

And if I may make a world broadcast I wouldn't advise anybody else to tangle with them either.

ON BLACK AND WHITE BALLS

Some weeks ago I wrote a little piece about a maiden lady called Miss Young, who used to live in this house of mine and died in the house immediately across the street, and who interested me rather because of a certain enigmatic quality she had.

Since I wrote that I have learned so much about Miss Young (and I do thank the people who wrote to me) and her background and ancestry—she was a direct descendant of Horatio Nelson, for instance: which explains the beaky nose she had and her hooded, rather avian eyes—that now she haunts my house more blatantly than ever, which I like, rather: she's a nice ghost and very good company.

But also I inherited Miss Young's cat, a rather elderly maiden lady herself, tortoiseshell, who spent some days and nights up the chimney and under the house until she got used to us and the kitten Jeoffrey and suddenly took to the open fire and the television, and, sad to relate, some incontinence in domestic hygiene: it's all right, I say, she's old and possibly entitled, since this is the house she grew up in.

Anyway, that isn't really the story. It was only that I was telephoning a friend and telling her about how I had acquired Sabrina Fair (that's the name of the incontinent old tortoiseshell) and my friend said, in what, I thought, was rather a grim tone of warning: 'Now you be careful, Charm, love. Don't you go writing anything about the Aborigines. They'll give you one.'

I wish they would. A little one. I'm a fool for little ones. So just in case there is the remotest chance that they will give me one (I've only got a kitten to sit on my lap now, my lot being too big for that sort of thing and mums' laps being specially designed for sitting on) I am going to write about the Aborigines.

102

And I am doing this because with my dear friend Faith Bandler, and my even dearer friend Toni (who has been my best friend for twenty-something years, which is a long time) I went last week to a seminar, conference—call it what you will—of Christian ladies of various denominations on the upper reaches of the North Shore of Sydney—what they call, I do believe, the Blue Ribbon Belt—and I went blazing with anger.

I had been having a bit of a go at the telly a couple of nights before, and I watched a representation of George Orwell's *Animal Farm*. And that pig Napoleon (whom I actually saw dining out at one of those North Shore restaurants in the middle of the petrol strike when the parking lot was so filled with Jags and Mercedes that we, in our more humble vehicle, had to go three blocks down) had caused to be written on the wall: 'All animals are equal but some animals are more equal than others'.

And after that I watched our own prime minister accepting the curtseys of a group of Aboriginal debutantes—pretty ones (and doubtless chosen for their prettiness?) in long white dresses, and gloves, and carrying equally pretty posies—at a ball especially arranged for them, and I thought I might throw up.

Why does there have to be a ball especially arranged for them? Why can they not make their curtseys at the usual balls for debutantes?

Why don't we, in fact, have a real Black and White Ball? It is a thought I give you with fierce pleasure.

I watched those kids, shy and pretty and dressed up in their long white gowns, holding their pretty posies in their white-gloved hands, rehearsed to the point where they stepped lightly and slowly on the arms of their equally rehearsed partners, mimicking what is, anyway, a fairly sickening and absolutely deadly bourgeois ceremony, and I thought: Yes, but what comes after, you pretty little things? La Perouse? Who sailed into Botany Bay, said '*Merde alors*' and sailed away? What will you do with your long white dresses? Put them away in tissue paper and lavender? Can you afford the tissue paper and the lavender? Where are you going home to after this pretty occasion? You actually shook hands

103

with the prime minister? Did you feel like fainting with pleasure?

Well, as I said, I was ready to throw up with this mockery, this condescension, this patronage and paternalism, when, most fortunately, my friend Faith Bandler appeared on the screen and restored sanity and decency and dignity by talking about housing for Aboriginal people, and talking with her usual wit and elegance and high good humour: the debutantes' ball had only amused her, where it had made me (and my dearest friend Toni too) spitting mad.

So, still spitting mad, and still with Faith laughing, we went together to the conference, or seminar or whatever, of Christian ladies in the Blue Ribbon Belt, which I was to open, and did, still in anger and no proper Christian spirit.

Faith made a good speech, and Dulcie Flower made a good speech too, but Toni and I, eating meat pies and custard tarts after on a brick wall in the sun, had a couple of things to say to each other (we've been saying things to each other for so long that we almost don't have to say them).

And Faith had said: 'You cannot do anything for the Aboriginal people unless you love them.' And Toni and I couldn't wear this one. We said (munching our meat pies): 'We won't be morally blackmailed into loving people because their skins are black. We will love black people proportionately as we love white people, or yellow people, or children, or dogs, or cats, or whatever.' We said (now on custard tarts): 'Nobody is going to blackmail us; not even Faith, whom we love.'

There was a lady at this conference, seminar, whatever it was, who, in question time, raised an argument about tribal burying grounds, and why they should be important. After all, she said, very few of us still retained our family homes. And my dear friend Toni—and forever I will bless her for this—said, very properly and raising her hand to ask the question: 'Didn't we ever think that the only culture we have in this country is the culture of the indigenous people? Might not tribal burial grounds be part of it? Would you tear down the Parthenon,' she said, 'because it is a sentimental relic of older times? Would you tear

104

down Saint Peter's? Or Saint Paul's? For God's sake,' she said (speaking of course to Christian ladies), 'let us hold on to what is left.'

Anyway, we talked about it over the meat pies and the custard tarts, dangling our legs in the sun, and we decided on justice rather than emotion (I will never forget as long as I live a real nappy-headed Negro called Hakim arriving at my house in a loin cloth with two peacock feathers in his hair and a poor Welsh parson's daughter trundling barefoot behind him with a knapsack on her back and a baby on her hip).

I don't care whether people are black, or yellow, or a mixture of both, or something in between. If they are nice people I like them, and if they are nasty I don't.

But the important thing is that they are people. And I think we had all better remember just that one little point.

ON THE RIGHT OF DISSENT

Everybody has said everything there is to say about Mr Askin's little blunder already, so I don't need to say any more, but now there is Mr Willis banning a play he hasn't even bothered to see and talking about 'hippies' and the 'lunatic fringe' and I think he is blundering too, and I am being very thoughtful just now about authoritarianism. Australian brand, I mean. Paternalistic brand, I mean.

Father knows best.

But does father know best really? Complacent father, smug father, slippers-and-pipe father, well-fed father, I-know-best-father, you-follow-in-my-footsteps-son-and-everything-will-be-all-right father?

Maybe son doesn't want to follow in your footsteps, father. Maybe, just maybe, son wants to think for himself. And maybe also—I've got news for you, father—daughter does too.

And it's just too easy, father, to say 'Ride over the bastards', or to label anybody who disagrees with you 'hippy' or 'lunatic fringe' or 'pseudo-intellectual' or 'quasi-intellectual'. You are being arrogant, dear papa, without any justification whatever. You are being dismissive, dear papa, without any real thought about what you are dismissing. And that's not really wise, papa, because there are forces stirring in this world—oh, surly if you will—but intelligent forces, angry forces, frustrated forces, and oh so powerful forces, papa, that might rock you out of your complacency. And quite soon too.

Never underestimate the power of the intellectual, papa. Quasi or pseudo or lunatic fringe. The only exciting things that have ever been done in this world have been done by people who think. I know that's disturbing, but it happens to be true.

Why do you think that a large majority of the Christian peoples of this world are called Protestants? Because, papa, they protested. There was a man called Martin Luther, once, a long time ago, and he protested. There was a man called Martin Luther King, once, a short time ago, and he protested. There was a group of English colonists in a country called America, once, who protested, and, by protesting, made the mightiest nation in the world, to which you genuflect these days, papa, with some sickening sycophancy. There was a group of frustrated and angry and hungry French, once, who protested, and by protesting, changed the whole pattern of European civilisation: and it wasn't banners they were carrying, dear papa, it was heads on pikes. There was a group of Russians once—raging dreamers they were—who protested, and by protesting made the other mightiest nation on earth.

There were coal miners who protested, and pit workers who protested, and railway workers who protested, and carders and spinners and weavers who protested, and there were women too (please remember papa that you have daughters as well as sons) and they chained themselves to railings and kicked policemen and were force-fed in gaols because they were protesting.

And where do you think we would be—what sort of society do you think we would live in—if there weren't people brave enough to protest? Not the 'lunatic fringe' or the 'pseudo-intellectuals' or the 'quasi-intellectuals', but people who think and get fed up and exercise their democratic right to protest. If nobody had protested in the past, there wouldn't be any democratic rights. If nobody had protested, our little kids would be down in the mines and the pits and in the factories for ten or twelve hours every day, our men would still be working an eighty hour week or more, and no woman would have a vote. We would still be living in feudalism and slavery. That we are not is only because people protested.

As far as I know, no injustice has ever been overcome, no wrong ever righted, by putting up with it, or by meekly accepting the dictum that father knows best. I may be wrong—some outraged people tell me I am sometimes—but if there is anything to distinguish man from the brutes, to lay the foundation for his singular dignity, it is his very singular faith in absolute and eternal values, in justice, in his own rights as a dignified human being—not as a child to be soothed and patted and scolded, papa—and against this nothing has ever been set, nothing has ever held any weight, not his own freedom nor even, at times, his own life.

Oh, 'lunatic fringe' if you will. When you are counting the heads, papa, count mine. Brown it is, and rather turbulent. I think the lunatics of the world have rather a regal air, and a style I admire. (I do admire style intensely, and hope I have a certain style of my own.)

You may think there is nothing regal in students lying down in the middle of a city street. But at least it has more style than somebody saying 'Ride over the bastards.' The students, at least, were brave. I like bravery. It makes my heart sing. And they were within their democratic rights to protest, if they felt like so doing, as their ancestors have protested through generation after generation. And I repeat and repeat and repeat that nothing has ever been accomplished without protest.

I would suggest, papa (papas?)—Australian variety, I mean—that you have a bit of a thumb through history and philosophy, and even current affairs in Europe (about which you seem to be singularly ignorant, or singularly insulated) before you construct your no doubt admirable theories about 'pseudo-intellectuals' and 'quasi-intellectuals' and 'hippies' and the 'lunatic fringe'.

I think, after the manner of artists, you should make some preliminary studies. I think you should consider a little more gravely the world in which you live. I think you should not rely so absolutely upon the safe phrase and the safe cliché and sit smug and complacent (those are terribly overworked words I know, but I'm overworked too and can't for the life of me think of better ones) saying: 'Father knows best.'

Among the cunning bargainers, hucksters and investors, the

astute and slippery profiteers of the markets and the bazaars (we read about them in our papers every day—caught out—sprung, if you will—and that is apparently their only sin: to have been sprung, I mean) the protestants to me have a positively princely gait and carry their heads high.

Lunatic fringe? Oh, but lunatics with their colours nailed to the mast. Brave colours.

Perhaps it might all be foolishness. But, as I said, the foolishness has a style and a manner and a creed, and nothing has ever been done without it.

Dear papa, will you not consort, even in imagination, with plotters and revolutionaries, with angry souls in small back rooms? Will you not consort, even in imagination, with buffoons, with mountebanks, charlatans, sadists, pimps and procurers, as well as with priests and professors and solicitors and councillors and members of the RSL? You might learn something. How about consorting with a few hippies and pseudo-intellectuals and quasi-intellectuals? You might learn a little bit more.

You might, even—perhaps this is too much to hope—never use a thoughtless cliché again.

What Are We Doing It For?
     and What Will You Leave to Posterity?

        I suppose everybody comes up to this thing of what are
we doing it for.

        Moments like these:

        When the milk bottle dropped into the coupi.

        When the _nice_ thing breaks. It's always the
nice thing that breaks. The lamp in Hydra. The really
gorgeous dress that gets the cigarette burn. The Greek
amphora. The door knockers. The Greek shepherd's bag with
the nasty child plucking all the XXX thongs out.

        Kitty coming to Hydra and using up all the water
supply in the cistern on her laundry and George going down
inside the thing and wallowing round and dropping the torch
into the mud just as he heard Kitty's voice above asking
"But darlings what are you doing it for?"

        Moments of despair with children.

        But how many people have a distinct purpose
beyond survival and immediate comfort? Education of
children perhaps. The driving thing of giving your own
children a better chance than you had yoursel. Does this
work out. Is it right, for instance, to make things easier
for them.

        Older civilizations seem to have a deeper concern
with the flow of generations. This probably derives very
strongly from peasant societies, where life is so close to
a common denominator of living that survival becomes both more
chancy and more urgent and can be best achieved by a very
fixed pattern of _past proof_.

        The salt mines in Western China are actually
subterranean reservoirs of brine, which is pumped up through
bamboo drills to the surface where the brine is evaporated
into salt. A Chinese will spend his whole life putting down
a new drill, and his son will do the same after him, so that
two generations are working entirely for a third generation,
because the mine begins to produce only for the original
miner's grandchild.
                  the Katsikas family.

The above and following page are sections from two pages of notes
for 'What Are You Doing It For?' (cf. p.37). Handwriting: 'The
Katsikas family'. (The Greek grocers referred to in the essay.)
National Library of Australia MS 5027

Dostoevsky, on the surface of it, was more obsessed with gambling than with writing, and for long periods only wrote to try and get out of debt and back to the gaming tables.

What we can really leave to posterity are only memories of us really, and possibly a few anecdotes. You can have a whole human life of struggle, with its multitude of problems, and be remembered only for one drunken escapade.

Money doesn't seem to come into it -- you can't take it with you -- although a great many people do seem to be obsessed by the acquisition of riches to be passed on. Yet the strange thing is that few people are remembered well. A lot of philanthropy is a sort of guilt thing, I suppose. Like Nobel, who is so stricken by what is done with his explosives, that he leaves money for a peace prize. And the great tycoons of America like the Rockefellers and Carnegies and the rest who seem to have to sublimate in good works for posterity a certain guilt about what it cost to make their fortunes.

The old tombstones of the last century in Connecticut and Massachussetts almost all carried the legend "He Amassed Wealth" instead of the usual "Rest in Peace". Now in fact much of this wealth was acquired just after the Civil War, when a great con trick was played on the South by the carpet-baggers selling wooden nutmegs.

Transcend

It is pretentious nonsense to
believe the work you do will
live after you. It might, but
then again it might not.
History is going to judge that,
Not you.
They say the Lion and lizard keep the courts where
Jamshed gloried to drank deep,
And Bahram, that great hunter, the
wild ass, stamps o'er his head
And he lies fast asleep.

I am Ozemandias King of Kings
Look on my works ye mighty and
despair.

The first quotation is from Fitzgerald's *Rubaiyat*: 'They say the Lion and the Lizard keep/ The Courts where Jamshyd gloried and drank deep:/ And Bahram, that great Hunter—the Wild Ass/ Stamps o'er his Head, and he lies fast asleep.'
Second quotation from Shelley's *Ozymandias*: 'My name is Ozymandias, king of kings:/ Look on my works, ye Mighty, and despair!'
National Library of Australia MS 5027

Somewhere between glaxies and electrons.

TIME.

It's abouttime. Don't know how many people have said to me lately
"There's never time any more." or "Oh, if only I had time I would
do so-and-so and so-and-so."
Time for what, anyway?
Ecclesiastes. A time for every purpose under heaven.
A very good poet, Ecclesiastes.
But poets have been going on about time since there were poets.

Quotes.

So let's have a bit of a think about time.

It is a peculiar unstable quality. It doesn't move evenly.
You know how when you are waiting for somebody or something time
abolustely drags. Time crawls. When you are happy and busy and
excited and interested time flies.   Rate of healing of wounds
And as you grow older time begins to race along.
Time's winged chariot hurrying near - and yonder all before us lie
deserts of vast eterntiy.

This world was created *≸* /✗✗✗ million

Vast geological ages. Millions and millions of years.

Man has been on this earth for, ✗✗✗ thousand

A great deal of time has passed.   Passed what? Has it passed us?
Or do we flow along with time -- a great many quotations compare
time to a river flowing -- but if it is flowing and we with it it
must have stationary banks -- like past, present, and future, which
would mean that everything is fixed and determined, and if everythis
is fixed and determined of what use is our free will? Do we even
have free will?

And another thing, you know. Our idea of eternity. "e will all
meet again in heaven - or the other place -- but who are we going
to meet? We are ourselves from the moment we are born until the
moment we die. Is it our young selves ✗✗✗✗✗✗✗✗ who are to exist
forever, or our middle-aged selves, or our old selves? And when
we are reunited are we even going to recognise our loved ones? Or
are we going to all of ourselves.
And still another thing - people longing for eternity when they
find so much of this life boring. The people who do things to "fill
in time". "To pass the time".

The above and following two pages are the first three pages of notes
for 'On Tick and Tock' (cf. p.265). Page divisions have been adjusted.
National Library of Australia MS 5027

Common sense tells us that everything is real only when it is
"now", in the present moment. Reality is served up to us in thin
slices of now. Like watching a film of which every frame arrived
from nowhere and turned into nothing. "~~Unxxfxxkxx~~ Unbron tommorow
and dead yesterday, why fret about them if to-day be sweet." And
common sense is so wedded to this view that if someone says they
have had a glimpse of the future, common sense will denounce them
as charlatans, as mystics are denounced for claiming to see back
into the past.

The opposite view is that everything, past, present and future is
solidly there. We experience things in time because our Now, so
to speak, goes steadily forward, as if we were travelling through
a dark landscape with a searchlight. In fact we invent time to
explain change and succession.
But how can we throw our searchlight onto the future in front of
us, or use it to illuminate the past behind us?

If all our consciousness is is a torch moving along a back alley,
what is the point of having it?

Somehow we exist "in time", in spite of its irreversibility.
          The moving finger writes etc.

Well, all that is about inner time. To live our lives in this
society we also have to have an outer, or public time. We have,
most of us, to live regular lives. There are people for whom this
works very well -- regular periods of work -- regular periods of
rest. There are other people, often creative, who work best in
long ~~waa~~tained bouts, followed by long periods of idleness. It
would be nice if society could come to terms with this one. But
society has to be regulated by public time.

Primitive societies had no need ~~fxxxkkxx~~ to measure time. Sunrise,
noon, sunset were all they needed.
It is only when society becomes a little more complex that man
needs to measure out his day. Men with fields to till and to harves
and animals to care for could not afford to be quite so negligent.
Men with regular work, and a little bartering to do, needad to
divide up their days farily accurately
The first measuring would have been by shadow -- a shadow stick/ in
the ground.
More complex civilisations, enormous structures designed in part
to determine equinoxes. Great Pyramid is one. Stonehenge is
another.
Shadow clock in Egypt two thousand B.C. a right-angled bar with .
the T raised up a bit, and the bar engraved with the hours.
Forerunner of the sundial, which I still think to be the most
charming clock of all. rab mathameticians in the Middle Ages.
Hours are Time's shafts and one comes winged with death.
I count only the hours that are serene
I shall return, thou never.

113

Handials, reading the time by the shadow cast on your thumb by a
held stick. Hand horizontal, left hand pointing west before noon,
right hand pointing east for afternoob,

Astralobes -- very pretty - back to the Greeks - first measure
the altitude of the sun and note position on the zodiac circle --
Chaucer wrote a treatise on the astrabobe in the 14th century.

Egyptians also had sighting rods to record the transit of the stars,

16th centruy nocturnals, or night clocks, sighting on the stars
again

Hourglasses, to record a specific length of time. As a sermon,
for instance. A marked candle. ᵤater clocks. Oil clocks.

Pendulum clock.   Mechanical clocks from 14th century.
pendulum invented by Galileo in 1581.

First patent for an electric clock filed in 1840. Don't like 'em.

Men knew what month they were in before they knew what time it was.
There were calendars of a sort before there were clocks. 3,000B.C
in Mesopotamia. A measuring of seasons, I suppose really.

Fairly convenient arrangements for measuring hours days and months,
What John Donne called "the rags of time" we haven't tamed and
domesticated time itself yet. It is full of supprises.

Whether people have inner clocks.

Some men seem to be aware in a mysterious way how much or little
time they have at their disposal. Develop their talents early
and work and live in a frenzy and die young. While other develop
late and do their best work in the long slow years,
as if they knew they had lots of time and to spare.
Or whether perhaps the early starters die young just because of
that frenzy of work.
But none of this belongs to public time -- a much larger
idea of time.

J.B. Priestley.   Man and Time.

J. W. Dunne. An Experiment With Time.   Time as a fourth
                                        dimension.

Have never worn a watch myself.

Precognition in dreams.

Dunne hard-headed military engineering type. Not a mystic. No
secret love, as most of have, of the mysterious. I can only
follow him so far, and then his mathematics beat me.

DISSENT AND PROTEST.

1. Democracy founded on the right of dissent, or the right of protest.

2. Phenomenal vitality of Athens -- strength and inspiration for Golden Age was deomocratic form of government. Athenian Assembly open to all free male citizens of adult age, regardless of income or class. It met 40 times a year. Anybody could speak about anything, providing he could command an audience. Council of 500 - all citizens over 30. Paid and served for a year. Inner Council of 50 met every day and adminstered the Government. Changed 10 times a year. No one man remained in power long enough to entrench himself. ████ 10 Generals elected directly from assembly . Served a year. Could be re-elected. Pericles.

3. Such a system can only exist in a small and intensely civic-minded population. Every citizen speaking for himself.

   Pericles: Here each individual is interested not only in his own affairs but in the affairs of the state as well ... we do not say that a man who takes no interest in politics is a man who minds his own business; we say that he has no business here.

4. If there had been no dissent, and no protest, civilisation would never have advanced twoards any sort of democracy. America a democracy. How did it become a democracy. Through dissent and protest. Bloody, violent protest. 1781 was the year when modern Europe was born, and the American evolution was the prelude to the French Revolution in 1789 -- it wasn't banners on poles then, but heads.
   Irish Rebellion -- Wearing of the Green. Not pretty.
   Russian Revolution. ⎞ British were only expelled from India
   Hungarian Revolt. ⎠ finally by violence, in spite of Ghandi

5. Workers -- ordinary working men -- have never won a single benifit without protest, without fight if necessary. There is record of terrible violence from the other side, the side of management, the side of law and order. Welsh Miners, Midlands Potteries, workers in the cloth trade ridden down by troopers. No management has ever freely given a concession. Wat Tyler.

6. How far do you think negroes would have got in their fight for equality with fighting? And there is evidence there too that the violence is from the side of law and order -- the boots and the truncheons, the fire hoses, the police dogs.

7. Protestantism. Means just that. Protest. Martin Luther had to put up quite a battle, and suffer persecution. The Hugeonots in France were killed, massacred, or sentenced to slavery in the galleys.

Notes for 'On the Right of Dissent' (cf. p.106).
National Library of Australia MS 5027

115

ON THEN AND NOW

In a new biography of Thomas Wolfe, written by Andrew Turnbull and published by The Bodley Head, there is one paragraph that fascinates me.

Apparently Wolfe often imagined himself conversing with the immortals, and this paragraph (page 60 if you want it) describes him in conversation with Shakespeare in a tavern, eating a cold pork pie and washing it down with sack.

Of course Wolfe is projecting himself back, time-machine style, from the twentieth century, and of course Shakespeare, universe within universe that he was—is?—accepts this with absolute equanimity. There is nothing new to him under the sun. Wolfe has provided himself with proofs: photographs of the Tower and the Strand in their modern dress, and a postcard of the *Aquitania* leaving Southampton Docks. But Shakespeare doesn't need these. He accepts it all, and is interested, in a calm but thrilling and thrilled sort of way, in what modern science has accomplished, in the power of the press and mass communication media, the march of literature, and—naturally enough—his own reputation in the modern world.

But then he asks: 'And the pox?' And Wolfe tells him that we cure it almost infallibly these days with an infusion in the blood, and Shakespeare is relieved.

I was stung with that absolute sting of recognition at this paragraph, because I travel by time machine myself. Very often. It was a habit I got into when I was quite a little girl and first fell in love with Andrew Marvell. Afterwards I fell in love with Herrick and with Suckling, and Lovelace (I've quite got over him since I've learned a little more about the part he played in those wars he left Lucasta of the chaste breast and quiet mind

116

for: better he'd stayed at home it seems to me), and I had my Byronic period, and even—shamed as I am to tell it—my bit of a fling with Browning (I thought at that time, in the overweening arrogance of youth, that I had a fair chance of snitching him from that dreary hypochondriac Elizabeth Barrett).

And I had my Shakespeare period too. A little reluctant, I was, because the man was small and bald, and I like them tall and hirsute, but then, I thought, he is a genius and you can't overlook that even if you have to overlook him—at eye level, I mean.

And golly it was fun suggesting to them themes for poems to be written in the future, and you don't know what lovely ones I am entirely responsible for. Actually inspired.

And then I fell in love with John Donne and haven't looked at another dead poet since. Not in that particular way. I am faithful in my fashion.

I must admit that what has always troubled me about time machine travel is the problem of transporting sufficient quantities of make-up and mink eyelashes and antibiotics and all those little odds and ends we women find quite indispensable these days. What would happen, I thought, if I had a cavity in a tooth? Would I need to have them all capped first for absolute safety? If I meant to stay for some time in another century, that is, and I suspect I would, being a glutton, as they say, for punishment, and also insatiably curious. Would it also be in the interests of safety to have tonsils and appendix removed first? (I am one of those odd creatures who has never had anything removed—except a tooth, and that made me cry because I don't want to lose any little bit of me.) And could one transport the Pill? Enough, I mean, to last out the possibilities of adventure.

I remember that sometimes, on cold winter nights on the island of Hydra, huddled over charcoal tins, we all used to play this game of time machines. And at that time not one of us had running water—you dragged it up from the well in a bucket. And not one of us had a flush lavatory—we had Turkish squats and an earthenware jar with a tin dipper. And not one of us cooked on gas—we cooked on charcoal, or, if we were very sophisticated, on messy little kerosene burners that were always blowing up in our faces. And there was no electricity, and our houses were lit at night with lamps and candles.

Now among our numbers there was an Irish writer, married to a marvellous Australian girl called Nancy, and this Irish writer, on one of our time machine jags, said with great earnestness and yearning, flopping his fine pale hair about him: 'For myself I fancy the eighteenth century. I have always thought, myself, that I would like to live in the eighteenth century.'

And Nancy said, flopping her thick dark hair about her, and howling with laughter, mouth square open like a young dark witch: 'You fool. You *are* living in the eighteenth century.'

Anyway, after Thomas Wolfe and his lovely conversation with Shakespeare I was ruminating on all this, and having a bit of a giggle to myself about my own imagined conversations and passionate love affairs with long-dead poets—because if one travels by time machine one always turns up in another century as one of the privileged, not one of the peasants: one turns up as a king's mistress or a mysterious Grey Eminence, not as a frowzled tousled sluttish chambermaid, or the limping ostler at the inn—and I thought to myself, now supposing one did it another way? Supposing one imagined oneself arriving back here, now, from some remote time in the future?

What would one find?

No Shakespeare.

Who would one really want to meet?

Nobody.

Don't you think that is sad? Einstein is dead, and Bertrand Russell is very very old, and I suppose, in the inexorable course of nature, won't be with us that much longer, and I can't think of anybody else I would want passionately to meet. The Beatles? No. Elizabeth Taylor? No. Mary Quant? No. I think I would have liked to have met Martin Luther King. But he's dead, violently and irrevocably, and I can only meet him now in imagination. I think I might have liked to have met Gandhi, and Churchill, and Nehru, and Mao (and I am forever envious of my husband because he did meet all of them: 'I walked,' he said, 'with Gandhi by the river Ganges.' And added, thoughtfully: 'Under a black umbrella.' I could spit.) And the Powys brothers are dead, and I should have liked to have met them. And James Joyce is dead, and D. H. Lawrence is dead—and I shouldn't have liked to have met either of them—and T. S. Eliot is dead, and at least I did meet him and he is the only non-disappointment among contemporary poets I have met.

Now I wonder, ruminating on all this, I wonder what the shape and size of cities have to do with it. London in the time of Shakespeare and the great Elizabethans was smaller than Wollongong. In a span of eighty-three years Athens produced 463 immortals from a population of less than 100 000, of which all but 30 000 were slaves. Is the soul and spirit defined and liberated by having places to walk around and talk around? And eat around, and drink around? Aristotle's rule for the perfect city was that it should be small enough for the cry of a single herald to be heard by all the inhabitants. 'A common life,' he said, 'for a noble end.'

Ah well. If I came back from some future time, even as one of the privileged, I know I wouldn't find Shakespeare. Shakespeares don't grow in this anonymous sprawl, and there is no Globe and no Mermaid Tavern where you might eat a cold pork pie and wash it down with sack, and talk and talk and talk.

So, failing that, if you will excuse me, I'm going to pack my cosmetics and antibiotics, and have my appendix out and my teeth capped, and get me right back to 'Jack of the Town'. John Donne, that is, before he got so passionately holy, that is, and while we could still understand each other so well.

119

A TALE OF TWO CITIES

Irwin Shaw wrote a very good story once called *Two Days in Another Town*, and I could very well take that title for this particular article, excepting that it wouldn't be strictly accurate.

'One and a Half Days in Another City' would be more like it, but then it wouldn't sound as rounded and finished. Rather messy, in fact. In fact I am rather messy, so perhaps it is suitable.

It is two years since I was in Melbourne last, and then it was only for a very formal luncheon and back to Sydney in time for dinner. I know that people do this all the time, and not just between Sydney and Melbourne, but between London and Paris, and Paris and Rome, and Rome and Athens, and think nothing of it. To me such carefree streaking about the sky for the sake of a meal is quite alarming, particularly if the meal turns out to be much the same as you could have had if you'd stayed at home, excepting that it is served (sometimes) in a different language. I think I would get my cities mixed.

Two years ago I still had Melbourne and Sydney mixed. Both, after Europe, were equally strange and equally familiar, and when I was young I'd had good times and better times in both cities, and bad times and worse times, and I'd fallen in and out of love in both cities, and worked in both cities, and dreamed very young and completely impractical dreams, and sometimes howled my eyes out. When you are young I don't think the surroundings matter much.

But even two years ago I could not understand the much publicised rivalry between Melbourne and Sydney, or the nuances of difference that make some Melbournians flee north: not to something, I've always felt, but from something. I know a man who declares that all Melbournians straying interstate should be repatriated, and I'm not quite sure what he means but there is a passionate sincerity in his statement that makes me consider it quite gravely. It might be segregationist policy, or something more profound, of the order of which Laurence Sterne wrote: 'It must have been observed, by many a peripatetic traveller, that Nature has set up, by her own unquestionable authority, certain boundaries and fences to circumscribe the discontent of man: she has effected her purpose in the quietest and easiest manner by laying him under almost insuperable obligations to work out his ease, and to sustain his sufferings at home.'

Anyway, after a further two years of living in Sydney, Sydney has become home for working out my ease and sustaining my sufferings, a city too familiar to be seen excepting upon dazzling occasions when one chokes suddenly on the beauty of the spread of the harbour and the towers of Mammon rising and the inconsistent contours of hills, highs and lows and ups and downs and the little terrace houses swinging over them like absurd frilly shoulder straps. Wanton somehow.

So that this time I went into Melbourne with a sharp bright shock, like walking into a pane of glass. (I know what I'm saying because I did that once, literally, in a ruffled train and long red gloves, at the Festival Hall in London. And with Royalty present. I ask you. I was knocked out cold and had to be revived.)

I don't mean exactly that Melbourne knocked me out. But it shook me. Not only is it a different city from Sydney, but it might be, almost, a different country. The air was different— crisp as a stalk of celery at the early morning hour of my arrival. And the light was different—softer, pinker, more diffuse. And I had forgotten the visual impact of flatness. After Sydney's gullies and hills, where one becomes visually accustomed to high skylines crenellated with towers, or deeply nestling clusters of domestic dwellings, and practically all streets swoop or soar dramatically, Melbourne seemed to have been ironed out by a celestial flatiron determined to smooth out every crease and wrinkle for the sake of neatness: it was odd not to see higher or lower than the end of a street, blurred a little in that soft diffuse light. Intriguing, in a way.

And domestic architecture is different. Melbourne terrace houses do not look quite like Sydney terrace houses, although the lace balconies are there, and the careful restorations—even Victoriana is transmuted somehow by the light or the consistent horizontal of the streets or by some minor deviations from the standard terrace pattern that I was not sharp enough, this time, to spot precisely.

My programme was too jam-packed with appointments to allow wandering (which suddenly and excitedly I wanted to do), but there was just time to sit in a coffee house in Collins Street and watch people go by for a while, and, yes, they looked different too. More restrained? More quietly elegant? The girls were wearing much shorter miniskirts than their Sydney counterparts, but the effect was one of young spring freshness, faultless taste, and the most careful attention to grooming. All right, perhaps they look ever so slightly *assembled*, but I think it is true that Melbourne women are smarter than Sydney women, and I suspect that they take their make-up off every single night before they go to bed and brush their shining hair every morning and never never wear stockings with runs, or accessories that don't match. Golly!

But it was later, after the meeting and the speeches that were the purpose of my visit, that I truly realised that I was in another city. Another country maybe? My hostess lives in a beautiful beach house more than twenty miles down the Bay, and we drove there along the flat flat highway, with all those new groomed houses and English-type gardens on the one side, and the flat flat bay and the flat flat sand and the wind-twisted, salt-encrusted ti-tree on the other, and the two sides of the highway were utterly incongruous, although I thought that you would have to have and hide behind an alien garden or join the Flat Earth Society just to cope with the visuals. And when the sun, all squashy crimson, was dipping down into the flat flat bay, we had drinks and watched a little boat rowing out of it towards us, like a walnut shell on pink lemonade, and no, it wasn't like Sydney Harbour, but it was beautiful too, and strange, and comfortingly familiar as well because of the children tugging our skirts and demanding attention and potties. I could live there.

She (my young hostess) had assembled for the evening a group of people whom I have wanted to meet ever since I came back to Australia. And this was the queer thing, and disturbing—not in any unpleasant way, I mean, but exciting and intoxicating, and confirming my suspicion that I was indeed a stranger from Another Place. Their references were not my references, their jokes were In jokes, Group jokes, Melbourne jokes, the events and the Christian names they chucked about casually happened or existed in outer darkness as far as I was concerned. It was a different language. A sort of shorthand. Opaque to me, but stimulating to the point of my wanting desperately to learn it, as a few years ago I was forced to learn Sydney language for the essentials of communication.

Stay longer, they said, and we will do this and see that and take you to meet so-and-so, and I wanted so much to stay, and to listen, and to learn, but I knew even then that I had already chewed on as much new food for thought as would likely give me mental indigestion, so I firmly jetted out of Flat Land and back to the dramatic hills and canyons of Sydney, and the In jokes and Group jokes with which I am familiar, and the careless girls wearing their minis slightly raffishly. And it was different. Very different.

But perhaps I can learn that other language. And perhaps I can have two cities, and two groups, and two sets of excitements. And be equally stimulated by both. But differently.

It occurs to me that I have never been to Canberra in my whole life. I think I might work on that.

ON NOT SEEING
AMERICA HURRAH

The taxi driver, a man of late middle-age and grown-up family, and liberal in his way, said he thought That Play might be shown without moral danger to selected (or did he say selective?) audiences.

'Ah,' I said, 'but who would do the selecting?'

He said he didn't know about that, but he thought that university people and doctors and folk of higher education and that would not be likely to be adversely affected by it. 'But if you just leave it an open slather for anybody . . .' he said. 'Well . . .' he said.

So I asked him if he thought that the anybodies and everybodies who had not had the benefit of higher education lived in a state of innocence concerning the act simulated on the stage and the words alleged to have been written on the wall.

And he said, puzzled but dogged, no it wasn't that. Those words were bandied about in hotel bars and on work shifts every day of the week. There were some jokers, he said, who couldn't say two words without one of them being of only four letters. He didn't approve of it himself, but he thought that half the time they didn't even know they were doing it.

'Well then,' I said, 'if they are so used to those words, how can they be corrupted by seeing them written on a make-believe wall on a stage?'

And he said that was different, wasn't it. Written up in public like that in front of everybody like a ('excuse my plain speaking but you seem broad-minded') public convenience. I had no idea, he said, just what was written and drawn on the walls of public conveniences.

124

I said I did have a rough idea. And that, as I understood it, there were considerably more ordinary Australian citizens who attended public conveniences than attended theatres.

But, still dogged, he still maintained that it was different. 'Written up in front of everybody like that.'

I asked him if he knew what the play was about, and he didn't of course. All he knew was that two people went to a motel room and wrote dirty things on a wall, and that was obviously enough for him and shouldn't be shown to anybody except selected (selective?) audiences. But he was a liberal man in his way, and as I left the cab he thanked me for the interesting conversation and—cautiously and embarrassedly—asked the question I had been waiting for. He didn't suppose I had seen the play myself?

'No,' I said, very weary. 'I haven't.'

He seemed relieved. One knew certainly that it would have shocked and distressed him profoundly to think of any woman, even a 'broad-minded' one, witnessing that (to him imagined) scene in a public audience.

But then I have to imagine it too, since apparently I am not allowed to see it. I missed out on its first full performance because by the time I was aware of it, it had already been banned.

And, much to my chagrin and frustration, I just missed out on a private performance of the controversial scene in Melbourne, although big, clean-shaven men, studiously polite men in anonymously grey-suited pairs cropped up, uninvited, at the house where I was being given a dinner party two nights after the amateur performance, and again, the next day, rose ponderously from an elegant sofa at my entrance into another house where I was being given lunch. (At least it might have been the same pair, or it might have been an entirely different pair, but they looked the same, and their object was the same: to persuade my hostesses to make statements.)

So it was with alacrity that I accepted my son's invitation to queue with him for a Sydney performance, sponsored by the most reputable and distinguished academics, politicians, and men of arts and letters. We arrived two hours before the doors were

125

to open, just to be safe, and already the queue stretched down the stairs, along the street, and curled back and around in a giant U shape through the enormous parking station next door. Groups were sitting on the concrete floor picnicking on hamburgers and chips, and although many of them would be, by their clothes and youth and ebullience, classifiable by authority as 'hippies' or the 'lunatic fringe', there were many older people too, unimpeachably respectable as to dress and deportment (I don't suppose eating a hamburger out of a paper bag or drinking coffee out of a thermos in a cold parking lot is considered lunatic, even by authority), and at intervals along the queue there were big clean-shaven anonymously grey-suited men studiously reading newspapers: they looked familiar. Police cars and vans screamed up outside, lights blinking. It was rather exhilarating. Some kids passed a bottle around. We ate hamburgers.

Half an hour before the doors were due to open the queue had looped out of the parking station and stretched, four deep, right down the block, still punctuated by the big, clean-shaven, anonymously grey-suited men studiously reading newspapers (how on earth do they get them to look so alike: they must take a course in conspicuous camouflage). If it was cold in the parking lot it must have been icy wind-driven hell in the street.

I think I anticipated what would happen. When the doors opened a couple of thousand people broke queue and stampeded. It was terrifying. I was swept by the sheer weight of bodies up against the garage wall, and pinned there, quite helpless, elbowed and butted and buffeted and trampled over and practically suffocated. I remember thinking madly: All this for a bit of graffiti? And then my son, who had been swept on somewhere else, fought his way back to me, and with our companions we elbowed and pushed our way through the surge and out into the street, bruised and defeated, and that taxi picked me up finally on the windswept and freezing corner of an empty street some blocks away.

And it wasn't until I was safe in my own warm kitchen, shaken and battered a bit, that I could think sanely again. That terrifying stampede had not been for the sake of a bit of graffiti at all, but for the sake of a fundamental adult liberty to make one's moral decisions and judgments for oneself. Aching all over, and still thwarted of the play, I thought a lot about obscenity. (I suppose one reveals something important about oneself by what one considers to be indecent.)

I thought of the obscenity of starving refugees in Asia, of famine victims in India, of dying Biafran babies, of children maimed and mutilated, of Vietnam despoiled, of young boys, loved and loving, being made, against their wills, into the approved and official murderers of a people who in no way have offended them. I thought of those same boys murdered themselves. I thought of burned and torn and diseased human flesh, the dead bodies of raped girls. I thought of condoned graft and corruption, of callousness and brutality and viciousness, I thought of all the obscenities that are being perpetrated all over the world that we can read about quite openly or watch on our television sets. I thought of Czechoslovakia and shuddered, and went to bed and couldn't sleep.

Last Friday night I was asked to yet another performance of *America Hurrah* in an audience composed entirely of invited guests, who were to be a television forum afterwards. But the controversial last short play, being banned, could not be performed. So, having no opinion of my own on its obscenity or lack of it, I was not qualified to discuss it.

But if I am to judge anything by the two plays that preceded it, or from the argument and discussion by the people who had seen all three, I suspect strongly that the whole trilogy might be highly moral. I will even go further and call it a morality play, in the medieval sense of the word. To us Australians it might even contain a dire warning, as the horrifying medieval plays in the time of the Plague warned. This too might happen to us if we continue dehumanising ourselves. We might turn into grotesque papier-mâché or plastic dolls who make a parody of the human act of love but get their kicks from writing dirty words and viciously destroying everything about them.

But of course I don't know really. At my age, and with all

127

that travel, and all that reading, and all that experience accumulated painfully, I am still not considered to be adult enough to judge for myself.

(Incidentally, I knew all those words when I was a snotty schoolkid.)

THE CHARM OF OLD HOUSES

Last Sunday I bought seven houses. At least I think it was seven, although I may have changed my mind about a couple of them towards the end of the afternoon.

They were beauties, every one. Romantic hulls redecked and furbished, sandstock bricks or stone cleaned down, discreet frilling of iron lace and delicate pillars frosted white, tubs of flowers and orange trees strategically placed to emphasise or enhance a wide verandah. And one I bought, sandstone that one and very old indeed, had been rejuvenated completely with an austere treatment of oiled wood, so you couldn't really tell if it had been built a hundred and fifty years ago or excavated from Ur of the Chaldees, or dreamed up by a very clever architect anticipating tomorrow.

I think I liked that one best of all. There was a great swooning bush of winter-flowering jasmine, and a very old wisteria vine nubbed with the first swellings of little buds. I sighed for it.

Anyway, even if I can't buy them all, or live in them all even if I could buy them in reality instead of imagination, it always makes me feel very queer and emotional to see an old house being restored instead of bulldozed down. Old houses are uneconomic, unfunctional in the contemporary sense, even downright uncomfortable if you haven't got the money to lay out on a lot of ingenious and expensive alterations, but they have vivid personalities and a sturdy honesty of construction that moves me deeply, even when they are in half ruin: they were built to stand and shelter generations.

Well then, I bought all those houses on a Sunday afternoon drive, and that was such a pleasant old-fashioned thing to be doing. Peaceful, as if tomorrow was as secure as one once believed

129

it to be, as peaceful as it seemed to be when brilliantined young men called for girls scented freshly with old English lavender and took them driving in family cars begged for the occasion. And Sunday afternoon then had a sweet heaviness about it, an undemanding drowsiness after the excitements of Saturday night and the ritual Sunday baked dinner. Sunday afternoons were decorous and formal really: boys were just as likely to propose, parked in the dappled silence of a bush road, as they had been to proposition the night before at the Palais de Danse, heated with the ecstasies of the quickstep and the smells of fly-tox and floor wax and Evening in Paris.

But the houses I wanted this Sunday afternoon belonged to other Sunday drives in buggies and sulkies and gigs and broughams, to sprigged muslin and parasols and button-up kid boots and polished harness and lavender gloves, and gem scones with fresh cream and strawberry jam for high tea after.

The friend who took me Sunday-driving had bought one— bought one really, I mean, not the way I buy things recklessly in my head—and it was perched high on a sheer cliff face over dilapidated boatsheds. A Victorian house come down in the world. A poignant house of original modest stateliness, but now deteriorated into a nostalgic shell, bedraggled at the lace hems, patched and peeled and shored up, shoddily partitioned to accommodate yet more temporary tenants. I wondered, prowling as soft as could be through the abused grace of empty echoing rooms, boarded up to damp and musty gloom, whether the tenants too had been going down in the world. Or coming up? Who was Tony, who had written over and over again on the cracked plaster that he was a good boy? In red too. Was that a bit of despairing whimsy, or a last desperate appeal to the Fates? There wasn't a fireplace in Tony's room.

But there was one in the original dining room, marble and iron and snot-coloured tiles, and somebody had lived there who liked paintings (or even painted paintings) because the dingy old walls were chequered with paler oblongs and bits of fluff and dust clung sadly to skew-whiff picture hooks. Only the paler

130

oblongs were quite small oblongs really, so whoever it was didn't go in for massive oils. Water colours probably. Maybe gentle seascapes, with that view. Was it a maiden lady, or a finicky bachelor? Somebody who really appreciated the high ceilings and the plaster mouldings and rosettes, and the three long windows that must have let in so much light before they were boarded up. And still on the wall there was part of a Japanese paper cut-out clinging tenaciously to its tack—faded red. A bridge, was it? A sampan? And was it torn like that viciously or only hurriedly?

I know that it will be lovely again, that house, after terrifying expenditure, and reluctant compromise, and exasperation with plumbers and electricians, and appalling shocks as to the real state of the floorboards, and sleepless nights as the cost of the dampcourses mounts inexorably and the balustrade of the staircase proves to be unsound and foreign workmen chip the marble of the fireplaces in the confident belief that such useless old things are to be sealed in anyway, and that eventually the house will own its owners and dictate to them the style and period of chairs and tables and beds and sofas and impose upon them its own restored and vibrant and stubborn personality. The owners will compromise, but the house won't.

I know this, because I've been through it all. Twice now. And I swore that I would never let a house own me again.

But they are so eloquent, these old houses pleading for appreciation, like old beauties in rags and decay and poverty who still wear their bones and the memories of their conquests with such unquestionable authority that one never doubts their right to do so, and pays homage. And fantastic bills for restoration. And mortgages the rest of one's life in their service.

And still prowling softly softly through that old, abused and battered house that now owned my friend, I remembered—oh, so many years ago now—sitting in a window embrasure a metre thick and gracefully arched and looking through a vista of low wide arches and mildewed walls rising out of little symmetrical mounds of powdered plaster and cat-droppings, and dirty grey stone floor-flags, worn like silk, and great hewn rough beams,

131

and it was another friend then, who had discovered an ancient set of dentures in an even more ancient cupboard, rank with mouse dirt, who sat beside me, clacking the grinning teeth in his hand and regarding the receding ruined caverns of my newly acquired house with the most sweet and contemplative smile.

And he said—how truly I didn't realise then: 'It's best like this. It will never be as beautiful again as it is now in your imagination. Now you can achieve the consummation with a thought, with a blink of your eyes. The vision is still flawless. Safe,' he said, 'in your skull, my dear.'

But, being arrogant and filled with confidence, I did not heed him, and after ten years of unremitting labour and loving service, broke my heart on an exacting house which was just beginning to flaunt the full authority of its restored beauty when I had to leave it for somebody else to enjoy. And I swore I would never do that again.

But peacefully, drowsily Sunday-driving through the dizzy warm spring afternoon I just wondered—looking at other old pampered beauties of houses flaunting their restored charms— where Tony, a good boy without a fireplace but with a lonely imperative to write things on walls in red, might be now.

I'll bet he's in the most modern home unit, built on the site of a bulldozed old house, and tricked out with central heating and a bar in imitation leather and buttons to press and switches to switch, and lots and lots of lovely hot water. At least I hope so. Because I think that's what he wanted.

For myself, I live in another old house. And it owns me.

IN PRAISE OF THE GP

I have wanted to say something about the medical profession for weeks now, while all the erudite people have been deliberating and pontificating and the would-be transplanters have been straining at their moral leashes, and the medical expertise has been pouring into columns and columns of print.

There has been a prevalence of witchdoctors.

But we've had the old flu wog in our house, and naturally called in our GP.

We've called in our GP fairly often in these last few years, but never lightly or hysterically, and only when we really needed help, and always bearing in mind that he is overworked and tired and doesn't get enough sleep and has problems and a family of his own to worry about and probably never gets to sit through one whole meal without frantic or panic-stricken interruption.

As a family of chrysalids, every one of us biologically involved in becoming something else, older or sicker or more sadly mature or bursting into adulthood or just sparking raggedly into first bloom, time-clocks all out of synchronisation with beastly flesh and not one of us resigned (we're a stubborn lot) to the inexorable laws of nature, we could not do without our family doctor.

Because that's what a good GP is. A *family* doctor. In every illness he considers the whole unit, and how one component of it might be abrading another. And why. And in treating one he actually treats all.

Maybe we've just been lucky to land upon a family doctor we love and trust implicitly. I have heard sad tales from more unfortunate people who have got themselves medically entangled with cold consortiums, devastatingly efficient and completely impersonal, the hasty dispensers of bleak patented miracles that

133

neither warm nor hearten nor encourage, but only bring temperatures down and aseptically clean up infections.

It's not that I'm against asepsis. Or scrupulousness of hygiene. But I never had any dealings with the medical profession until I had my first baby, and that was because we were poor, and doctors' visits expensive (ten-and-six it was then), and my mother had a big red book and sublime confidence in the efficacy of friar's balsam and senna tea and antiphlogistine poultices (or bread and sugar ones) and treacle-and-sulphur doses and Epsom salts and lysol and old sheets torn into bandages, and I don't think we suffered from the want of a doctor all that much.

But when I had my first baby I had it grandly in the biggest and most modern hospital in Sydney and they were all so damned efficient that they would have aseptically amputated all the joy from such an experience if I hadn't been as stubborn as I am. I still remember with a shudder how they slammed the lift doors in my husband's distraught face while they conducted me coldly and efficiently to the upper regions of pain and glittering reflectors and hard trolleys and horrific steel cases of instruments in the sterilising and great clocks ticking out the seconds and the minutes and the hours and white masks and intricate apparatus of unmentionable intent and impersonal clinical questions and muffled screams and groans coming from other rooms and complete disapproval of the fact that I had painted every toenail a different colour so that I would have something nice to look at. It was a torture chamber.

I had my last baby in my own bed in my own house, with no anaesthetics or reflectors or clocks or masks or clinical questions but a hell of a lot of gentleness and kindness and warmth and encouragement and my husband boiling water in the kitchen (to keep him busy: I'm on to that water-boiling lark now), and after it was over the other kids came in all shining and radiant to see their new brother—and no glass between. And the adults involved—the new mother included—all got slightly sloshed, on happiness, I think, as much as ritual champagne.

I don't know that I would recommend that for every mother,

but it does have something to do with the way I feel about GPs. Dispensing warmth and kindness and sympathy and understanding as well as pills.

They are in a terribly equivocal position these days. And very low in status on the medical totem pole. The knowledge explosion has exploded just as violently in their field as in the educational or the scientific. No single person, and I will throw you Leonardo and Burton, and Hippocrates himself, could ever keep up with the spate and torrent of new discoveries. Doctors are being forced to specialise, to contract and narrow themselves to a single branch of study, and in narrowing themselves narrow, unfortunately for us all, the broad humanity which is the essence of the Hippocratic oath they all took once.

'Whatever house I enter, there I will go for the benefit of the sick . . .'

As a family we have been lucky with our GPs. I was just remembering the family doctor we had in Athens who treated us by remote control. He taught me how to use a hypodermic, practising on a potato, so that my sick husband could come home to our island with some chance of proper treatment. That doctor was a little sandy ferrety sort of man and he smoked eighty cigarettes a day and kept his records on the torn backs of the packages and never sent bills and believed, quite truly, that he was on earth, and privileged to be so, in order to heal people.

I shovelled on to him alcoholic bums and terrified young girls and proud and agonised old ladies, denying the death-fear, and he took them all, and healed them if he could, and soothed them if he couldn't, and never reproached me for my trespass upon his time and his tolerance.

And he said once that if he had three sons he would make the cleverest and coldest a surgeon, and the warmest and kindliest and sloppiest a GP. 'A healer,' is what he actually said. And I said: 'What about the fool of the family?' 'Oh,' he said, 'I'd make him a gynaecologist.' And we laughed ourselves silly.

At Epidaurus, under the western slope of the mountain Kynortian in the Peloponnese, there lie the ruins of the ancient

135

shrine and hospital of Asclepius, who started all this. And on the island of Kos, just off the coast of Turkey, there grows still a very old plane tree (not old enough for what they claim, but perhaps seeded or sprung from the original) under which a healer called Hippocrates once taught. A disciple of Asclepius, he was, and dedicated to the art of healing. And in 2000 years what he set down is not only without parallel, but a model of what clinical records should be.

But the important thing to me is that he never forgot his humanity and his obligation.

'Life is short,' he wrote, 'and art is long, the occasion fleeting, experience deceitful and judgment difficult.'

Therefore, now, let me set down my praise of the ordinary general practitioners who are game enough to tackle all that. Who bring to ordinary people like me comfort and consolation and reassurance.

If the breed dies out for want of appreciation, or more tangible rewards in specialisation, the families who rely upon their family doctor are going to be the poorer. In love and trust and confidence, I mean. As if such sonky emotions mattered any more.

ON NOT ANSWERING LETTERS

On the subject of letters I've had a couple of very plaintive little ones within these last two weeks. Gently reproachful. Puzzled even. They go something like this:

'I wrote to you on such and such a date about such and such a matter, but since I have not had a reply must suppose that the letter went astray.'

There is no need to suppose anything of the sort. I'll take a bet it is on my desk now, somewhere in one of three stacks, each equally mountainous and weighed down respectively by a set of goats' bells, a river pebble, and a rusty bolt from the buggy of the Kelly family.

On the corner of every letter in the first stack is scrawled firmly: 'Answer'. On the corner of every letter in the second stack is scrawled—less firmly—'Try to Answer'. And on the corner of every letter in the third stack is scrawled absolutely nothing. Even my optimism won't carry me that far. Because if, as is being borne in on me quite inexorably, I haven't got Buckley's of even reducing the first stack (more being added to it each day), let alone rolling up my sleeves and whaling into the second stack (which is actually the most interesting stack because not one of the letters is begging specific questions or asking for information or advice or issuing invitations to speak at this luncheon or that or to open festivals and fêtes or to address meetings, but just extremely interesting letters from extremely interesting people whom I would love to answer: I can't get near that lot), then what on earth am I to do about the third stack?

Burn it? I can't. If all those people took the trouble to write to me a letter of commendation or praise—or censure if it comes to that—they deserve the courtesy of a reply. Theoretically, that is. But the credibility gap widens daily. I am like a politician making promises to myself with my tongue in my own cheek. Tomorrow, I say. Tomorrow. Phooey. Tomorrow there'll be more.

Why do I not employ a secretary? Because, upon my word of honour, I cannot afford one. Besides, there are very few of my letters that could be answered by a secretary. The invitations, perhaps, but what could a secretary write to the enchanting old lady who is saving a crooked sixpence for my daughter's wedding, or to the whimsically contentious young one who has thrown down a gage to me on prior possession of John Donne? She says he wrote 'Busy Old Fool' for her, and I say he wrote 'Busy Old Fool' for me. Or to the lady who also owns a cat called Jeoffrey, named from the very same very obscure poem by Christopher Smart. Or to the letters filled with personal and family reminiscence, valuable human and historical stuff, worth exploring further. Or to the senders of manuscript and poems asking for comment and advice (I feel terribly guilty about those: I try, but reading manuscript takes time and extreme concentration).

The point being that I *love* my letters. I can't get out to the mailbox fast enough in the mornings to see what the day's bag is. The only way a writer can judge the depth or degree of his communication is by the response it evokes. It's like an exciting conversation. I say this. You say, yes but. And ideally we should be off, thrust and parry, poste and riposte. But not even D'Artagnan could thrust and parry with quite so many people at once. The very thought is exhausting.

I even like *writing* letters. At least I used to. I used to fancy myself rather as an eighteenth century lady of wit and charm and negligible domestic duties seated at a silk-polished escritoire with lots and lots of cunning pigeonholes and secret drawers and sticks of sealing wax and intricate seals and a finely wrought sandbox and a jar of quill pens and a single rose in a fine glass vase, and my taffeta sleeves rustling secretively as I scribbled scribbled scribbled delicious confidences and spicy observations to the wittiest and wickedest people (taking great care, of course, to make a fair copy of each letter in my own journal in case

138

my *bons mots* should be lost to posterity).

Oh, but that is a far cry to the set of goats' bells and the river pebble and Kelly's bolt.

I am trying to remember how long it is since I wrote a letter to one of my friends abroad. A year? Eighteen months? Something like that. Through lack of communication they have been metamorphosised (is that a word?) into Other Worlders. When I try to imagine them I find I am making them up, piece by piece, quite laboriously. Actually they don't exist at all.

I am not being flippant, or grizzling about all this, but in fact any freelance writer has quite a considerable amount of secretarial work to do on his own account. I have a filing cabinet which I am forced to keep in order every day or I would never know to what I am committed or who paid me for what or what might be deductible when the tax man cometh. I have a receipt file and I have a bill file and a bank file and a contract file and two dozen other files as well, and I have a diary for deadlines and a Teledex that has to be kept scrupulously up to date. I have a filing system for carbon copies and another for tear sheets. All this takes more than five minutes out of every day, and is boring to boot.

Come to think of it, most of my writer friends are, and have been, men. And they always have devoted and efficient wives who look after all that bit for them and put fresh flowers on their desks as well and call them for meals. I do think that if the wife of a writer is a writer herself she should be allowed a wife too. Just a little one. No, I'm not becoming a perverted and nasty old lady. I would just like to be free to get on with my business. Which is writing.

Because I am a housewife like any other. I do have a cleaning lady twice a week but that is the extent of my domestic help. And houses, as any woman knows, don't run themselves. If there are to be meals the meals must be planned for, shopped for, prepared, cooked, and cleaned up after. If there are to be clean clothes in the closets the clothes must be washed and ironed. If the bed linen is to be changed somebody has to change it.

139

Also, one cannot have a family and pretend they don't exist. They do, imperiously and demandingly, each with his own problems and his own particular claims for attention. And I cannot sell them short for a heap of mail, no matter how fascinating the mail is. That's for career ladies, of whom I am not one.

If I could take one whole day off every week I could clear it all up and keep clear. But I cannot afford one whole day a week. Nor even half a day a week. And if I had a whole day free each week there are so many things I would like to do, like taking a ferry ride, or going to the zoo, or sitting on the beach with a book, or browsing through bookshops and boutiques, or stripping down my sitting room chairs, or covering cushions, or planting more trees, or just visiting a friend.

However, writing this I have made one resolution. Today I will go through those piles and fish out all the invitations and at least have them off my conscience.

But the next time any of you are puzzling, pen poised, about how to fill up the requisite two pages of duty letter to parents or grandparents or godparents or aged aunts, will you think of this poor Sisyphus, eternally rolling her paper ball uphill?

Only, I would hate it if you stopped writing to me.

LAMENTABLE BROTHERS

Last week in Sydney was Freedom from Hunger Week, and I suppose that is why I am writing about hunger this week, not believing that one single special week is enough time to remind our well-fed selves that about half the population of the world goes to bed hungry every night. Bed? How stupid and complacent of me. Most of them don't have beds. And one of them dies every nine seconds.

If anyone is nosing out obscenity those facts should be obscene enough for even the most ardent of our professional or self-appointed public moralists.

In fact the necessity for a special Freedom from Hunger Week seems to me to be quite an obscene necessity. We sent our donations, some of us ate a starvation meal and grimaced and said: 'Doesn't it taste awful,' and then we responded generously enough to the Sunday doorknock appeal, and went back to our Sunday roast dinners or barbecues with good appetites and virtuous consciences.

The Australian Freedom from Hunger Campaign have actually collected five and a half million dollars in the last five years (I don't know how much extra they garnered in the special Obscenity Week), much less than the cost of one F-111 of course, and such a sum seems so piddling and inadequate for all they want to do that I for one feel dreadfully uneasy.

I did have a most informative and frightening pamphlet on world hunger, with masses of statistics and figures and percentages, but as usual in my enthusiasm for causes I loaned it to someone who never returned it, which is just as well really, because I find such staggering statistics to be eventually quite meaningless, and I have been sitting here trying to imagine hunger.

Shamefully, I can't. Not really. I don't think anybody who has never been hungry can. And I suspect that is the root cause of our apathy towards the problem.

I mean, I am hungry right this minute. And I know exactly what I am hungry for. Specifically, two particularly luscious and perfectly ripe pears that are at present chilling in my refrigerator. I am hungry for those pears and a pint of fresh cold milk. And my doctor is very pleased with me that in my third week of (ironically enough) Asian flu my appetite is at last improving.

But I know, certainly, that that has nothing to do with real hunger. After all, the pears and the milk are there, tangible things, mouth-watering, just waiting for my pleasure in eating them. And I had a grapefruit and two boiled eggs for breakfast, and I know my daughter is cooking (ironically again) curry and rice for dinner and we had a conference on my bed this morning about whether she should buy fresh meat or whether we should be frugal and use the leftover chicken and lamb in the refrigerator: it's likely to be thrown out otherwise: the cat is awfully finicky about his food.

These are shameful things to write, and I feel shame at writing them while I am threshing about and trying to stretch my imagination to the point of comprehension. And failing. I know that if I saw one starving child my heart would turn over and I would do anything, anything, to nurse that child back to health and strength again. But all those millions are beyond me. They become amorphous, beyond the reach of my imagination, beyond realisation. Finally a set of statistics.

I have a photograph here of a little Chinese girl. It was taken during the last war on the railway platform of the provincial city of Liuchow, and when the man who took the photograph focused his camera the little girl was alive, and when he clicked the shutter she was dead. It is the photograph of a dead little girl. Very dead. She looks like a rag doll, a gawky rag doll, but pretty really, with square-cut black hair and great big stary black eyes. The eyes look surprised. She had walked all the way from the city of Kweilin to get to that railway platform, through hundreds of miles of drought-stricken country where whole battalions of soldiers were down on their hands and knees in the fields, grubbing for grass roots to keep them alive. I suppose, having got so far, that little girl would have to be incredulous when death took her anyway, between the focusing of a camera and the clicking of its shutter.

They do say that you don't really die of emptiness, even having been empty for as long as four weeks. You die of diseases that are sometimes quite respectable ones but are usually indecent. Obscene if you like. Tuberculosis and cholera and influenza and pneumonia and rat-bites. If you have lived for five years or ten or if you're lucky maybe thirty-five on millet or maize or lentils or rice or black beans it is more than probable you will have picked up one of the deficiency diseases on the way, the diseases where chronic hunger disguises itself as feeble-mindedness, or feeble-bodiedness, or blindness, or impotence, or such complete dullness and apathy of mind and body that you are incapable of helping yourself and become a dumb sitting duck for insidious microbes and parasites. Nature is cruel as well as prodigal. Perhaps that's why the starving of the earth reproduce themselves at such a prodigious rate.

Trying to realise hunger I have been forced to come a little closer to peoples I understand. I have been reading about the potato famine in Ireland, which halved the population by immigration and starvation. In the worst period 15 000 Irish people were dying of starvation every day. And I've been reading about hunger in nineteenth century England, hunger which began the Ragged Schools and Dr Barnardo's Homes, and hunger in eighteenth century England which filled the gaols and overflowed into the Hulks and then into the transports which colonised Australia.

But the really mad thing is that hunger in the world today is unnecessary. The earth is being used only partially. It is quite possible, with present scientific techniques and agricultural skills, to add millions and millions of acres of cultivable land to the world's potential larder, with improved irrigation to grow two or three crops a year instead of single crops, with improved fertilisers to double or treble crops.

The Freedom from Hunger Campaign work with their so inadequate funds on this basis—helping people to help themselves. Restoring dignity and pride to our lamentable brothers. But it is too big. Much too big. It is a matter for governments, the same governments who, pinched ever so slightly, cut down first of all on what is nicely called 'foreign aid'. The same governments who can litter heaven with the remains of their satellites and spend billions on military hardware and personnel.

It is mad mad mad. The same governments could, if they wished, put a meal into every hungry stomach in the world. In the meantime it is left to individual organisations like the Freedom from Hunger Campaign. They must break their hearts at how little they can accomplish. But even a little, I suppose, is better than nothing at all, and so we have Weeks, Obscenity Weeks, as though people aren't going to be just as hungry this week as they were last week, and next week too, and the week after that, and next year, and the year after that.

Come to think of it, I don't believe I want those pears and that pint of milk just yet. They might choke me.

THE PLEASURE OF LEISURE

We have just been celebrating in anticipation the six-hour working day with another nice long weekend. Or rather, the Olds who still remember their militant union days might have spared a passing thought for the reason for the holiday. The Youngs, I suspect, just had a long weekend. And maybe a lot of the Olds did too, the fierce teeth of militancy long since drawn in exchange for a set of plastic clackers, so much more convenient, really, and quite adequate for the softer fare of affluence.

Still, what with garbage strikes, and postal strikes, and transport strikes, and teachers' strikes, there are evidently still a lot of militants about one way and another, and I have no doubt that the six-hour day will eventually become a reality.

And after that we will celebrate the five-hour day, and then the four-hour day, and then the three-hour day, until the day we find that in the meantime automation has snuck up behind us good and proper and everybody will have to fight for job permits to enable them to work at all. Jobs by lottery, maybe, or as prizes for competitions to be discovered in the breakfast cereal or on the backs of dog-food packages.

Not that I'm against a six-hour day. I was brought up in a strong labour and union atmosphere, and you don't shrug off your origins easily. Actually my father was only militant in conversation, being a hedonist by nature and finding fishing more to his liking than union meetings, but he paid his dues regularly and had Strong Opinions, upon which he discoursed lengthily and passionately. (I was wrong to use the word 'conversation'. He probably never had a conversation in his life: at least I never heard anybody else get a word in.)

I have just discovered from an old friend of his, who is a

marvellous discovery in himself, and a discovery made through this column too (I'll never grizzle about letters again), that they were apprenticed together in Derby, England, to the Haslam Foundry and Engineering Company at the turn of the century. They earned four-and-sixpence a week for a working day from 6 a.m. to 5 p.m. with three-quarters of an hour for breakfast and an hour for lunch. They did a seven-year apprenticeship and advanced in wages one-and-six a year until the last year, when they were advanced two shillings. So, at twenty years old, they were earning fourteen shillings a week.

But what to me is most interesting—no, not most interesting, but most apposite to what I'm writing about—in this fabulous communication from my father's friend, is the fund of anecdotes he offers about playing whist at the mess table at mealtimes, and swimming in the Derwent River, and boy apprentices lugging in their cricket gear to the foundry so they could play on Chester Green at dinnertime, and going to the YMCA, and learning chess, and the fun they had visiting the Royal Agricultural Show on complimentary tickets wheedled out of my grandfather, and a family secret I never knew—my father used to be a choirboy. I wish I could charge him with it: he never let on to us, not a single word in all those words he used so dogmatically.

For adolescent boys who were worked hard and had pretty little leisure they seem to have crammed it with activity. Participant activity, I mean, not spectator activity.

In 1908 my father's friend came to Australia, and my father followed him in 1909. After all sorts of jobs they landed up in the canefields at Mackay in Queensland, where they lived in a barrack room with two collapsible hessian bunks, no bedclothes, and a plague of fleas. They had breakfast at six, were in the field by six-thirty, and worked, with a lunchbreak and a morning and afternoon smoke-oh, until six o'clock at night, and until noon on Saturdays. For twenty-two-and-six a week.

I am not for a moment recommending this as a desirable set of working conditions, and no damn wonder my father became a theoretical and conversational (?) socialist.

But it comes back to leisure, and enjoying what precious bit of it one can get. I know my father, until the last year of his life, enjoyed every minute of his with a pleasure that was probably the closest he ever got to sensuousness, and I was thinking about this, and wondering how much people actually do enjoy their leisure these days. I can think of hobbyists, gardeners, dedicated handymen, the yachting fraternity, fishermen, and not many others.

Theoretically we all have so much of it now. But practically, do we? In the urban sprawl a lot of people spend at least an hour—a smelly, nightmare hour—getting to their work, and another hour getting home again. At the weekends there is the car to clean and the lawn to mow and the maintenance jobs to be done on all the possessions still on hire-purchase, and the Saturday morning shopping, and heaven knows what else.

It is almost impossible for ordinary wage-earning families to exist in even the basic degree of affluence without both partners working, or the man of the house taking two jobs. (I come across taxi drivers constantly who are driving spare time to supplement incomes inadequate for their families' growing needs, and widows who have to work, under the lap and fearful, because they cannot possibly live decently on their stingy pensions, and so many many wives who spend all their leisure time catching up on housework and maintenance put aside because they have to hold down jobs through the week.)

So where have shorter hours got us in terms of real leisure? Everyone seems so hurried and harried and twitchy these days that the most they can make of their leisure is to blur it away with alcohol or collapse torpidly in front of the television, which doesn't demand any participation whatever.

Of course there are weekends, with hideous traffic and crowded beaches and fretful children and all the enormous effort required to get out and away to anywhere that's the least bit peaceful or pleasant. In New South Wales we've just lost some of our northern beaches to mining development, sewage effluent has fouled up others, and there's not all that much left, assuming that one thought it worthwhile spending hours of leisure packed white-hot and bumper-to-bumper to get there. On the whole it seems less of a strain to stay at home and get one's wind for the next frantic week.

I've just been reading about one of those ant-heap industrial-domestic satellite projects in America, where the men had actually achieved a five-hour working day, the shortest in history, and were blessed with all the leisure any working man could dream of. They came home early in the afternoon with hours and hours of complete freedom to do anything they chose. And their wives said that for the first two weeks they tinkered with their cars and played Mr Fixit around their apartments and took up squash and golf again and fooled around with plans for inter-apartment-building baseball matches or talked about keeping racing pigeons. And after that they dropped one activity after another and yawned and yawned and took naps in the afternoon and too much liquor with the boys or sat around watching daytime television and criticising their wives' management of the household. (The wives, of course, hadn't had their own working hours reduced, so were probably jaundiced about the whole situation: what woman, hurrying through a busy day of planning and meals and housework and ferrying kids to and from school, wouldn't be jaundiced at a great sluggish lump of male lolling around the place and telling her how to be efficient? It's a wonder there wasn't a break-out of ice-pick murders.)

But what happened after a month was that practically every man was moonlighting at a second job, simply because they were bored out of their wits with so much leisure and didn't know what to do with it. Would that happen here?

Oh, happy happy happy the man whose work is his hobby, and who lives in blissful innocence of the frenetic rat-race for more and more yet. That really doesn't seem to have made people happier at all.

THE TWILIGHT ZONE

Waiting time is always an uneasy time. A curiously helpless time. Deprived of any possibility of action even the most optimistic spirit flickers like a flame deprived of air. Time drags. Indistinct possibilities—perhaps inimical—prowl the corridors of one's mind. The ghosts of old fears walk. New fears shudder suddenly into sharp relief and are subdued only partially or uncertainly, leaving disquiet. Nerves jump.

Waiting time is like twilight, indeterminate yet prescient, before the lights blaze on and the night declares itself.

I feel all this very strongly now as the world waits for the American presidential elections and whatever the subsequent declaration will be. It seems certain that not much will be as it was before, but how momentous will be the change, and in what direction? How deeply and irrevocably will we be affected? Affected we Australians must be, and I think more importantly than by anything that happens in our own electorates.

Whatever we say or do now, whatever we hope, whatever we fear, we are powerless to influence even minutely the dramatic action of the awesome American extravaganza currently on stage and whirling in a frenzy of hysteria, violence, hatred, vituperation, threats, promises and predictions to the end of the act and the moment of disclosure.

And as at all truly consequential moments in history it is suddenly and devastatingly clear that whatever is to happen started happening a long time ago, while ordinary people, unwitting and uncaring, went about their ordinary affairs in standard pattern blinkers, blind to everything but the narrow personal path they had chosen to follow. Or had been, all unknowing, pressured into following.

149

In 1913, for high society, life was still a continuous fête of dinner and balls and opera and ballet, carriages and coupés, country weekends, the shooting season, the Henley Regatta, satin and tulle and diamonds and deep décolletage, immaculate shirt fronts, black satin revers, and faceless servants who knew their places and valued them. How could those privileged people have believed, in the golden feasting and dancing of high summer, that they were dancing into an abyss, prepared and waiting long before, that would swallow up a whole generation of European youth and a way of life that would never be recaptured?

In the year of the Wall Street Crash there was dancing too in the 'world made safe for democracy', more frenzied, less gracious, perhaps even a little hysterical, but they do say that in New York that year the sunsets were blood-red, the most beautiful that had ever been known, coloured so gorgeously by the good soil of the Midwest blowing away into dust.

Munich I remember by my father's drawn face and his restless pacing through the house at night and his frightening outbursts of anger against those simpler, more complacent or optimistic neighbours and workmates who expressed perfunctory relief and got on with their business and beer and betting as usual.

When the Mongol horde swept out from Tartary I suppose the watch-fires on the towers of Kiev burned with a bright reassurance, and sleepy sentries warmed their hands and yawned and dreamed of food and liquor and willing girls.

And here in Australia ordinary men go about their ordinary affairs still, as if nothing were happening, or as if whatever is happening is no concern of theirs.

Since 1914 ordinary men, mostly decent men, have slaughtered something like one hundred million other ordinary men, and their ordinary women and ordinary children too, with bullets and bayonets and bombs and flames and slow starvation and gas ovens and more refined forms of torture. And ordinary men have come back from the slaughter to live out their ordinary lives and die their ordinary deaths, convinced that the slaughter was necessary for the betterment of the human race. Or of one

150

particular portion of the human race, self-designated to be served the biggest and richest slice of the cake no matter who has to make do with crumbs only, or stay locked out from the feast altogether, noses pressed to the windowpane.

Never has there been a time like this for the angry and frustrated stirring of the scrabblers for crumbs and the entirely crumbless, humiliated finally into boldness, and demanding a fair share. A fair share of food, of education, of housing, of medical facilities, of the benefits of the new marvels of sophisticated invention. Demanding a fair and equal right to civil liberty, to freedom of expression, to justice, to human dignity. Demanding a fair and equal voice in the portioning out of the cake.

It is a dreadfully uneasy time, filled with the sullen muttering of the discontented, errupting into painful spasms of violence and brutality that breed more violence and brutality. Fear engenders repression, repression engenders hatred, hatred discards reason. Men brave enough to teach reason and tolerance do so in the foreknowledge of the assassin's bullet; a country like Czechoslovakia which liberalises harsh laws is brought to heel by force. The cold war warms up. Riots and looting are everyday occurrences. National looks at national with ugly intent, whipping up an orgiastic pitch of hatred. New and bitterly determined forces emerge, student power, black power, and the terrible power of the utterly deprived. Punitive clubs and batons and fire-hoses and gaol sentences check them only momentarily, politically evasive words and derogatively dismissive labels check them not at all.

These are signs and portents. Signifying chaos? Or annihilation. Conflicting voices scream conflicting messages and threats and warnings, and like medieval Europe we rush to the millennium as to the end of the world.

Or we wait, helpless of action, incapable of influence, in an indeterminate twilight of waiting, prescient with the advent of change. When those gorgeous sunsets flamed behind New York it would have been of no use to have recognised in them the good soil of the Midwest. The dust bowl was already a reality.

And over the next few weeks the threads of history will draw together inexorably into a pattern that will inevitably create a new series of conditions for the existence of the human race on this planet.

What will the pattern be? It is too late already to go all the way with LBJ. LBJ isn't going anywhere any more excepting back to the ranch. Perhaps wisely, he got off.

Where might Hubert Humphrey demand that we should go? Or Richard Nixon? Or Spiro Agnew, friend of military dictatorship? Or George Wallace, bent on 'law'n'order' at any punitive price? Or—God help us all!—Curtis Lemay?

Every one of these aspirants to dizzying power and terrifying responsibility is committed publicly, globally, to change. Each of them screams, hoarser and hoarser with the effort of making himself heard: 'The old way has failed us. I will lead you a new way.'

A way to enlightenment, justice, some hope of harmony? A way to further repression? A way into Armageddon? A way back to the Stone Age?

Put away your placards, kids and long-hairs and quasis and pseudos and ratbags and irresponsibles and arty types and the lunatic fringes. You might as well save your breath and your energy for the moment. You can't do anything now but wait.

THE VOICE OF
RESPONSIBILITY

At this time when the in-fighting between the conservative elders of our tribe and the impatient young is getting rather nasty, it is interesting that the obviously more swinging elders of Britain have thought it fit to lower the age of legal responsibility in their tribe from twenty-one to eighteen years.

I suppose, in our usual follow-my-leader fashion, and after the usual time-lag, and in spite of predictable outrage and consternation from the traditionalists, we will eventually tag along and declare our eighteen year olds to be adult too.

Young artisans, apprentices, bank clerks, typists, trainees, embryo executives, hooligans, vandals, rape packs, schoolkids, and practically the whole student body of our various universities will be, in this event, entitled to a political voice in their own futures.

And since their futures are likely to be much longer than the futures of the ruling elders perhaps it is just that they should have the opportunity of saying their say in the shape of things to come at the polls instead of having to howl protest and dissent in the streets in order to be heard.

As long as they don't have any political voice they can be dismissed with ridicule and contempt, or sternly subjugated in the interests of their elders, just as women were dismissed with ridicule and contempt, or sternly subjugated in the interests of their male overlords, before they fought their way through to recognition as fully fledged members of society, and won—violently enough—the right to vote. And won also the novel status of political importance to the seekers-after-votes, who had to execute a chagrined about-face from contumely and disdain to outright wooing. From the lofty self-satisfactions of disapproval to the invidious position of having to ask for approval themselves.

There is, of course, something a little incongruous, even zany, about voters going to their voting in school pinnies, blazers, flat hats and hair ribbons. In this time of ever-protracted education there would be a sizeable group of young citizenry saying their say in the management of society before they had ever properly contended with it, and while they were still wholly dependent upon their discredited elders.

One does not discount for a moment the very real concern of the educated young in the future of their country—which is their future—or their idealism, or their passionate sense of justice, or the freshness of their ideas. But until their ideas and their idealism have been tested against the abrasive realities of fending for themselves in the market places of a society something less than Utopian, they are theorists only.

Still, they are considered to be old enough to drive lethal automobiles, old enough to drink intoxicating liquors publicly or privately, old enough to become parents, old enough to be held responsible for their actions by the law, old enough to put on their country's uniform and kill other people, old enough to be killed themselves. It is not so very long ago that a number of schoolboys went straight from their desks to the cockpits of Spitfire planes, and very grateful their elders were to them too.

And since students are the members of the community who suffer most directly from the inadequacies of our penny-pinching education allocations, the power of their vote might force politicians to pay more realistic attention to educational needs instead of grudgingly doling out the minimum ration of dollars (although well-oiled with soothing unction and sweet promises at election times, it's true) as they have been inclined to do up to date, not finding it necessary to consider the opinion of the voteless student body, or the voteless trainee teachers, further than to reprove or punish any attempt to voice complaint.

Nor should one forget that not all of the eighteen to twenty-

154

one age group are students. Many of them have been contending in the marketplaces since they were fifteen or sixteen and have already acquired some experience of the ways of the competitive world and the real value of the dollar. They have probably, also, formulated some ideas of their own based on their experience which might be worth consideration.

I have heard it put forward that the years of limbo between leaving school and coming of age are so very dangerous for young men and women at the peak of physical maturity and mental agility precisely because responsibility is always being urged upon them on the one hand, and denied them on the other. I don't quite see how anybody can learn to use responsibility without having responsibility to use.

But what is most interesting about this age group is that they are completely innocent of the somewhat muddled and constricting mythology of their elders. To the young the First World War, the Second World War, and even the Korean War, might well seem as dim in time as Waterloo or fabled Agincourt. Historical events. Like the Great Depression their parents go on about when they are lecturing the young on ingratitude. Or the Australia of Henry Lawson, and mateship, and pioneering, and rugged individualism, and rough diamonds with picturesque personalities, and damper and billy tea and swaggies.

These are a new generation in a new time, and much more at home in it—never having known any other time—than their elders, who are still nostalgically dragging the chains of past traditions and past moralities and past social patterns and attitudes through the here and now, where such encumbrances, even though cherished, are sometimes hampering. And mostly irrelevant in a changed and ever more rapidly changing society.

There would be, obviously, many young people too immature, selfish, stupid, feckless, scatter-brained, or loutish to use the power of the vote seriously and responsibly. There are many adults already enfranchised who are also too immature, selfish, stupid, feckless, scatterbrained, or loutish to use the power of the vote seriously and responsibly. And there are many citizens who are

155

just too old and feeble-minded to use the power of the vote responsibly. I suppose that's one of the weak spots in the democratic system of one citizen one vote.

But a young vote might blast some fresh air through the cobwebby dovecotes as well as ruffling the smug old doves into activity and attention to the needs of this large section of Australians.

Anyway, it's going to be interesting to see how it works out in traditionally conservative and newly innovating Britain. You never know, it might prove to have been a really good idea.

FIZZ!

It seems very suitable at this time when Jackie Kennedy, the uncrowned Queen of America, has bestowed her hand and her heart on Aristotle Onassis, the poor Greek boy from Smyrna (admittedly ageing, and no longer exactly poor, but what the hell: it is a classic fairy story as fairy stories go and should do much to encourage and inspire other poor Greek boys) that the other supreme gift of American civilisation should simultaneously be bestowed upon the land of myth and magic.

With the acquisition of Coca Cola as a bonus to the acquisition of Jackie, things might begin to go better at last. Or go different, anyway.

Greece has held out stubbornly for a good long time against the benefits of this mysterious beverage of secret formula and extravagant claims. This in itself used to be refreshing. In a different way, of course.

After all, the Greeks had plenty of refreshing drinks of their own, whose ingredients and properties were known and officially passed as harmless.

How well I remember the gaseous pleasures of *gasoza*, chlorophyll-green or the faded pink of old-fashioned corsets, psychedelic orange or innocently clear except for the fascinatingly restless jostling of the bubbles imprisoned in the bottle, and served so icy cold that the tastebuds were momentarily anaesthetised and it was several seconds before the sticky coating of sweetness was apparent in one's mouth or the bubbles exploded convulsively in one's innards.

In that unsophisticated time *gasoza* was often manufactured as a backroom enterprise with Heath Robinson machinery salvaged from heaven knows where or improvised from heaven knows what. Colouring, flavouring and sweetening were variables. But it didn't matter much as long as the maximum quantity of gas was pumped in.

Then there was *vanillia*, beloved of children, who spooned the great white lump of vanilla paste around and around in the glass of ice water until it softened and then sucked and dribbled over the spoon, to the detriment of their clean clothes, the despair of their mammas, and the delight of the outsize wasps homing in on the sweetness. And *vissinatha*, a liver-dark decoction of cherries—or was it mulberries? Healthful anyway, and recommended earnestly for all childish ailments, like the rose hip syrup we used to queue for on the National Health in London after the war.

Later, with tourism and growing sophistication, the Fix beer monopoly began producing really delicious and unfizzed fruit drinks—orange and lemon and apricot and peach and apple in season—and the other soft drink manufacturers apparently got clued in or invested in new machinery because soft drinks generally became dependable. In fact they became very good. I think someone passed the word to soft-pedal a bit on the gas pump. The adventure of opening a bottle of *gasoza* was gone, of course, but you can't have everything.

But the tremendous consumption of soft drinks—five hundred million bottles a year I read somewhere—was, and still is I suppose, a public consumption, a pavement consumption, to be sipped by dressed-in-their-best women and children at little iron tables under a scalloped awning at the evening hour of promenade. The men were more likely to be sipping *ouzo*, while the linked young girls, as soft and ripe and downy as peaches themselves, paraded up and down, whispering delicious secrets to each other and tossing braids like thick glossy bell pulls for the benefit of the foppish young bucks with sideburns and keychains, strolling on casual inspection tour.

And the bubbles fizzed and the sugar-sodden wasps fell drunkenly into glasses or crawled in spilt pools of *gasoza* where the last rosy light was caught in little winks, like diamonds.

Summer and soft drinks and soft intent of slowly passing girls deliberately re-passing the sleek moustaches, the pointed shoes, the twirling keychains. I don't know that Coke would really have added anything to it. Or will add anything to it, although I have a disturbing image of the evening promenade speeded up to the demented pace of a TV commercial, and I'm not at all sure about that!

But what did add to it—and added to everything in Greece—was water. Clean water, pure water, cold water, served with all food and all other drink as a matter of course. A bottle of soft drink, a cup of coffee, a glass of brandy, was always accompanied by a glass of water, sweating with chill. A meal was accompanied by a glittering carafe. Every household icebox had a water tank built in, so there was always ice water on tap.

In fashionable urban Kolonaki or in some shepherd's hut remote even on a remote island the first refreshment a guest was offered was a glass of cold water, precisely centred on a ceremonious tray. In Kolonaki the water would be accompanied by a glass of liqueur or a little saucer of jam. In the shepherd country there might be a few choice figs, picked with the dew on them, or prickly pear fruit peeled of spines, a handful of almonds, a plate of raisins. It didn't matter. It was the water that was ritual, ceremonious, elemental, and anywhere away from a municipal water supply the guest was expected to comment on the sweetness of it, its purity and freshness, and his host's good fortune in having access to such an excellent spring.

Any Greek will swear to you that he can detect the subtle differences between water from two different springs. I am not sure that palates can be so fine, but that is what they claim, and men have come to blows about the respective merits of certain springs and wells. There are towns that are famous for nothing but a sweet pure spring, whose magical properties will draw invalids from hundreds of miles away, and barren women, and ageing men seeking renewed vigour.

Adders of one sort or another may abound, but the water is eminently drinkable, whatever Baedeker may have suspected, and whatever some timid tourists suspect now, cautiously rejecting the sparkling water for something safely bottled, even to clean their teeth.

Oh, the sacred springs of Greece! Haunted by gods and weeping nymphs and myth and magic and legend ever renewable, ever recoverable in the cold gushing crystal of their lovely waters. Poseidon forever strikes his trident against the sunbaked rocks of Lerna in Argolis to make a spring for beautiful Amymone. Pyrene forever weeps inconsolable tears to make the fountain at Corinth. Castalia forever flees Apollo at Delphi. On the island of Poros you can drink the deathless waters of Poseidon. Springs disappear, other springs gush forth miraculously, moved by earthquakes that remind you Poseidon is still busy with his trident.

I daresay there will be some new myths springing up now. With the advent of the beautiful nymph Jackie, beloved of the demigod (satyr?) Aristotle, there came the magic waters of Coca Cola, whose secret is kept safe by the high priests of Big Business forever and forever. And there came also weapons in plenty, even for reluctant warriors, tanks and guns and bombs and other instruments of destruction, powerful in war.

Oh dear, I can't go on with this. I just hope like mad the beautiful nymph Jackie doesn't prove to be Pandora.

NOTES FROM UNDERGROUND

With examinations in progress and the school year winding up to its nervous end, a horde of young people are about to be launched into the Great Society to sink or swim, according to their native wit and the real worth of the education to which they have been submitted for the last twelve years.

If they are to be valuable members of society one would sincerely hope that they have been encouraged—at least in their senior years of secondary education—to criticise that society constructively, to express their ideas for improvement, innovation and reform freely, to be politically aware and argumentative, and to take an active role in the government of their own school communities while still a part of them. One would sincerely hope that they will be launched from their schools as highly critical, alert, mentally creative and socially conscious individuals, armed with more than the piece of paper that certifies only the amount of set instruction they have been able to absorb towards the end of slotting nicely into safe and untroublesome conformity.

I wonder how many schools in Australia do so encourage the young men and women in their charge to think outside the purely academic curriculum, to question and criticise and discuss and debate the society which they are about to inherit, its morals and manners and customs and taboos and institutions, and the dependability of such things as life rafts in the face of a turbulent full flood tide of social change. I wonder how many schools even permit, let alone encourage, open discussion of the education system itself, or welcome suggestions from students for immediate or long-range improvements.

And I suspect that such schools are rare indeed. If they exist at all.

Lately I have had an interesting communication from an organisation of secondary school students in Melbourne called Students in Dissent. This organisation differs from Secondary Students for Democratic Action, while supporting it, in that it is presently underground, from necessity I don't doubt for a minute, but perhaps from choice as well, as being more exciting that way as well as less vulnerable to punitive action.

I know that all schools have always had secret societies with esoteric passwords and code names and vows and symbols and elaborate rituals and regalia. (If you think about it there are a lot of supposedly adult and publicly unshakable pillars of rectitude and decorum who still play at secret societies with the unbridled appetite of children.) But I don't want to denigrate, even by inference, Students in Dissent, which seems on the face of it to be an organisation both purposeful and responsible, and not at all like anything I remember as going on under the old Assembly Hall at Wollongong High.

They (he? she?—I don't know) sent me a whole swatch of underground news-sheets, not only their official sheet 'Tabloid', but also a selection of the independent news-sheets that are quite suddenly being roneoed off in high schools or under high schools or in the nicest suburban homes all over the Melbourne area. Apart from a certain rather flamboyant and revolutionary style to the titles—'Ubique Underground', 'Folklore Underground', 'Treason', 'Sentinel Underground', 'Reform', 'Fallout', 'Pravda', 'Peon Underground', 'Tirade', etc.—what impressed me most after a diligent reading was that there were so many of them and they displayed such damn good sense. A bit of student cheekiness bubbles up irrepressibly once in a way but on the whole one is inclined to wonder why their headmasters aren't standing up and looking smug and taking credit for having produced such remarkably intelligent, lucid, provocative and stimulating young people.

What their headmasters are actually doing (by my reading of the news-sheets) seems to be precisely the opposite. There are fulminations, cries of 'menace!' and 'manipulation!', 'sinister

162

outside forces!' and 'gullible minds!', there are threats of expulsion (in the case of Michael Eidelson a suspension carried out) and—most alarmingly—security police investigation of at least two sheets, 'Pravda' and 'Ubique Underground'. That one is really nasty to think about. Police intimidation in schools? Where on earth is the Great Society heading? Isn't it about time that there *was* some criticism of this sort of repressive action, so frighteningly reminiscent of the totalitarian way that these same students are taught to abhor in contrast to the democratic way where freedom reigns and everyone is equal and entitled to express his own opinion as long as it is the opinion of entrenched authority?

And what are these subversive, gullible-minded, manipulated young undergrounders saying that is so menacing?

From 'Ubique Underground': 'The adage (no doubt a wise one) that rules should not be made unless they can be enforced is too often taken to mean that any rule must be enforced and too infrequently taken to mean that there shouldn't be a rule. In other words, the *reasonableness* of a school rule is not enough debated.' (The italics are mine.)

And from 'Tirade': 'As a basis for discussion we put forward the following positive programme of immediate reform . . .

1. The SRC *should be given a more prominent role in school administration, while being limited to students from senior school.*

2. Forums *to discuss protests on the many trivial issues linked with administration, e.g., boys' long hair, restrictions on girls, etc.*

3. Freedom to form political clubs *if students so desire, and these to be free of staff interference.*

4. Religious instruction *should be made optional for seniors.*

5. Some freedoms *now granted to Form 6 should be extended to Form 5 as this would break down the exclusiveness surrounding matriculation students at present.*

6. Student-run meetings *or discussions to replace many of the unnecessary and petty Monday morning assemblies.*

163

7. More communication *between students and staff, and more freedom generally.'*

Also from 'Tirade': 'Students should ask themselves what they are achieving in schools, and what their role is in relation to the system. Student revolution is not the answer, as this system would simply be replaced by another. A questioning critical attitude is the vital thing, so that no administration will be permitted to feel secure and so self-assured that it can adopt a conservative and unchanging policy.'

From 'Tabloid': 'Social action can mean two things. (a) It can mean the patching up of the effects and results of our society—results such as poverty, neglect, lack of education, etc. This type of social action is called Social Welfare. (b) Or it can mean the abolition of those forces in society which make Social Welfare necessary—it can attempt to abolish those forces causing poverty, lack of education, etc. This type of social action is called Social Change.'

Oh, you wicked wicked children! Your business is to be meek and obedient, to recite on Monday mornings that you love God and your country and honour your flag, to speak when you are spoken to, to swot up facts and figures and figures and facts for the purpose of passing examinations, and to leave such vexing questions as human rights, social change, civil obedience or disobedience, and even your own education to your elders, who know best. Even if they can't go backward as far as they would like, at least they will do everything in their power to prevent a new generation from going forward. So watch it, and always remember that everything is for the best in the best of all possible societies.

For myself I can't see any reason why you shouldn't be freely and articulately above ground, but then I suppose you might qualify for being run over or having your scholarships taken away or being denied your education altogether.

Thanks anyway for inviting me—however dangerous to myself by implication or contamination—down under.

BEWILDERED ON
THE BOURSE

'Bourse,' says my dictionary, is a 'name given to the place, in foreign countries, corresponding to our (Stock) Exchange, where merchants and financiers meet to transact business.' It also says something of the low Latin root of the word, meaning 'hide (stripped off and tanned)'.

There now. I'd always imagined that the Bourse was one single particular street somewhere, cobbled, with solemn old buildings of rosy brick and curved white plaster mouldings, and all lit with the calm light that old prints have.

I'd never thought exactly where this street might be. My sense of geography at the best is shaky and at the worst utterly baffling to my family and friends, who cannot understand why I persist in locating Spain on top of France, or get so terribly confused about ports of call on sea voyages. So I had never been so bold as to assign my Bourse a particular city or even a particular country, unlike the Rialto, of which I have an actual photograph with myself under a striped umbrella drinking something out of a long glass and looking pensive, possibly because I had just been through a very tiresome hour persuading a banking gentleman that an Australian travellers' cheque was valid money. The Rialto had let me down. 'You'd do better on the Bourse,' I was probably saying to myself.

I have been moved to pinpoint the Bourse more exactly by the current world crisis in finance. What with trembling francs and tottering pounds and stubborn marks and dithering financiers and incomprehensible economists, it is disappointing to me to have my solid and dignified Bourse, so satisfying to the imagination, reduced to hide stripped off and tanned, or just any old foreign stock exchange. Because I've been to one of those (stock exchange, I mean) and came away convinced that everybody inside was mad. I'd had some sort of crazy notion that if it were only *explained* to me I would be able to sort bulls from bears as well as the next one and even come to some sort of simple understanding of the real nature of money, which is quite as mysterious to me as geography, in spite of the fact that I need money more than I need geography and have found that the heedless use of the one has more far-reaching consequences than the insouciant use of the other.

I still don't know what money is, apart from being the root of all evil, as some pious folks would have us believe, or not being everything, as others say more moderately. Secrecy and shame and guilt hang around it and furtiveness, either through not having enough of it, or through not wanting to reveal what an amount of it one's got.

'Money,' wrote the economist Ralph G. Hawtrey, 'is one of those concepts which, like a teaspoon or an umbrella, but unlike an earthquake or a buttercup, are definable primarily by the use or purpose which they serve.' Further, the *Encyclopaedia Brittanica* states firmly that 'money is anything'.

Well, if that's the closest the experts can get, it's no wonder that currencies reel and tremble and shake and flounder about, let alone poor bemused people like me, who still can't grasp the principles of the gold standard or Fort Knox or why all those ingots have to be shuttled around from vault to vault. How do we know the ingots are gold, anyway? They might be bars of salt or peanut toffee or sawn up railway sleepers for all anybody is going to tell us. Stranger things have been used as money before this, sheep and oxen and elephants and skulls, pigs and palm nuts, feathers, cowrie shells, handfuls of nails, gunpowder, slaves, serfs, or those colossal millstones that were used by the islanders of Yap as negotiable lolly. (I am very proud of knowing that Yap is in the South Pacific, although I have never met a Yappese, and do not know if millstones are fluctuating these

166

days or devalued or holding steady or out of circulation altogether.)

Anyway, millstones don't seem to be any sillier than those bundles and bundles of dirty crumpled paper that used to pass as a foreign concept of money. How gingerly and unconfidently one handled it, representing as it did thousands and tens of thousands and hundreds of thousands of monetary units—in other words two cups of coffee, a tip for the waiter, a museum catalogue, and half-a-dozen coloured postcards. And which traveller has not eventually been stuck with pockets or purses full of leftover lira, gulden, drachmas, dinars, escudos, roubles, shekels, taels, yen, or even a stray zloty or two? (I bought some leftover drachmas once from a traveller in London, only to find when I tried to use the stuff in Greece that all the noughts had been dropped from all the currency in the meantime.)

The one thing I know about money is that it sticks to some and not to others, by what principle of monstrous inequality I don't know. Contrary to Scott Fitzgerald's profound conviction I've never found the rich to be noticeably different from the rest of us. A Rothschild I knew, who might justifiably have indulged in a bit of swank, actually lived in a Thames-side pad (sparsely furnished at that) at Whitechapel, and often seemed hard-up for spending lolly. Millionaires, at least the ones I've met, have turned out on acquaintance to be about as amiable or dim as lesser beings, although perhaps they went in for wives rather more extensively than most men can afford to do, and were either meaner or more ostentatious about tipping (whichever way was bound to be wrong, as one of them rather sadly pointed out to me: he was very sensitive about it).

And yet they must be different, because they have the stuff and I don't. Also they keep the stuff and I can't. The knack must lie in knowing how many rupees go to the krone from day to day or hour to hour or bolivars to the rial and where the ingots are stacked this week and what is happening on the Bourse. It seems a terrribly risky game to play, particularly at the moment when you can't put your trust in any sort of money because it's likely to turn into something else entirely by tomorrow.

I suspect they are wisest (if not presently richest) who put their faith neither in paper nor banks but gold pieces in their socks stowed under the floorboards, or well-set skulls piled in the loft, or pigs or elephants or bundles of feathers or jawbones or herds of yak or bricks and mortar or diamonds or olive groves or palm nuts or anything else evidently tangible and negotiable. Millstones, even, if you happen to be Yappese and millstones are steady.

Then you needn't fret yourself about the precise location of the Bourse nor whatever madnesss is happening there with francs and marks and dollars and levs. You'll have a little something with which to barter when all that paper stuff collapses. Even something with which to ornament yourself. We're bound to get back to barter and ornament sooner or later. Sooner, I hope. I will feel much safer.

A PRIDE OF LIONS?

I was asked to write something about Australian men. But nobody has specified precisely what sort of Australian men I am to write about. And they do come these days in all sorts of shapes and sizes and degrees of confidence and sophistication and weights of chins and bellies and rumps.

Actually I do think Australian men are getting a bit rumpy in this generation. That's not really a criticism, only an observation. I don't object to solid hindquarters on either men or women. Or horses if it comes to that. Sculptural, in a way. Those great white rippling Percherons ploughing through the poppies in fragrant French fields.

Well then, since I am Australian born (and bred, I suppose, if you can call my rather zany upbringing breeding: although my father did say we all had fine wrists and ankles and therefore might class ourselves as thoroughbreds; he did loathe women who were, as he said, 'beef to the heels like bull-calves') obviously I did my first practising on Australian men. There was nothing else to practise on in a small Australian country town.

And they were young quarry workers and farm labourers and a few taxi drivers cruising down the coast for Sunday larks (our town had the reputation for the prettiest girls on the Illawarra coast) and a stray commercial traveller or two. Or even three, if I am to be honest. And very worldly the commercials seemed too at the time.

In fact, I suppose, I practised on anything handy in pants. From the moment I could distinguish. And I think I distinguished quite early.

But of course I had no standards of comparison then, apart from literary ones (Byron and Marvell and Lovelace and Keats

169

and Shelley and that lot, and the gloomier and more thrilling Russians: Raskolnikov sent me quite wild), and current film stars, of whom, perversely, I romantically preferred Conrad Veidt ('there's a lighthouse shines across the bay'), and Peter Lorre and Claude Rains, when all the other girls were swooning for Robert Taylor. I didn't tell the other girls, naturally.

But my very first romantic attachment was to twins who were called—I know that I will never be believed—Honk and Donk. They used to bring me sticky sweets when I was eight and endeavour to lure me down into the aloe cubby we had on the beach. And after Honk and Donk came the Bawny Crab (I swear the name is true) who died, poor boy, of the lockjaw, contracted while pinching the obligatory number of little brown eggs for me through the rusted wire of his mother's hen coop. And then there was Tom Fly (whose sister was called Flossie Dog), and Geik and Splonge and Googles. And Dai who was of Welsh parentage and nicked lots and lots of chocolates and tinned peaches from his father's grocery shop. And Eric who had been to America and showered me with a fortune in cent pieces and all his scout badges.

And writing this I wonder what sort of Australian men they grew up to be (excepting the Bawny Crab, who didn't get to be grown up). They were country boys of working-class parentage and mixed ancestry—their fathers were Yorkshiremen and Derbyshiremen and Welshmen and Cornishmen and men from Ireland and Scotland—but my father was a Derbyshire man too so it didn't seem strange. They were loutish lumpish boys, I suppose, with big soft ears and great mottled hands, clumsy and slow, and they had bad teeth and no education and inarticulate yearnings towards grace and beauty and stifled ambitions towards they didn't know what and no prospects whatever excepting the quarries or the farms or the steel mills or, if they were clever enough, a place in a bank or behind a grocery counter or on a butcher's cart or in the post office, and a war which they couldn't have predicted but which liberated so many of them into travel and romance and adventure and more intoxicating thought-patterns than they could have dreamed of then. Even in the aloe cubby. I have an idea that wars—and I am against them—hold some sort of clue to Australian men.

They will all be middle-aged now, and the fathers of families, and good members in standing of the Leagues Club or the RSL. They will be Sunday fishermen and weekend gardeners, members of the Shire Council, and their names will have been reverted from the wild and whimsical nomenclature of childhood—Honk and Donk and Geik and Splonge—to the staider names of baptism. Contracted, naturally, in the Australian way. Keith and Alan and Bruce and Harry and Vince and Cec and Dave and Christy, and they will have been married comfortably and complacently for twenty years or more to the girls called Molly and Valda and Isobel and Joycey and Sylvia and Thelly and Audrey and Gwen, and they will all have modest cars and modest bank accounts and modest houses jam-packed with plastic and modest dreams for their children, so much better educated than they were. Or maybe they have raging dreams for their children, who are bound to let them down.

Now, I may be quite wrong about this, but I don't think there was a Sir Lancelot in the whole bunch. Or even a potential Sir Lancelot. Tirra lirra never sounded, however muffled, by the rank and reedy creek that flowed sluggishly beneath my splintered window, although I listened for it desperately enough and performed prodigies of imagination in trying to transform coarse country adolescents into parfait gentil knights.

I know it is not wise to generalise—it may even be impertinent—but I don't think Australian men are good at the Sir Lancelot bit. A girl needs a phony Hungarian count for that, or a Jewish poet with eyes like ripe olives, or practically any cosmopolitan con man with a bit of the real flair for the game.

It is a flair, after all. Because what Australian men, however worthy, seem to lack, is any real sense of the romantic or the erotic. As a game, I mean. As that delicious knowledge of a pre-ordained conspiracy between the sexes that European men are born with. And I don't mean bottom-pinching either, but

171

something much more subtle—the whatever something that enables a short, bald, tubby French boulevardier to turn on one sweet slow heavy glance in passing and make the dowdiest middle-aged English spinster walk like a young queen, nonchalantly tossing her hair.

It is a very vibrant and very sensuous quality, a very melting quality, and I like it rather much myself. Because above all it is completely confident.

I think I might be beginning to generalise after all, and that is presumptuous on my part, but if I could just be allowed to sneak in one generalisation I do believe that Australian men are terribly unconfident about their own masculinity. The Lord knows why. But they seem to be so sensitive of their virility that they must constantly prove it. Not to their women, however, but to their drinking and surfing and sailing mates, their weekend mates with whom they engage in constant competition—of physical strength, mighty oaths, beer-swilling capacity, and Arabian Nights tales of erotic conquest. They protest too much.

Just on observation I would believe that their mistresses are mechanical ones—boats and cars and lawn-mowers and handymen's toolkits—on which they can lavish (and do) passions that their wives never knew existed. To watch them tinkering with mechanical innards on a blithe Sunday morning is to avert one's eyes hastily.

I was just thinking in passing that if you can have collectives like a cry of players and a gaggle of geese and a flock of martlets and a flush of roses and a pride of lions and a school of barramundi and a boil of prawns, what collective could you apply to Australian men? A boast of Australian men? A swagger of them?

Now, my great and glorious period of Australian men was in wartime, when it was fairly simple to transform them into romantics. Lancelots abounded, vowing vows and throwing down gages and begging for hair ribbons to wear over their hearts. Australian men were still lean and slouchy and brown in those days (poor damn Depression kids that they were) and under the emotional stress of partings came up with the occasional poetry of inarticulate men, poignant beyond telling. Tirra lirra rang like a tocsin through those years, and even such a glutton as I was glutted with eternal vows and perfect red roses and locks of sandy hair and regimental numbers and sets of airforce wings and champagne corks and the Song of Songs. And silver chains for my thoroughbred ankles.

Well if they were capable of that sort of abandonment then they must be capable of it now. Perhaps it is the women who are at fault. I don't like to suggest that, having feminist leanings myself.

And of course I know nothing, or next to nothing, about the new generation of Australian men. They may be Lancelots all. I've been married to one of the old breed, lean and slouchy and brown, for more years than I need to confess, and we have three nice children and are paying off a nice house and I don't think I would know quite how to react if you put me back on the boulevardes again, or into the aloe cubby with Honk or Donk, or sighing out of my splintered window for tirra lirra by the rank and weedy creek.

Actually I think men are gorgeous. I adore them, and couldn't bear to be deprived of one around. My mother used to say, wickedly I thought, that they were only forked radishes anyway, but I will settle for that, as long as they sing tirra lirra occasionally. Whatever nationality they are.

And when I am a little old lady in lavender lace I will say with absolute certitude and Dorothy Parker: 'There was never more fun than a man.'

THE BIG BREATHALYSER

A *Plague on Your Children* it was called, and I don't know what the rating of the ABC's *Impact* series is, but I hope it was high for that particular programme, and fear that it probably wasn't, and would earnestly beg a repeat showing for the instruction, edification, and stomach-turning of those who didn't see it.

I had much the same reaction to it as long ago I did to the film *Horror in Our Time*, which so hideously documented the newly disclosed world of the concentration camps for the stupefied and incredulous to see and note well and remember.

And I thought then that that was the foulest thing I would be likely to see and emotionally digest and accept in my lifetime. But I'm not sure now. The concentration camps had happened. Were past. The plague on our children is still in clinical preparation. The foulness is being stored in canisters and containers all over the world, the nerve gases, also the scientifically seeded and cultured germs of the most loathsome diseases ever visited upon unfortunate humanity—diseases such as anthrax and smallpox and the medieval plague and spotted fever and others (148 were possible, I think it was said).

But where credulity boggles and breaks down is at the evidence that this monstrous production of future affliction is not in the hands of The Invaders, diabolically preparing the great wipe-out before taking over, but human men and human women with human smiles and human eyes and human voices articulate in explanation. At least they looked human and sounded human on the television screen, but they can't be. Can they?

One has to assume that these doctors and chemists and scientists and research workers and laboratory assistants have not been coerced into their abhorrent activities, as were the brutalised and degraded attendants upon the gas chambers and ovens, although outwardly the set-up looked hauntingly familiar. There were the high wire fences, the warning notices, the guards, the slavering watchdogs, the checkpoints, and the enclosure within the enclosure. The death factory.

The advantages of plague and pestilence as a weapon in modern warfare were explained unemotionally to viewers by an American general. Plague and pestilence destroy only life. Not property. Existing installations and communications systems would remain intact for the immediate use of the conquerors, protectively gloved and masked and briefed in decontamination, so that everything could go on neatly as usual. Everything, that is, except the twitching victims.

Plague and pestilence without warning, invisible, odourless, spread on the prevailing wind over fields and farms and towns and cities and little villages. One deep breath one sweet blue day and the suppurating sores come next. Or the blisters. Or the spasms. Depending on the choice of the aerosol released. There are a variety of choices.

Viewers were privileged to watch laboratory animals dying horribly under conditions of scrupulous asepsis, and the antics of a dog under the effects of a nerve gas. Not lethal, in this case. And she'd forget after, they said, as she collapsed drunkenly in a corner and raised her muzzle and howled in agony. She'd forgotten the times before, they said.

As in the concentration camps, there were giant incinerators for the burning of carcases. Only in this case the carcases had to be sterilised before destruction to avoid the risk of contaminated smoke blowing out of the chimneys. All decontamination procedures were strict, lengthy, and involved. One was all too frighteningly aware why.

There was further film of sheep also dying horribly but out in the open and not under laboratory conditions. They seemed to die the same way as the laboratory animals. American sheep, they were. One gathered that a test in some scientific laboratories might have got out of control. Something went wrong, perhaps.

Oh well, I suppose they can't be 100 per cent certain. And there was an island off Scotland that had been used for an anthrax test on other sheep a few decades back. The test was successful, in that all the sheep died to plan, but the island still won't be free of deadly contamination for another hundred years.

And flushed out Vietnamese, of course. Gasping and choking. Nerve gas? A doctor said that thirty per cent of the adults and ninety per cent of the children died of respiratory collapse. The Yemenite victims we saw were rather nastier visually. They were seared and blistered by something or other. Something very unpleasant.

Then there were some detailed shots of human bodies polluted with smallpox and bubonic plague and spotted fever. Telling, those shots. One did indeed think of one's children immediately, and with anguish.

This is better than The Bomb. Because even small countries can manufacture enough virulent germs to contaminate large countries effectively. It makes things fairer all round. One aeroplane or one ship can release enough aerosol to fix the population of a whole city. As the American general explained, sickness would be spread pretty evenly through all classes of people in all categories of employment, so that even if only thirty per cent got an effective dose the city would still be crippled. And he did stress that there would be no destruction of property, unlike The Bomb which makes such a mess of everything.

Not all the aerosols in current manufacture or storage are lethal to human life, of course. At least, not immediately. Nobody seemed to know about the side effects, or the long-term effects. There are the defoliants, which merely reduce forests to deserts and arable land to bitter waste. And there are the aerosols of temporary effect—the so very useful tear gases and riot gases—and we all know how handy they've been to the forces of law and order.

Only, once you start using aerosols, even of temporary effect, might you not be tempted, in rage and hatred, to try something more lasting? Particularily as it is so conveniently there already, neatly stored. They said blandly, in human voices, that those racks and racks of hermetically sealed canisters of scientifically cultivated pestilence were not meant for use. What are they meant for then? Why are they there at all? Why are such vast sums (America alone is spending a million dollars a day) being invested in scientific complexes of sterile chambers filled with gleaming pipes and tubes and vats and seeding belts and experimental apparatus, all locked away behind the high wire and the warning notices, the guards and the checkpoints, and the leashed dogs prowling the perimeters?

One accident. One slip. One moment of ordinary human fallibility. One deep breath one sweet blue day . . .

Perhaps that sad hero David Vincent has been right all along. Perhaps it is The Invaders that are so carefully preparing a plague on our children. I still can't believe those people are human beings.

THE MAGIC CARPET
OF LEARNING

Last week I was one of a party of press and radio and television people who were invited by the Minister for Education, New South Wales, to inspect a very new primary school built to serve the needs of children from the very new housing estate of Tregear, on the outskirts of Sydney.

It is good to be able to say that it is a very beautiful school indeed, and I believe that it will still be a beautiful school in fifty years time, functional and functioning, and that generations of children will be happy there. It has the look and feel of that sort of school.

But what impressed me most, through the speeches and explanations and the questions and the inspection of pagoda roofs and cool eaves and sliding classroom walls and mobile furniture of admirable and imaginative design, was a thing the headmaster said, standing in the big raftered library which is the focal point of the school complex, top-lit and carpeted softly and darkly from wall to wall.

He said: 'There will be people who will say that the carpet is an unwarranted luxury. In fact, it is very practical. And besides,' he said, 'the children can sprawl on the floor and prop their heads on their hands while they're reading. It's the best way to read,' he said.

And I thought that was just about the nicest thing I had ever heard a headmaster say. To lie down on a soft dark carpet and sprawl and prop your head on your hand and lose yourself in a book. Of course it's the best way to read. And I thought too that these were very fortunate children to be so encouraged from

178

the beginning to associate reading with pleasure and comfort and relaxation, and not only the acquisition of information. Perhaps these children from a raw new housing estate, many of whom have changed dwellings and schools also four or five or six times already, will be the unlikely nucleus of a new clerisy.

Clerisy is a lovely word for which I am indebted to the Canadian writer and critic Robertson Davies (recently in Australia) who uses it himself in *A Voice from the Attic*, out of fashion as it might be, on the grounds that it has no familiar synonym.

'The clerisy,' he says, 'are those who read for pleasure, but not for idleness: who read for pastime but not to kill time: who love books but do not live by books.'

The clerisy, one suspects, are rare birds on the contemporary scene, where most reading is read for immediate profit and instruction, for information, for facts, and where fiction, unless of the sensational or semi-documentary kind ('faction' I have heard it described) is regarded with more than a little suspicion as being frivolous and time-wasting. It is more acceptable, more publicly erudite, to carry a volume on early Egyptian sarcophagus scrapers, say, than to be caught on the 8.15 with a paperback of the latest Muriel Spark. No, not Muriel Spark. She's fashionable, and fiction is all right if it's fashionable, although early Egyptian sarcophagus scrapers are better.

Also, it seems to be considered desirable these nervous days to read as rapidly as possible. There are courses that can teach you to assimilate whole paragraphs at one bolt and clumps of words at a mere flicker of the eyes. Gollop gollop gollop, flick flick flick, and you've done that one. I can see that this might be quite a handy accomplishment for busy people who have to deal with a lot of documents, or for the anxious digestion of the daily news, the company's yearly report, the relevant article in the financial quarterly. But it has nothing to do with reading enjoyment. Nothing to do with a kid sprawled on a carpet, head propped on hand, lost in a book. (This is such a pleasant picture that I keep coming back to it. Pleasurably.)

As a very fast reader myself I have often cursed my own facility, simply because I hate coming to the end of the experience of the particular book I am reading. That is why, probably, I am such a glutton for very long books, and trilogies—those three-course reading meals—and why I re-read my favourites over and over at intervals of months or years, recapturing the first intense emotions and every time experiencing new ones, so that it is always stinging, fresh, illuminating, like the most satisfactory love affair. And reading is that, I do believe.

Robertson Davies says that the best of novels are only scenarios, to be completed by the reader's own experience. 'We shall find nothing in books,' he writes, 'which has no existence in ourselves.' But in reading we can find ourselves, if we go about the matter gladly, with attention, responsiveness, and in no great hurry.

A friend of mine told me that she could never have properly or fully understood her own family background if she had not read Henry Handel Richardson's *The Fortunes of Richard Mahony*. Certainly I know that I would not have understood mine without the light shed upon it by D. H. Lawrence's *Sons and Lovers* and all his other stories of the pits and collieries, and lately, with painful recognition, by Christina Stead's *The Man Who Loved Children*.

I think this might be developing into a plea for the reinstatement of the novel, and if so I shan't apologise for it. I discovered the novel when I was eight years old, sitting (or sprawled? yes, it had to be sprawled) on the woodheap with my back against the sun-hot tin of the wash-house, chewing grass stalks and convulsed with the chaotic splendours of King Arthur's court as evoked by Mark Twain. I have been discovering the novel ever since, with passionate pleasure, distress, wonder, exhilaration, amusement, and floods of tears. And although I have read, and do read, history and biography and philosophy with profit, enlightenment, and often delight, it has always been fiction that has moved me most deeply—almost as deeply as poetry—and to which I return to lose myself, or to find myself, in those tumultuous worlds of the imagination.

Anyway, I am happy to leave the self-improvers to gobble

up facts and figures and formulas and short-cuts to material betterment as rapidly and anxiously as they may. Jolly good luck to them, and I hope they get to the quid or the well-stocked mind or whatever it is they're after as quickly as they wish. I shall take my reading pleasures more self-indulgently, in a more leisurely fashion, and at least until a public burning of fiction is introduced in the interests of progress I shall refuse to carry a novel in a plain wrapper.

And I shall think with great pleasure of kids sprawled on carpets, heads propped on hands, lost in books. That was just about the nicest thing I've ever heard a headmaster say.

A GRACEFUL GIFT

The other day Cedric Flower, a friend of many years, brought us round a copy of his new book, *Duck and Cabbage Tree*, as a Chrissy present.

Cedric's Chrissy presents have always been graceful gifts. We count among our treasures an alphabet book that he and his wife Pat made for us one Christmas in London when we were all young, with drawings by Cedric and verses by Pat. It must have taken them weeks to concoct, and contains such gems as, 'The Seine was put on Paris ground to grow those lovely bookstalls round', and 'The reticent English are modestly reared, but really their clothes are something quite weird'. And, 'Into this world there came the novelist, and why not knowing, nor willy nilly wist'. A telling touch at the time, and as time has passed more telling and willy nilly wisty than ever.

Pat, as everybody knows, has been concocting books ever since, but *Duck and Cabbage Tree* is Cedric's first if you don't count the alphabet book, which wasn't for public consumption anyway, although it should have been, and we've shared it around through the years until it has become a little tatty at the corners and we've had to put it away for the sake of our grandchildren, who will be mystified by it.

Anyway, *Duck and Cabbage Tree* is for everybody, which is nice. It is not, repeat not, a cook book, although cook books sell so well these days that the ambiguity of the title might work in the author's favour. And maybe he'll do a cook book next; it would be certain to be a pretty and witty one and to include some quite surprising recipes.

Duck and Cabbage Tree is a pictorial history of Australian clothes, from 1788, which was the beginning, to 1914, which seems to be the end as far as Cedric is concerned. One gathers that after that wearing apparel ceased to be fun or even interesting.

You might think that a history of Australian clothes is a meagre sort of vein to explore. And stopping at 1914 you don't even have the phenomenon of the Menzies suit to analyse. But even a quick riffle through the masses of gorgeous plates (if they weren't so well documented and authenticated I would swear that Cedric had run them all up himself) makes one wonder why nobody thought of doing it before.

'After all what is fashion?' asked Oscar Wilde. 'From the artistic point of view it is usually a form of ugliness so intolerable that we have to alter it every six months.'

Ah, but if you are dumped, or are born, willy nilly wist, at the ends of the earth and many months' sail from the stern dictatorship of fashion's vagaries, you probably have to invent your own, out of sheer necessity, convenience, and the materials to hand. And the results are likely to be interesting.

One of the materials to hand was the cabbage tree, that curious upturned mop of palm that still survives the developers here and there along the east coast. There's one in a backyard a few houses down from us and we pray for it in every high wind (and Cedric rushed out to the back deck to have a bit of a gloat over it). There used to be a couple more on the high ridge opposite, but progress did for them, more's the pity. If I had been around I think I would at least have stripped the leaves, just on the off-chance that there might be somebody who still knew how to weave a cabbage tree hat.

Cedric's great-grandmamma, widowed in Wollongong, wove them as a business, and a pretty good business it must have been too with the market price at ten pounds a hat. It was such an elegant bit of headgear, wide and flat-brimmed like a gondolier's hat and very finely woven, and the crown decorated in the centre with a woven star or anchor, and a ribbon tied around. And durable too in this harsh climate. Burke and Wills packed thirty cabbage tree hats into their exploring luggage (although Burke made his public exit from Melbourne more stylishly in a conical black hat, blue coat, and red shirt).

Maybe the durability of the hat, rather than its simple elegance, was responsible for the high price. When you bought a cabbage tree hat you bought it for your own lifetime and the lifetime of your son and your son's son too. A few originals survive even yet, hats, I mean, as well as cabbage trees.

I was thinking that a revival of such a stylish and sensible piece of headgear (not cabbage tree, certainly, but straw) would be very nice and decorative on the Australian male scene, instead of those ghastly little snap-brim things that make even the most comely masculine head look deformed. And white duck trousers, and Crimean shirts, red for preference, worn with a sash maybe. It's time our men reverted to a distinctive national costume. Once upon a time they were noted for their originality. On the Californian goldfields our lively lads were named the Sydney Ducks for the trousers they wore, made of a strong untwilled cotton, hard-wearing stuff that used to be worn by eighteenth century sailors and was considered most suitable for convict transportees. Duck might have become a colonial fashion out of utility, but a very distinctive fashion it was.

The bushrangers, expectably, were somewhat more hip in attire. Johnny Gilbert wore buckskin trousers with polished boots and leggings, a jewel-studded vest with a cravat, and stuck his pistol through a red sash. His hair was long and oiled and he must have been a smasher. Johnny O'Meally too wore buckskin breeches and high boots, but seemed to have been more modest about his upper wear. When killed he was found to be wearing three Crimean shirts and a white comforter. Why three? Was he cold? Did he not possess a smart sack coat like Johnny Gilbert?

If this book is more concerned with male fashion than female it is not only because it's high time but also because Australian women didn't create for themselves any fashion that was exclusively and originally their own.

They were lucky for a while in that early trade was with India and China, providing cottons and muslins and light stuffs that were ideal for the climate, although one gathers that the suitability

184

of a fashion had nothing to do with the adoption of it. Then as now the nitty creatures hankered after the latest mode, and the arrival of a ship would bring all the women rushing to see what the new arrivals were wearing. As Cedric writes, they were less adventurous than the men.

He thinks they probably needed the reassurance of fashion to keep them sane. 'Life in a slab hut became more bearable in a shape made fashionable by Queen Victoria or the Empress Eugénie. Under the circumstances,' he says gently, 'it seems more heroic than ridiculous.'

The men were comfortable. The women were not. Ah well, that's all reversed now. The cool mini-shift and the loose skinny skimmer have become to all intents and purposes national dress for Australian women, while the once-dashing male throttles himself—even in the tropics and as a ludicrous accessory to a pair of shorts—with a collar and tie.

I would advise him to invest in *Duck and Cabbage Tree* for some stunning sartorial ideas. And everybody else too. Not just as a plug for a good friend, but because the book is a pure joy, and a lovely Christmas gift.

I SHALL NOT WANT

Well, now we're over that again and can tune down our oscillating metabolisms, say from full panic to only normal panic, at least until next week anyway.

I do hope that the celebration was worth the preliminary panic after all, and all the thought and organisation and planning and headaches and hangovers, and that the cleaning up isn't too formidable, and that all the people who said they weren't going to bother this year changed their minds at the last minute and bothered as frenetically as anybody else. They usually do.

And now that we've had the candles and carols and gifts and feasting and family reunions, and we've been surprised all over again to find ourselves gushing goodwill in spite of everything we said beforehand, and will no doubt say again, we should all be feeling—if not actually in a state of grace—at least a little more benevolently disposed towards the mad sad erratic human race to which we so surprisingly belong. There might be something to it after all. A lot of quite extraordinary people have thought so, including Jesus Christ.

Admittedly we did not choose our human condition, but since we are landed with it we might as well be loyal to it, just in case there is more value to this peculiar experiment in existence than often appears.

But being loyal to human existence means being loyal to all of it, and of course it is difficult for us who exist in a more or less privileged mode to recognise or accept the value of human existence that is so degraded and demoralised as to scarcely seem human at all. The Biafrans, for instance, could be rejects in the experiment, as could most of the peoples of Asia, of India, of Latin America, or any other of the two-thirds of the human

186

company that look like being discards for want of sustenance. No peace or goodwill for them, or turkey-and-pud either.

Even if some of them can summon the incredible will that must be necessary to want to cling to life under such appalling conditions they are unlikely ever to realise their human potential of creativeness, humour, laughter, love, generosity—those best parts of our human dole that somehow make up for the rest and even, if only occasionally and unexpectedly, give us an intimation that we might yet be capable of being nicer creatures than we had supposed.

Most of us felt something of this yesterday, and today we're still trailing a few wisps of our better and more generous natures. Or if we're not we ought to be.

Traditionally this is the day of collection boxes, when we are supposed to distribute gratuities to the people who have served us obligingly through the year—the postman and milkman and the garbage collectors and those other collectors who are dignified now, I think, by the title of sanitary workers and perhaps don't leave a Christmas poem the way they used to do. But if indeed these people have been obliging through the year (and there are many who would quarrel with that) we've probably distributed our gratuities already: besides, they're all off duty today, maybe polishing up their smart new cars or lolling on the patio.

Still, tradition is tradition, and before there ever was a Boxing Day or a postman either, alms-giving was an obligation. In medieval England every house had its alms-scuttle for donations to the needy, every traveller of degree carried an alms-coffer as part of his luggage, every religious institution had its alms-house attached, and wealthy households employed a full-time almoner to supervise the distribution of its considerable charity.

Perhaps they had more faith in the possibilities of the human condition and the value of it than we do now. Certainly they were more religious, and considered charity as part of their Christian duty. There was no condescension or patronage in the giving, and no shame in the taking. The proper spirit was humility on both sides, and if a bit of graft crept in, or penitential bargaining

187

with the Lord (as with King John, who used to compound for breaking rules of abstinence and fasting by feeding hundreds of the poor at a time), Christian duty was still Christian duty, and it was the duty of everyone to contribute whatever he could towards the feeding of the hungry and the clothing of the naked and the relief of the distressed. Your fellow-man was your fellow man and nobody questioned it.

Oh dear. But the scale of human misery was probably so much easier to comprehend then than it is now, when what most of us feel in the face of our unfortunate fellow men is only utter helplessness.

It would be simple if we could take the broken meats from our Christmas tables as they did then, or empty the refrigerators bursting with leftovers that are going to be a bore to the most ingenious housewife before she's through serving them up again and again some different way, and distribute them personally, or through an almoner, to the hungry of the world. I am sure every decent person would do so gladly.

There are still some rare ones who have managed to retain this sense of personal involvement with the needy and the hungry and the oppressed, but usually they've done it by giving their whole lives to it, and that's beyond most of us. We might wish to be as good as that but we know very well we're not, and we've got our own lives to live anyway. Besides, our stomachs turn up so easily, even at newspaper photographs of the diseased and the deformed and the mutilated: we could never endure a confrontation with the real thing.

So what we've got left is only money, impersonal and unsatisfactory, but necessary to our contemporary almoners— the relief organisations—if they are to get on with their dedicated work of feeding the hungry and clothing the naked and relieving the distressed. I know that everybody has spent too much already, but I believe that most of us could tip up the alms-scuttle and still find something there to put in an envelope and send to the Freedom from Hunger Campaign or the Save the Children Fund to help those splendid almoners to get on with it.

And not penitentially, or to compound for self-indulgence and gluttony, or even in the name of charity, which is a beautiful word sadly debased, but in common justice.

If we believe in human existence that is. We have to be loyal to all of it and have faith in the experiment, which might, after all, have more value than is presently evident.

DEATH BY MISADVENTURE

Criminal abortion is indeed a grave and terrible subject, and all responsible adults must be glad that, in the press and on television, it is again under discussion. Discussion is good. Indignation is good. Anger is good. Nothing yet was ever accomplished by resignation, no set of circumstances ever bettered by the willingness to submit to it or put up with it.

The Victorian police surgeon, Dr John Birrell, has estimated the annual total of criminal abortions in Australia at 90,000 and has stated his belief that one conception in every five is terminated in this way. It is therefore a practice so general and widespread that it must be regarded as just one of the risks implicit in woman's situation.

It is a criminal act. But who is the criminal? The woman who seeks deliverance from the callous demands of nature, the doctor who helps her from compassion or uses her dilemma for gain, or the law which makes a relatively simple operation clandestine and therefore open to abuse?

Enforced maternity brings into the world wretched unwanted infants. All the world now accepts the necessity for contraception in some form. The fact that all the world does not accept the necessity for abortion rests on a dubious moral point, and if such a morality condemns women to shame, degradation, secrecy, sterility, and sometimes death, what is one to think of it?

Human life is sacred, says morality, and fortified by this argument, proceeds to sacrifice the life of the mother to the life of the unwanted foetus.

Abortion must be necessary if for no other reason than that so many women undergo it in such appalling circumstances.

That the circumstances are so appalling is the fault of the law.

In countries where abortion is legal it is under control, and standards of medical skill, hygiene and after-care can be maintained to safeguard the health of the unfortunate woman who has surely suffered enough in making her terrible decision. For I do not believe that women make this decision lightly or callously. It is for most a traumatic experience, and that mental anguish should be heightened by shame and humiliation as well as physical anguish turns what is already an ordeal into a punishment.

A punishment for what?

It is interesting to note that the majority of abortions are performed, not on young girls 'in trouble', but on married women who are already mothers, who love their children, and wish to restrict their families for the family's benefit, in accordance with accepted modern social teaching which urges parents to plan their families and sets up birth control clinics to the end that unwanted children should *not* be born. Even with advanced forms of contraception complete safety is still uncertain and accidents— as the town gossips used to say with such pleasurable smirks— happen in the best-regulated families. So the wife and mother, the pillar of her home and the respected member of the community, becomes a potential criminal because she has been 'caught'.

If she is in a good social and financial position she will find it relatively easy, crime or no crime, to find expert assistance. Of course at a price. And a price which has nothing to do with the actual expense of the operation, but might be regarded more as 'risk-money' on the doctor's part (at the best), or as extortion by the patient (at the worst). Fortune favours the privileged as always. But even at her most privileged a woman seeking an abortion is a suppliant, and under the best possible conditions the operation is still performed secretly, furtively, in complicity, and as a moral and legal transgression.

If her financial position is not good she will find it more difficult, she will need to beg and cringe more abjectly, she will have to turn to people of more dubious qualifications, be denied the boon of anaesthetic, suffer excruciating pain, risk internal injuries, and be bundled out into the street immediately afterwards as something not only undesirable but positively dangerous. If she has the support of her husband she will find even this severe torture more bearable than having an unwanted child.

Then how much more pitiable is the plight of the unmarried girl, who, having made a 'mistake', must at all costs conceal it from her employer, family, friends, teachers, or become an object of pity or scorn. Unmarried mothers are still, to our abiding shame, the subjects of lewd jokes and smoke-room sniggering.

If she has a lover he might marry her. More often than not he urges her to 'get rid of it'. The relationship may have been casual and ended before she was aware of her pregnancy. In these days of sexual licence she may not even know who the father is.

She might, if she is lucky, be taken under the protection of the lover who will find out an address and pay for the operation. She might have an experienced girlfriend who knows where to go. More often than not, even now, she is most dreadfully alone, and in her terror and ignorance lets weeks and even months go by or resorts to quack pills, making the abortion finally more dangerous and painful than it need have been and increasing the risk of serious illness, sterility, and even death. And girls still commit suicide rather than become unmarried mothers.

One thing is certain. No repressive legislation will prevent women terminating pregnancies they do not want. Surely it is in the best and truest interests of society to accept this, as it has been accepted in so many other countries already, where abortion is no longer considered a crime but a social safeguard, carried out under strict controls, safely, and without stigma, when circumstances warrant it.

This is not to belittle the value of human life, but to dignify it.

For surely it is a little ironic for the law to be so nice about the rights of an unwanted embryo and at the same time put the lives of twenty year olds into a lottery barrel?

ON GETTING YOUR NAME
IN THE PAPER

•

When I was a girl it was considered to be quite a thing to get your name in the paper. Local paper, that is. The metropolitans were out of our ken. News from a distant star.

Marriage would get your name in the paper. (The bride, formerly Miss Euphemia Macauley, wore a gown of ivory satin and carried a shower bouquet of cream roses. Etc.) Death also. Or competitive sport. Or being chosen May Queen. Or elected alderman. Or winning the knot-tying at the Scouts' rally or the belt-and-reel at the life saving carnival. Or giving a shower tea or being presented to an imported dignitary at the Coming Out Ball in the Oddfellows' Hall. Or taking part in the annual physical culture display.

Later there was a war and you could get your name in the local paper by being wounded or coming home on leave. Or dying.

Our local reporter was called the Tin Hare, for the extraordinary speed of his gait as he scuttled from council chambers to drill hall to wedding reception to garden fête, and he must have been a kindly man—or timid—because he never, as far as I can remember, named a name in his stilted columns without respect and approval and due formality, or raised an issue that would raise a single eyebrow. Scandals might have been common knowledge and ginger hot but no breath of them ever scorched or sullied the bland four pages of our local. Posterity, thumbing through, could well believe us to have been the dullest collection of gigs and hayseeds that ever existed.

But perhaps the Tin Hare had something at that. My local

papers are now metropolitans, and I read the names in them with some unease. Even alarm.

Who is one to trust any more?

Oh, it's not Mr Sin or the strippers or the passion-slayers that worry me. But here are doctors and solicitors and company directors and members of local government—the very pillars of our society—getting their names in the papers for being hauled into courts of law, accused of graft and chicanery and double-dealing and heaven knows what-all.

And beautiful soft women scuttling through their umpteenth love affair or marriage as fast as the Tin Hare used to scuttle on his innocuous reportage. (I'm not at all against beautiful soft women scuttling, but for heaven's sake not with your name in the paper. Scuttle softly.)

But what beats me is that these very same names in the papers are the first and the loudest to denounce the young as pseudos and quasis and subversives and phoneys and irresponsibles.

Mercy! The young have their names in the papers too. Day after day, and sheet after sheet. And they have their names there— not for chicanery or graft or double-dealing or being pseudo or irresponsible—but for accomplishment. Their names are there for hard and consistent work. School Certificate. Higher School Certificate. First year uni. Second year uni. Third and fourth year uni. Arts and Med and Law and all.

It takes twelve years to matriculate. And I've seen them, as you've seen them, sweating out that last month or so, losing a stone in weight, crashing with bronchitis or flu or neuralgia, not eating and not sleeping, half blind with tension headaches, surrounded by mountains of books and texts, and pushing and pushing themselves to get through to their names in a list in the papers.

Pseudos they might be, and subversive, and intransigent. And arty too. I've been agin them as much as I've been for them. And perhaps they will, in the course of time, develop into doctors and solicitors and company directors and members of local government and get their names in the papers for being hauled

194

into courts of law on charges of graft and chicanery and double-dealing and consorting and heaven knows what-all.

But just now at this time of year, their names are in the paper for good work consistently done. Hard work. It's frightening, sometimes. So very much depends on it.

Or their names are in the papers on casualty lists. Wounded or dead. Why? For a cause that most of us agree is no cause at all, and if they don't agree they have their names in the papers again. Like young Zarb, and young Simon Townsend before him, and young William White before him, and all the young men who said: 'No. I won't.' And took the consequences. And got their names in the papers.

Just personally, I would like for every doctor, solicitor, company director, stockbroker or member of local government, every actor, actress, huckster, hood, estate agent, loose lady going through her umpteenth love affair or marriage, every pillar of society who ever got lumbered at it—bad luck!—to go through the names in the papers.

There is little Emmelene, and Rosemary, and Roberta, and Esme. And Christopher and Robin and Adam and plain John. Their names are there because they did something, not nasty or to be brazened out, but something to be proud of. And they got their names in the paper for it.

The Tin Hare would have had no trouble with them. Names and addresses would have been all. And scuttling round he would have got them, with no breath or whisper of ginger hot scandal attached to them.

I love names in the papers actually. I think of posterity thumbing through. But I also think of the Olds, contemptuous of the Youngs, and I think of the white-faced Youngs, sick to the teeth with swot, and Olds sick to the teeth with sin, and Olds and Youngs getting their names in the papers. For various reasons.

I think I would rather have the Youngs.

A SENSE OF EASE

I never walked into my friend's sitting room but with a sense of refreshment and ease. It was that sort of room.

Not a clever room, or a decorated room, but calm and friendly and a bit untidy, and when you wanted to butt your cigarette or put down your cup of coffee there was always a table in exactly the right place, just to hand, with something interesting or pretty on it: my friend has been known to buy flowers or snuffboxes sometimes in preference to food, and amber beads, and old silver candlesticks.

There was a wall of books and lots of paintings and prints, and what furniture there was was graceful and old and comfortable and meant to be used rather than admired. The sofa and chairs were covered in fresh blue and white chintz, and there was a padded footstool for one of them in case you felt like putting your feet up. The windows opened onto trees and the sea beyond and the white curtains billowed and blew and innumerable friends or the newly adult and newly troubled children of friends, or friends of her children, slept on the window seat, after long hours of conversation in which souls were unburdened and laid bare on the coffee tables. It was a room for unburdening.

The other night I slept on the window seat again after long hours of that unburdening kind of conversation, under a pretty quilted eiderdown frosted very gently with pink flowers and with a salt breeze cold on my face and shoulders. And ghosts walked. Because my friend is moving, and the room was half dismantled.

The big bookshelves were gone, stacked plank to plank, and the books were packed in cardboard boxes labelled 'The Best Disposable Nappies in the World' and 'Seville Orange Marmalade', and where the bookshelves had been there were glass doors that one had never known were there, all ornately decorated with leadlighted symbols of red and green. Who on earth was it, one wonders, who was contracted to this suburb in 1912 or thereabouts to make bad Leonard French stained glass circles and riotous fireplaces, quite frenetic with cast iron and art-nouveu tiles? Why had one never seen before that my friend's fireplace, around which we had sat so cosily so many times, was actually hideous?

In fact the whole room was hideous. Shabby and shoddy and tired and dejected in the way rented flats usually are when they're cheap enough for the landlord to get away with the minimum of upkeep, or no upkeep at all. It is my friend's great gift that, always having had to rent cheaply, and never ever having had a place of her own, she can make ease and calm and even beauty out of rooms like these, with bits and pieces picked up at markets, or sometimes inherited, and patched up, re-covered, re-polished, and arranged so that every piece sits in its place as if it couldn't have possibly sat anywhere else.

And this is where the ghosts began to walk. Because I realised for the first time that the footstool for the blue and white chair was in fact a butterbox with a padded cushion on top. But not any old butterbox. It had once been my own butterbox and I had padded it in that time of young married life before one can afford to buy chairs, and my friend had inherited it, along with my other old tatty bits of furniture, when I had gone to England so many years ago.

And here I had been walking into my friend's pretty, calm room for the last four years, not even knowing my own butterbox, or that stepped set of shelves so very useful for putting things on as well as in, or the bulging wardrobe in her bedroom, painted over its veneer, that I had inherited from somebody else before she had inherited it from me. And the dining-room dresser that I had bought second-hand as a bargain not only because of its rather sturdy character but because I couldn't afford anything else.

And all this was very queer. It was difficult to know where

197

I left off and she began. Because when I had left these very ordinary and apparently unsignificant articles behind me they had been in a half-dismantled place like this. Tacks and fluff and darker oblongs where the pictures had hung. And piles of papers and documents on window ledges, and biscuit tins and wicker baskets and the last of the Christmas wrappings. And yellow paper laid thickly under the two pieces of carpet that you had never seen before to have been two pieces, probably because of the way she'd arranged her furniture.

And in all those years that I had been in other places in the world, acquiring other articles, abandoning them, dismantling again, building up other rooms with other things of a different character, starting again somewhere else, and making the long wobbly ellipse of experience that led me back to my beginnings, these old discarded bits and pieces had been going on quite quietly in daily use, but transformed by other voices, other hands, growing a patina of memories that were not my memories. Although my memories would have to be there too, under the new coats of paint and the blue and white chintz cover.

Lying there on the window seat under the pretty eiderdown I began to wonder about other pieces of furniture abandoned in other places or handed on, other rooms, once friendly and welcoming, stripped down to tiredness and shoddiness and tacks and fluff in between habitations and personalities. There must be bits of myself in daily use all over the world.

I had been very sorry about my friend having to give up this flat and her pleasant sitting room that had always given me such a sense of ease and refreshment. But of course I see what she will do now, being the way she is. She'll find some other crummy old place with hideous leadlighting and cracked mouldings and uncertain floorboards and she'll cover anything unpleasant with bookshelves and put down her two pieces of carpet and arrange her furniture in such a way that there is always a table to hand for the convenience of the person sitting in that particular chair, and there will always be flowers, and interesting small objects about, and ashtrays in the right places, and somewhere for a

198

friend to stay overnight. She has a gift that way. She takes her house with her wherever she goes.

And somehow it touches me deeply that there is a bit of me too in this atmosphere she creates. Like an old butterbox, padded, and so useful if you want to put your feet up.

ON BEING ALONE
WITH ONESELF

Like anybody else who for twenty-four hours of every day is surrounded by—embroiled in, part of—an interdependent society like a family, I have sometimes muttered to myself, in exasperation or frustration or sheer weariness: 'Oh, how I wish they'd all go away and leave me alone.'

And so they did. Not, I hasten to add, in pique, or to teach me a lesson, but quite fortuitously and separately they all went away. And for the first time in exactly half my life I was quite quite alone, as I had so often longed to be, really alone for a whole week that was mine to do with as I chose.

My plans were not dependent upon the plans of anybody else, my meals were not dependent upon other people's appetites, preferences, appointments or comings and goings, and my moods were not dependent upon other people's uncertain temperaments. There was no involvement, no demand, no interruption, no whirlwind of movement, eddy of activity, chatter of voices, slamming of doors, blaring of radio, calling of queries, rattle of coffee cups, flaring of anger, no snatch of careless song, and no laughter.

They went away and silence rushed into the vacuum of their absence and filled my tall house to brimming.

At first I dabbled in it quite cautiously and tentatively, not being certain of my ability to maintain equilibrium in such a quantity of the stuff, for silence, whatever it is, is not buoyant: one sinks in it rather than rises. Some sort of spiritual water-wings seem to be necessary. My heartbeats were audible and even my thoughts too loud. I felt guilty and furtive and slightly out of control. Nefarious even. As though I had no right to . . . to what? . . . to be alone in my own house? Or just to be alone? I felt apprehensive, in imminent danger of discovery, but by whom or what I couldn't have said.

There was the telephone, of course. And friends dropping in. And going out to a party or dinner. And some necessary marketing. I was not in any way cut off from human contact. But the normal and familiar human contacts seemed in some peculiar way to have changed subtly—almost to have become artificial—and in them I had the most curious sense of exposure, as though I was play-acting at being myself and not doing it very well. And always, after the voices and the laughter and the last goodnights, I would close the door and the silence would stealthily expand again to fill in the echoing pockets, and I would be alone in it, listening, waiting, and filled with an indefinable excitement.

I thought, I am myself alone at last, and I can do anything I please. What pleased me was evidently quite childish. Like making my breakfast on hock and iced peaches, served to myself quite ceremoniously with flowers and Beethoven quartets and nobody except Jeoffrey the cat to see, and he wouldn't tell. And lying in the bath for an hour, trickling in fresh supplies of hot water and extravagant quantities of cologne, and then going back to my great brass bed in the middle of the morning (the brass bed spread with the best lace-trimmed sheets) with a novel and a plate of fruit too beautifully arranged to be eaten, just as the novel was not actually to be read, because I was too intent discovering the scene to myself in the mirror. With satisfaction.

But of course these childish indulgences palled. It is probably not my nature to loll in bed in the middle of the morning, desirable though such a practice has often appeared in the past. What was more to my taste was spending the middle hours of the night, the really nefarious hours that are always potent with limitless possibility, in my study, going through old manuscripts and notebooks and letters and photographs, or just sitting in the dramatic shadow outside the exciting circle of the work lamp, listening to my own thoughts with astonishment and sometimes

201

dismay: it didn't seem to be myself thinking at all, but somebody else entirely. You just wait, I thought, until *she* hears what you've been up to. You'll cop it. And heard myself giggling defiantly.

Or in those hours I prowled from room to room very quietly, surprising things that had moved themselves from the places in which I had put them—an ashtray, a book, a jug, a shell. The house breathed and creaked and settled itself more comfortably on its foundations, not furtively, as it had done at first, but quite openly and confidently. Somewhere upstairs a door unlatched itself with a discreet click, a window chattered momentarily and was silent again. The refrigerator shuddered and hummed and there was a tune in it somewhere, and words, as there is in train wheels. The bathroom tap dripped with a sharp bright ping. The chimney shook down a little puff of soot and a card toppled slowly and significantly from the mantelpiece. I locked the doors and lit all the candles and felt mysterious and reckless and expectant, like a lady in a Gothic tale—the one who walked around in only her skeleton and all the family jewels.

I forgot to eat for twenty-four hours, and heard myself addressing Jeoffrey the cat at length and with excessive courtesy. Some mad story I told him, I don't know what exactly, but he seemed to appreciate it. I sat in front of the looking glass for an hour, staring at myself. I woke from a dream with tears on my face and there was no one to tell.

By the middle of the week the telephone tempted me almost unbearably—it wouldn't be giving in, would it, just to ring up somebody? Anybody. Or to turn the knob of the radio. Or even, because after all nobody would know, to switch on the television. Just for an hour? But I didn't. I had made no conscious pact with myself about the renunciation of these ordinary little props to the lonely, but I knew quite definitely that they were not allowed. Not this time, anyway. Not if I was to discover whatever it was. I stared at the telephone, begging it to ring. It lay stubbornly mute. It became a contest. Any other day, I thought wildly, the damn thing never stops. And finally, weakly, with sweat in my palms, I snatched it and gave in.

202

The house turned against me after that. Even while I was having that nice companionable chat on the telephone I'd known that it would. The high stool I was balancing on to reach the reserve tins of food in the top cupboard slipped from under me and I crashed most painfully. The sharpest knife cut my finger viciously. The big Portuguese basket deliberately spiked my leg. And I began turning all the lights on at night because I was scared. It wasn't at all nice to be alone any more.

They're all back again now, of course. Clattering and chattering and demanding and interrupting and involving me, and sometimes I wish they'd all go away and leave me alone. Because, next time . . . Why do I feel so strangely that there was some mysterious marvellous opportunity in all that silence? That I missed.

The *Herald* (Melbourne), 19/7/68, p.9: full page. (cf. 'Here There Be Crocodiles', p.97) Note juxtaposition of Clift and under 20 feature.

THE TRIALS OF BEING A WOMAN

PRACTICALLY every magazine, periodical or newspaper I pick up these days has an other article about women.

Their role in society. Their role in the family structure. Their role in the community. To work or not to work? To marry or not to marry? Conception or contraception? Submission or revolt? To band together or go it alone? Womanpower in action! Pow!

Every last part of us, from our minds to our innards, is under the scalpel for public dissection. Can it be — shush! tread softly — that we have become in-ter-est-ing? Not, perhaps, to be taken for granted after all?

It is true that commercial advertising still keeps us firmly in our places, Omo-ing our sheets and Handy - Andy - ing our floors, producing gourmet meals from tins and frozen packs and removing even the suspicion of aroma from such meals with a nifty spray can of spring flowers, polishing our furniture and cleaning our windows with the help of a cute wee gnome, and concentrating all our tiny minds on choosing the right brand of toilet tissue.

that astonished publicity when Professor Leonie Kramer was given a chair of literature at Sydney University, and Jean Battersby an official voice in the future of our culture.

What was there to be astonished about? They are very capable human beings, both, and splendid at their jobs, and to be congratulated. I suppose, on getting them. But why the fuss? Because they are women. And then I remember, sadly, that I heard Geoffrey Dutton, who ought to know better, referring derisively, on a television program, to lady novelists. Sinks the heart. Yet as half the human population we ought to be able to assert ourselves a little more forcibly. Yes, I know, assertiveness is not feminine, and assertive women are likely to find themselves being avoided, even by other women.

Assertive women m a k e other people uncomfortable and become themselves, the subjects of much ridicule and b a d jokes.

Women should be — oh dear — soft. Soft, quiet, dignified, serene, thoughtful, peace-loving. And that's not the stuff revolutions are made of.

Unwomanly

Revolutions are hard and angry and noisy and undignified as all get out. Think of Mrs Pankhurst's mob of terrorists and how undignified they were, how shrill, how violent. How unwomanly. Of course they got things done. But it has never ceased to amaze me that those ladies were brave enough to shatter the soft, quiet, dignified image with actual bombs.

All women's organisations since are mild in comparison. Their objectives are excellent. The broadening of women's horizons, more active participation in public affairs, equality of opportunity, civil rights, international relations, saving sons from slaughter, feeding hungry children, stopping wars.

But they are all going about it in a peaceful and dignified way.

Nobody to actually pouring acid in letter boxes or blowing things up or heaving bricks, although I did read that there is a new women's liberation group in America called WITCH — Women's International Terrorist Conspirary from Hell. Maybe there's hope there. If I am not actually advocating violence. Only having a little think about it?

There is another way. A hard way. But it could prove effective. Lysistrata took it long ago in ancient Athens. And the way is to use our very weakness — our handicap as it were — as a weapon. Go on strike. Deny those superior males their bodily comforts until they even things out a bit. No. It wouldn't work. There would be too many scabs in that union.

And of course it occurs to me that all these articles I've been reading lately in magazines, periodicals and newspapers are in women's magazines, women's periodicals, and women's newspaper supplements. If we are becoming interesting I'm afraid it is only to ourselves.

And on that depressing thought this lady novelist will get back to her kitchen. All the same I'd hate to think those commercials have actually got it right.

No change

A fighter for women — EMMELINE PANKHURST — the founder of t h e Suffragette movement.

MILITANT WOMEN from Save Our Sons movement demonstrate at the Square.

The *Herald*, 27/2/69, p.14: section. (cf. 'A Thought on Violence', p.232) The placard reads: 'Army's brainwashing methods must stop!'

CHARMIAN CLIFT on: The voices of Greece

Greeks' spirit is not tame

I have hesitated about writing anything on the Greek situation, mostly because I felt I didn't entirely understand it, and I have been afraid to write to friends there for elucidation since I might very well compromise them by doing so.

The voice of Melina Mercouri, stripped of property and citizenship, rings clear as a morning bell. "I was born Greek, I will die Greek: Patakos was born Fascist, he will die Fascist." One would

"When I am 'appy," she said once, "I explose. And when I am angry, I explose . . ."

not expect less than that from her. "When I am 'appy," she said once, "I explose. And when I am angry, I explose."

One imagines her to be very angry indeed, and that she will go on exploding. Melina's is the authentic Greek voice of resistance, the voice of Marathon and Salamis, of the pass at Thermopylae, of the Byzantine Constantine Palenlogus of the Klepths harrying the Turks from their mountain lairs through all the hundreds of years of Turkish overlordship, of the heroes of the War of Independence, of Metaxas' famous "No!" to the Italians, of the underground fighters who waged unremitting war on their German masters. This is the voice of people of the Dodecanese Islands, who, during their occupation by the Italians, painted their houses blue and white, the colours of the Greek flag.

Melina is, of course, a wealthy and famous woman, living in America, and it is perhaps easier to hurl defiance if you are not going to be seized for it and beaten up and hurled yourself into some terrible prison camp. All the same I do believe the note would

be just as clear and just as authentic if she were inside Greece, as the note of conservative Eleni Vlachou was clear and authentic in refusing, in spite of all persuasion and all threats, to publish her newspapers under censorship.

What the composer Mikis Theodorakis said in defiance we don't know, because he was nabbed pretty early and we haven't heard anything of him for a long time, excepting that when he was due for trial he did not appear and it was said he was in a coma, having most curiously developed diabetes a couple of days before.

One of the letters smuggled out of the prison island of Yioura to London last year states that prisoners were arriving in such terrible condition from Security Headquarters that the military doctor said: "But for God's sake! Were they beaten up by cannibals?"

But torture has never broken Greek spirit before. For 3,000 years they have been starved, beaten, burnt, roasted on spits, they've had their tongues cut out and their ears cut off, they've been blinded, enslaved, and for 3,000 years they have cried, "Freedom or death!"

The note is clear, authentic

And this is what I can't understand about the present situation. How can it be that they are so completely intimidated, or appear to be intimidated, as to accept a regime that has wiped out every constitutional liberty, and imprisoned liberals, humanists, intellectuals of even moderate persuasion, trade-union leaders, professors and poets and lawyers and the Mayors of municipalities, the aged and the sick, pregnant women and the mothers of large families, under the most appalling circumstances and with no right of appeal.

Even an ordinary Greek gaol is nothing short of frightful. (I know a European woman who spent three months in gaol in Athens and she said sometimes she thought she was playing Moll Flanders. She had a lot more grey in her hair when she came out, although, on the other hand, she came out speaking fluent Greek; she always did learn everything the hard way.) The prison islands are notorious.

Heroism

It is bewildering enough that the United States and Britain, as avowed enemies of Fascism, should accept the junta with no more than a "tut! tut!" of disapproval, more bewildering that Australia appears to approve of it so heartily that we deny a visa to anyone who is likely to speak out against it. But it is more bewildering that the Greeks in Greece seem to have taken it so tamely. I say "seem to have" because the resistance could be underground, as it has been so many times before, and if it is it could

any personal friends, so I hope desperately that security hasn't caught up with them yet, or they've gone to ground. I can't imagine them keeping their mouths meekly shut under tyranny of any sort.

In fact, I can't imagine any Greek keeping his mouth meekly shut. Every man is a politician and an orator. The most impas-

The p[...]

A newspaper report at the weekend said Sydney chemists this week were launching a price-slashing campaign to get rid of their "expensive image."

The general secretary of the N.S.W. Housewives' Association, Mrs K. Adami, was quoted as saying that prices had been going up for years and every chemist seemed to set his own price.

The president of the N.S.W. Pharmaceutical Guild, Mr R. L. Frew, said the guild would recommend to its members that the prices of 40 to 50 health and beauty aid products be lowered.

These products include such items as hair shampoo, hairspray, hand lotion, beauty soap, talcum powder, deodorants, suntan oil, skin creams and baby oil.

Mr Norm Thomas, a chemist in Manly, is the

The *Sydney Morning Herald*, 1/2/68, Women's Section (WS)
p.2: section. (cf. p.33) The photograph is of Melina Mercouri.

206

ICTATORS

"It was a sad day. Fascism had been tolerated for a whole year..."

Long live democracy!

"A democracy," wrote Aristotle, "is a state where the freemen and the poor, being in the majority, are invested with the power of the state . . .

"For if liberty and equality, as some persons suppose, are chiefly to be found in a democracy, it must be so by every department of government being alike open to all; but as the people are the majority, and what they like is law, it follows that such a state must be a democracy."

I was bound to be nosing around after definitions (and I found this one in Volume 7 of the Encyclopaedia Britannica, Junior-Educational) because a couple of Sundays ago I could have been discovered, rather surprisingly, on the stage of a leafy suburban cinema shouting "Long Live Democracy!" to some hundreds of people, with genuine fervour, and what's more, in Greek. Greek is a much more suitable language than English for fervour.

Now this is not the sort of thing I normally do, but it was a rather emotional evening one way and another, and a lot of other people were letting off steam, too.

International

One Australian poet recited Cavafy's "Waiting for the Barbarians" in English, another Australian poet said "Agia Sophia" in Greek, a Greek group sang Australian bush ballads, another group danced Zorba, a very well-known folk-singer belted out "Freedom," another belted out Cuban folk, the lights dazzled, the mike went on the blink, a slide of Melina Mercouri flashed on the screen brought cheers, and one of King Constantine, hisses and some cries of "Pig!"

There was bouzouika music amplified to torture pitch) and sweetly harmonised songs sung Greek style and unaccompanied. There were also speeches. It was a grand evening and we all enjoyed ourselves hugely

longer it was tolerated the more tolerable it would become to the Western world. Even token disapproval would very likely diminish with time, and it would even be possible that the colonels could be transformed into respected ornaments of the "free world." Such things have happened before.

To simple-minded people like me such things ought not to happen. Nations which declare themselves pledged to safeguard the principles of democracy, individual liberty and the rule of the law, should, in my view, honour their pledges. Or declare openly for fascism if that's what they intend to support anyway.

They might even have some arguments in favour of fascism that would be worth considering. Like Hitler built good autobahns, and Mussolini drained the Pontine Marshes. And the colonels have cleared up the festering corruption of Greek bureaucracy.

But is that enough? And is it even true? Why should one believe that the representatives

toleration of fascism is too high a price to pay, but then, as I said, I am rather simpleminded.

Troeller and Deffarge report that at the beginning of the last school term 6,000 children were rejected from enrolling at their schools because their parents had Left-wing pasts. Civil servants don't get jobs without signing loyalty oaths, or keep them if their relatives are politically active. Pressure is applied to anyone who visits a "Left-wing" doctor for treatment or consults a suspected lawyer. Those who hold the Greek flag in too much honour to display it compulsorily on holy days and colonels' days end up in gaol.

Suppress

In a new book by Stephen Rousseas and others, "The Death of a Democracy: Greece and the American Conscience," Rousseas quotes six Italian economists, who say, in part: "How is it possible for any army

The *Sydney Morning Herald*, 23/4/68, WS p.3: section.(cf. p.65) The photograph caption reads: 'It was a sad day. Fascism had been tolerated for a whole year...'

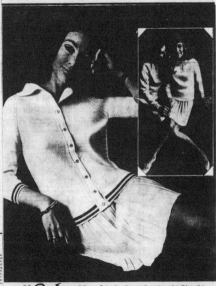

The *Sydney Morning Herald*, 1/8/68, WS p.3: full page. (cf. p.106) Note that by now the Clift essay has been moved across to p.3, with the Grace Bros advertisement.

The *Sydney Morning Herald*, 17/10/68, WS p.3: full page. (cf. p.149)
Photographs are of Hubert Humphrey, George Wallace and Richard
Nixon.

The *Sydney Morning Herald*, 16/1/69, WS pp. 2,3: full double page spread. (cf. p.200) Page 1 of the Women's Section was reserved for David Jones advertisements.

210

CHARMIAN ★CLIFT

On being alone with oneself

Showcase

Click! It's high-speed gaberdine!

play togs

LIKE ANYBODY else who for 24 hours of every day is surrounded by ... embroiled in, part of — an interdependent society like a family, I have sometimes muttered to myself, in exasperation or frustration, or sheer weariness: "Ah, how I wish she'd all go away and leave me alone."

And so they did. No, I home to add, in peace, or to book me a break, but quite fortuitously and separately they all went away. And for the first time in exactly half my life I was quite, quite alone, or I had to effort longed to be, really alone for a whole week that was mine to do with what I chose.

My plans were not dependent upon the plans of anybody else, my meals were not dependent upon other people's appetites, preferences, opinions, streams of coverage and goings, and my moods were not dependent upon other people's moods and temperaments. There was no performance to be mustered, no interruption, no whirlwind of movement, eddy of activity, chatter of voices, slamming of doors, blaring of radio, calling of queries, turtle of coffee cups, throwing of anger, no snatch of careless song, and no silences.

They were away and silence reigned with the vacuum of their absence and filled my new house to brimming.

Cautiously

Mute

Discover Grace Bros

take the plunge at Yamp Cove

Turn your back on your public and be the toast of the coast! They're putty in your hands since Watersun revamped the one-piece. Two at G.B's, all they're cut out to be in Bri-Nylon. The barer Bara mini-suit, white, navy, 32" to 36" — $18. Navy one-piece, red/navy/white super-doll tie 34" to 38" — $15.95

BRI NYLON *Watersun*

BROADWAY 2.0946 • BONDI 38 0422 • PARRAMATTA 635 0360 • CHATSWOOD 41 0111 • TOP RYDE 80 0533 • ROSELANDS 758 081

I like Sydney BUT...

By
JILL
BOWEN

Not summer suits!

211

The *Sydney Morning Herald*, 10/7/69, WS p.3: full page. (cf. p.306)
This was the last weekly piece to be published.

Charmian Clift – a tribute

"ANYONE for fish and chips?" is Charmian Clift's last article.

To me, its publication is the best tribute we can pay her.

The article epitomises her love of Australia – a love that was not blind to its faults, but great nevertheless.

I first met Charm through the pages of her book, "Mermaid Singing," a book which reactivated my own love affair with Greece.

For the past four and a half years, since she started her weekly feature in the "Herald" Women's Section, I have grown to know, admire and respect her.

Our ideas and ideals often clashed. This was natural in two people with rather forthright characters.

Suffice it to say that if Charmian Clift believed in anyone or any cause her loyalty was unswerving.

As the mother of three bright "youngies" –aged 22, 21 and 13 – she knew what it was to be classified as an "oldie."

But did she sit back and accept it as inevitable?

No. She met the challenge of youth as she had met so many of life's challenges. She came to grips with it, got to know what it was all about and became one of its champions.

Charmian Clift was the champion of many causes during her brief life, but most of all she was the champion of the underdog and the little people.

Let's hope that her words on their behalf will not be forgotten too soon.

MARGARET VAILE

Margaret Vaile's tribute to Charmian Clift, from the *Sydney Morning Herald*, 10/7/69, WS p.3: re-set and format adjusted.

LETTERS TO THE EDITOR

Vale Charmian Clift

SIR,– Charmian Clift has died.

So the announcer said. Just now. Aged 45 years.

Yet for all the sense of loss and tragedy of a life cut short there is also a profound surge of thankfulness for her life. From one small voice in the wilderness that is suburbia comes the heartfelt prayer that her family, who are mourning her death, will permit us to grieve a little, too.

I am not familiar with her novels, but each week her column in "The Sydney Morning Herald" reached us as sanity, a different perspective, giving to thousands of us who are vegetating (as our detractors put it) as we bring future citizens into the world and raise them to the best of our ability, encouragement to widen the scope of our vision.

She had courage, humour, compassion, honesty. And love. How she loved her country and its people! Otherwise why bother to take us to task? To George Johnston and your children, our thanks for being so generous as to share her with us.

ANONYMOUS
Blacktown.

SIR,– Not only was Charmian Clift in my opinion the best woman columnist, if not the best columnist Australia has ever produced, but she had a quality in her writing that left her readers feeling they had not so much read an article, as spent a few minutes with a valued friend.

It would be a fitting tribute to a fine writer if all her articles which have appeared in the "Herald" for the past four and a half years were collected in one volume. May we hope for this?

(Miss) J. HOGG.
Beecroft.

SIR,– Entirely because of Charmian Clift I became an inveterate reader of the Women's Section of the "Herald" over the past few years. The warmth, humanity, wit and wisdom of her weekly articles were a joy to read, and at times profoundly moving.

DONALD WEIR.
Double Bay.

SIR,– A sad hurrah for Charmian Clift – one of our most human and down-to-earth writers.

ELIZABETH
WEDLOCK.
Neutral Bay.

The *Sydney Morning Herald*, 12/7/69, p.12: re-set and format adjusted.

214

SIR,– In a world where intolerance, racial hatred and suspicion of anyone with conflicting views are so prevalent, she was a woman who not only possessed great artistic talent, but one whose identification with the things in which she believed was an inducement as well as a challenge.

I shall never forget the fierce anger with which she spoke of the criminal wrongs we white Australians have tolerated and inflicted on our black brothers and sisters.

She was a woman who, although not herself a convinced Christian, often shamed those of us who claim to follow Christ, and yet do so little because of our apathy or because, perhaps, we feel so little.

Charmian Clift's death has created a void which we cannot afford to leave vacant.

CLARE
SCOTT-MITCHELL.
Wahroonga.

SIR,– Her articles made Thursday's "Herald" a special pleasure; they were always well-written, topical or provocative, giving us new thoughts about places we knew, or sharing with us the delights of places that were unfamiliar to us; but above all it was her genuine enthusiasm for all she wrote about that touched us, and her ability to be unafraid of being herself.

(Mrs) SUE NICHOLLS.
Miranda.

SIR,– The passing of Charmian Clift was a great loss to the progressive Greek community in Australia, where she was known for her opposition to the military junta at present ruling Greece. As an honorary vice-president of the Committee for the Restoration of Democracy in Greece, she had endeared herself to the Greek people of this country. Every Greek democrat is mourning her premature death and is inspired by her example and her struggle for the dignity of man.

L. PASCHALIDES,
for the Committee for the
Restoration of
Democracy in Greece.
Sydney.

SIR,– Vale Charmian Clift!

Thank you for the privilege of knowing you through your weekly column, carried on often through so much adversity.

Thank you for giving us good literature to read that was not warped or cynical, but beautifully thought out and carried through to perfection.

Thank you for raising so gently many issues that the sterner sections of the paper so blindly ignored.

Thursday won't be Thursday any more for a long time.

ROSEMARY
MANCHESTER.
Sydney.

UNIFORM LEVELLER

The bill is for one grey suit, five white shirts, one pair of black lace-up shoes, one pair of white gym shoes, two pairs of white gym shorts, two blue T-shirts, two pocket badges, one school tie.

The extra pocket badge is to replace the one lost from last year's suit, which now becomes a spare for emergencies such as dry-cleaning or getting soaked through, and the tie is also an extra for last-minute morning panics when he can't remember where he dropped the other one the afternoon before. Oh yes, and talking of getting soaked through, there is a new raincoat as well. And socks. And underwear. And a sweater.

The cost is formidable, but there is no way of cutting it. He has grown so much in this last year that all of his old school gear is ludicrously too small, and there is no elder brother at school any more to hand things down. I suppose one could buy second-hand, but kids these days seem to be humiliated by this perfectly sensible procedure, spoiled little brats as they are, and one weakly goes along with their affluent attitudes. At least while one can.

And then there are all the textbooks, the exercise books, the pens, pencils, rubbers, rulers, pencil cases, instruments and instrument cases, plastic covers, and the Lord knows what-all in the way of little extras and refinements that are perhaps not strictly necessary but from a kid's point of view eminently desirable. And a lump contribution to the P & C.

The school he attends is an excellent one from an academic point of view, but it is certainly not a fancy one in terms of required clothing and equipment. Besides, it's free. At least the government says it's free. And why we dopey parents go on helping to maintain that particular fiction is beyond me.

If schooling is really free and a uniform really compulsory, then surely the uniform should be supplied. I never did hear of a soldier being asked to buy his own, and education seems to me to be an infinitely more constructive and worthwhile business than slaughter; but of course I could be wrong.

They do say that the whole purpose of school uniform is egalitarian and demonstrates our democratic way of life. Johnny shall not appear to be of a more affluent caste than Sam, or pampered Mary, who was given an MG for her seventeenth birthday, than poor Peg, who is sixth of twelve children and the household drudge out of school hours. Uniform, they say, is the great leveller.

But what happens in actuality is that the levelling is never downward to Sam and poor Peg, but always, and increasingly up to Johnny and Mary. I see in Australian school uniforms a high snobbishness, a visible and distinct caste mark, either social or intellectual, that brands not only the wearer, but also the parents of the wearer, and publicly slots them neatly into their proper station.

It is the reverse of egalitarian, for if the purpose of the uniform was truly egalitarian then every child at every school would wear exactly the same, with no distinguishing feature of any sort, so that nobody could tell at a glance whether the child in question was one of the brainy ones who had made a highly selective school, a dullard at a school of low academic repute, the indulged brat of wealthy parents, a Catholic or Protestant, or the child of military-minded folk mad for the discipline (to make a man of him).

I won't say that uniforms aren't attractive in their own curious way. The girls', anyway. One of the things that enchanted me on my return to Australia—enchanted me visually, I mean—was the posies of schoolgirls bunched brightly at bus stops in clumps and clusters of singing colour. I had never seen that before, or if I had I'd forgotten it.

I wore a school uniform myself in the Depression years, when great variations were permissible, black, navy blue, box pleats, cross-overs, short sleeves, long sleeves, stand-up collars, turn-down ones, and lengths from ankle to kneecap. The only standardised thing about those un-uniform uniforms was their exceeding ugliness: they were meant strictly to disguise the slightest hint of budding femininity and to render their wearers as bulky, clumsy and gawkish as it was possible for cloth and buttons to do.

So all those pretty, gay garments came as a surprise to me. Particularly as I was fresh from many years in Greece, where school uniform is of necessity much simpler. There all high school girls (at least those at state schools) wear a plain black button-through dress with a flared skirt and tightly belted waist and crisp white detachable collar and cuffs. A monogram designating the school is the only distinguishing mark. High school boys don't wear uniform at all, except for a regulation peaked black cap, rather rakish in style and embroidered in front with Athena's owl of wisdom, luridly, in sequins. The littlies at primary school, boys and girls alike, wear a blue cotton overall with white buttons and white collar. You can easily distinguish the sexes, though, because all boys' heads are shaved to bristly stubble (for hygiene) and all the girls wear theirs as long as it will grow (for beauty: to the devil with hygiene).

But then I am wrong about that too. Because there was—how on earth could I have forgotten this?—a special uniform for church parades, patriotic marches, the name-days of heroes, and such other splendid public occasions. The uniform was selected on some inverse principle that always baffled me, since the poorer the school the more elaborate was the gear required. So my daughter, who attended what was called, in our village, The Down School, had to be decked out on Sundays and feast days in a serge sailor suit of Edwardian design and maddening intricacy. The pleats of the skirt required about three hours of pressing, and the wild convolutions of blue braid that decorated the white nautical collar and cuffs were not, alas, colour fast, so that every time the collar and cuffs were washed—that is to say every time the dirty little beast wore the wretched ensemble—it was necessary to unpick every last inch of those miles of blue loops and wiggles and then to sew them all back again. By hand. Imagine forgetting that lot!

The little girls from The Up School marched in a different elaboration of blue pleats, and in addition wore on the tops of their heads starched white bows of such incredible dimensions that they looked like a fleet of helicopters taxiing along the waterfront: I always expected them to take off, vertically, and still carrying their laurel wreaths.

Funny thing. I bought myself a very cheeky dress just lately, and wore it to a party, where it was greatly admired. It is navy blue, with box pleats, and a white shirt front with a turn-down collar and a floppy red tie. Everybody said that it was terribly cute. Because it looked just like a school uniform. Oh well . . .

LAST OF THE OLD?

I didn't write anything about Australia Day this year because it always seems such a damp squib of an occasion that it is better perhaps to let it fizzle out without notice or comment. More polite, anyway, to just pretend it isn't happening.

So it was interesting to find that, for the first time, Australia Day made quite a respectable bang this anniversary. Interesting and surprising. Because it was not, after all, the stately set piece of the First Fleeters and other Heritage Worshippers that attracted attention, but the rather acrid fumes that hung about over a whole series of sharp explosions of query. Who are we? What have we done? Where are we going? And why? The questions crackled with a new urgency which I, for one, found stimulating after all the years of soggy self-congratulation, pious platitudes and official smugness that used to be considered not only suitable, but necessary, for public utterance on Australia Day. Advance Australia Fair, and all that.

It seems to be a good time to ask questions. This is the last year of the most violent and disruptive decade the world has ever known—the seditious sixties, the suspenseful sixties, the subversive sixties, and finally the sordid sixties—and the last year before we Australians set out into the third century of a possibility for a nation and a people, unique, distinct from every other people and nation on earth.

True we are still attached by an umbilical cord of habit and sentiment to old Mum England, but there is no real need to cut it since it is, in fact, withering away of itself. And that makes me remember that it is seventeen years ago today that the drums and tuckets sounded for a new young Queen and the dawn of a new Elizabethan age. And look what happened to that. Oh well, there was no foretelling then. The sixties were unimaginable. Just as well perhaps. We might all have slashed our wrists. Or taken an overdose. Opted out. Got off.

I wonder if there is any foretelling now. About the looming seventies, I mean. A lot of the old breed will die off. Digger breed. Alf next door. Mum in winkle-pickers who never did have much of an education and waited all those years for her 7th Divvy bloke to come home. A fundamentally decent and kindly breed, unimaginative maybe and sometimes even dull, but with nothing perverse about them. And another breed will take over, a new breed who will not be able to remember back beyond the sixties. Come to think of it, who can now without an effort?

That damned decade of human confrontation over the gaps of our own silly human devising. Black against White. Haves against Have-nots. Ins against Outs. Humanists against Materialists. Hawks against Doves. Students against Authority. Authority against Dissent. Respectables against Irreverents. Olds against Youngs. Intellectuals against everything. Very angry it's been, very violent, very self-righteous, with everyone being holier than everyone else and getting themselves arrested to prove it or beating up someone or being beaten up or defiling telephone booths and railway carriages or killing savagely and without provocation or freaking out in despair. And getting around the moon where the world, they say, looks small, and all of a piece.

And through all this we Australians have gone on regurgitating: we are young yet: we have the most marvellous climate in the world: it's a great place to grow up in: we have a glorious heritage: we have a glorious future (like just around the corner).

I don't know that we're so young any more. Youngish perhaps, but old enough to stop making youth an excuse for our dreadful irresponsibility towards ourselves and our inheritors. Old enough to stop indulging ourselves in one long lazy hedonistic weekend that is not a reward for any real achievement but only an endless public holiday, self-decreed and honouring nothing—excepting

221

our marvellous climate, perhaps, which is actually not marvellous at all, but brutal, savage, fickle and conducive of much skin cancer. Old enough to start doing things for ourselves, inventing things for ourselves, making things for ourselves, our own sort of things, I mean, and not bad copies of other people's things.

I don't know why one should be embarrassed at expressing some hint of idealism. Maybe because cynicism is easier, and of course more fashionable. But I don't see why it is not possible, now, to stop the sweet rot of hedonism and get back to breathing that high thin air of endeavour that is more bracing, really, and I believe would suit our constitutions better. It used to, anyway.

I don't see why we can't look after our aged and sick ungrudgingly, generously, and without that iniquitous and totally unnecessary Means Test. I don't see why we should accept poverty in this country at all. We ought to be outraged and ashamed that it exists. I don't see why we shouldn't have an education system that would be a model to the world and a guarantee for our own future instead of the shoddy, shabby, patched-up, creaking, clumsy structure that we put up with. I don't see why we can't call a halt to the vandalising of nature and begin conserving, intelligently, lovingly, and with a long-term plan. I don't see why we shouldn't be a proud people, and a creative people, and an original people, and an adventurous people, and a resourceful people. It's all at hand to do, and I am still idealistic enough to believe that we could do it, and be much the happier for the doing.

Only of course we'd have to call off the long weekend. And we'd all have to work harder. And think harder. And maybe share out more generously. Even do without some of the luxuries we are beginning to take for granted, be more frugal, tougher, self-reliant.

I've never thought self-esteem to be a bad thing, providing it is for self-achievement. It's better than being demoralised, which we might be in danger of becoming in the future as we are outpaced and outdistanced and outthought by more vital and less self-indulgent peoples.

That's why it was good to read those editorials and comments on this Australia Day. Maybe, just maybe, it might have been a really important Australia Day after all.

AS OTHERS SEE US

My friend Jo turned up the other day. I shouldn't have been surprised. She has been turning up all over the world for years now. Wherever I've been there has always come a day when quite unexpectedly but also quite matter-of-factly Jo has lobbed in. Wearing some little cotton shift picked up in the children's department of Marks and Spencers and a diamond as big as the Ritz.

Still, Australia is a fair lob away from Knightsbridge, even for Jo. I had a tremendous sense of occasion, although she found her way to me quite prosaically, by public transport, without the least fuss or bother, and all within an hour of her arrival in the country was parked at my kitchen table taking up where she had left off five years ago at another kitchen table in another country and another set of circumstances.

She seemed to think it the most natural thing in the world. 'Nowhere is far any more,' she said. And this was something of a corrective for me, who had been feeling for some time that that was exactly what Australia was. Far. Very far. Tucked away under the curve of the earth. At the bottom. I know that distance shouldn't really mean anything any more, but lately I've been developing some sort of defensive thing about being at the bottom of the world instead of on the top. Cut off from a lot of places and people and possibilities that interest me. Away from where the action is. Even, in a guilty sort of way, deprived. (Perhaps that is what a lot of other Australians feel, and could explain some attitudes?)

In fact, Jo supplied a lot of correctives. She did a great deal in a very short time and in a frankly tourist way, carrying a cine camera. She drove over more than 200 miles of coastline,

224

including the burned out bits where the bushfires had raged, she flew to Adelaide, she spent a day on a sheep station in the company of twenty-three Americans, she went to Bondi and Manly and Taronga Park Zoo and on a tour of Sydney's Opera House ('worth every cent and every million'). She surfed and was properly dumped. She went on a quick excursion into the Blue Mountains. She ate meat pies and fish and chips and then dined grandly at what we consider to be our best restaurants. She drank milkshakes and pineapple crush ('fabulous') and beer and sampled a wide range of Australian wines. She walked city blocks looking in shopwindows and pricing consumer goods. She walked suburban blocks looking in people's gardens and front windows. She talked to anybody and everybody and never stopped asking questions.

So through Jo I recaptured many of my first, and so very vibrant, impressions of Australia, and much that I have come to accept in these last years became novel again. There were pegs on which to hang comparisons and queries.

Why do Australian men dress in conventional business suits and collars and ties in the sweltering summer? Wasn't it possible to originate some more suitable form of clothing—a neat, open-necked bush jacket, say, with shorts? Or a loose, Indian-type shirt? And why such drab, dull colours in this light?

Why do women of a certain age and social caste wear so much expensive and uncomfortable finery just to meet each other for luncheon or tea? Why are their faces so often peevish or petulant or bored?

How is it that the young girls manage to look so cool and neat and groomed at noon on the hottest day? So shining of hair and clear of eye? As if, she said, they didn't have sweat glands at all. She said that in comparison London girls looked tatty and unwashed and plastered with make-up. (Then we followed a very beautiful girl for a block, and she was shining-haired and confident and walked like a young princess, but both bare elbows on those lovely brown arms were positively grubby and Jo and I were very disappointed: she let us down, that one.)

Why, asked Jo, do we call our excellent wines claret and hock and chablis and burgundy when we might give them new names, Australian names, and the chance to be proud in their own right?

Why weren't there more waterside restaurants, coffee houses, beer gardens? Why wasn't there more outdoors eating and drinking generally?

Climate, Jo, I said. Capricious climate. The winds that do blow. And the rain that does rain. All at once and without warning. Well, she said, they manage all right in Paris. With screens. Awnings. So I said perhaps the explanation might lie in some lingering puritanism in our natures that makes it slightly embarrassing for us to eat and drink on pavements in full view of passers-by. Or the conservatism of city fathers who declined to grant licences for such gay purposes.

Abundance staggered her. So much of everything. English clothes, Italian shoes, French perfume, Spanish lamps, Chinese embroideries, Japanese cars, Greek rugs. (Why, you can buy anything from anywhere in the world.) And prices. (So very expensive.) And kindness. (You must be the kindest and most hospitable race in the world.) And distance. (You can't imagine it beforehand, no matter how much you read.) And traffic lights and pedestrian crossings. (People are so incredibly good and patient about waiting for the lights to change.) And first-class hotels that don't quite make the grade, even at first-class prices. (What is it? Why don't they come off? Inexperience? Lack of expert staff-training?)

And the phenomenon of suburbia, so strange and to her inexplicable. Such an uneasy and uncomfortable compromise between urban and country living. All those miles to travel backwards and forwards every day just for the sake of a little box on a little fenced plot, with no focal point, no feeling of community, no distinctive character, no market place, nothing in fact (to Jo) that would make one box in one area more desirable than another box in another area. (If you stuck around a while longer, lady, I said, you would be corrected. Our fenced plots are the most important of our possessions. Our inviolable little

226

pieces of territory in this great empty land. Our security of tenure. You would have to learn something of the days of the squattocracy and the land-takers to understand what one tiny fenced plot means. Even now. And perhaps always.)

Jo flew out again after ten days. Still bubbling, excited, questioning, and with a list of books to read. She'll be back, she said, for certain. Or almost certain. Because she must see the Centre now, and the Territory, and the Barrier Reef, and the West. And if she can't come she says she will send her children as soon as they're old enough. She thinks it might be just the land for them.

A HOME OF YOUR OWN

The lady I am going to write about has a very lovely old-fashioned name, which I shan't put down here because it would embarrass her and that's the last thing I would want to do.

Besides, she might be afraid that the recounting of her story would involve her in official investigation and possibly deceit. I think she loathes deceit more than anything in the world, except flying, maybe, and thunderstorms, and spiders, and dark places. She's a timid little thing, really. She likes pastel colours and soft pretty clothes and soft pretty things around her and romantic music and a glass of sparkling wine on her birthday. A little homebody, born, you would say, to be looked after and cherished and protected.

Unfortunately there isn't anybody to protect her. Not any longer. She has been a widow since 1962. Her husband was a soldier. At least he was a soldier for ten years, from 1939 to 1949, and he served in Queensland and Darwin and Milne Bay and Morotai and Japan. Once she didn't see him for two years. But when he died in 1962, quite suddenly, of a tumour of the kidney, he was a civilian.

I suppose a tumour of the kidney can't be proved the direct result of war service. Although I don't see why that should matter. The man did serve his country for ten years, which is quite a slice of anybody's life. But beneficent authority, or Big Brother Inc., or whoever decides these things, decided in all their benevolence that the widow of this former soldier was not a war service widow, but a civilian widow. And this has proved to make a great deal of difference. Like the Means Test.

When her husband died she was left with two children—an adult son, and a teenage daughter. The son was on the point of being married, but the daughter was, of course, totally dependent. She had no income, the house was still mortgaged, and she was faced so suddenly with many expenses and bills, including the cost of her husband's funeral. So she sold the house and paid off everything, and when all was settled up she had $3000 left with which to devise a completely new way of life for herself and her child. Also a widow's pension of $37 a fortnight. (That did rise at one point to the magnificent sum of $41 a fortnight, but dropped again this year to $25 a fortnight when her daughter left school and went to work.)

Now, what she thought she would do was to use that $3000 as a deposit on a small home unit, and supplement her pension by a part-time job. She isn't afraid of working, and hates the thought of asking help or charity from anyone.

But here's where the vicious circle begins, and, as far as I can see, goes round and round forever, or until Big Brother abolishes that iniquitous and humiliating Means Test.

As a civilian widow she is not allowed to earn more than $128 a year. How on earth is anybody to pay rent on that, let alone instalments on a loan? If she could get a loan. Because that $3000 isn't enough capital to buy a home unit without a loan, and she can't get the loan without proving an income which in fact she is not allowed to earn.

Also, that $3000 in the bank, instead of providing a sense of some security to her, has recently proved to be an embarrassment. Because now that her daughter has gone to work and ceased to be a dependant, she is not supposed, as a civilian widow, to have more than $400 in capital. In fact, at the beginning of this year, her pension dropped to $6.60 a fortnight because of her bank account, which she has been nursing stubbornly as her one hope of re-establishment. Perhaps authority expected her to blue the lot on a spree. Or spend it on racehorses. Get rid of it somehow. Anyway, she's not allowed to have it. Perhaps, if she had had just the normal human amount of common cunning she might have put it in a sock and hidden it under the floorboards. But she didn't. She was honest, and so is penalised.

229

For some years now she has been living in somebody else's house. She rents a small kitchen and a bedroom which she shares with her daughter. Neither of them—a woman of middle-age and a lively teenager—has any privacy at all, no place to entertain their separate friends, no corner to be sick in, or sad in, or alone in. No place to think quietly, or talk quietly, or even to hang up their clothes without tripping over each other. And I don't care how strong the bond is between mother and daughter— and it is very strong in this case I do believe—such propinquity must be nerve-racking for both of them. And the rent she pays ($12.60 a week) is money down the drain. There's nothing tangible at the end of it. No security for sickness or old age or loneliness— and she has been sick lately, with a spell in hospital and a rather long and very tired convalescence, and of course loneliness will come too, because teenagers don't stay in the nest forever, particularly if the nest is a bit crowded.

All she wants is some little place of her own. With a bedroom for each of them, and a sitting room where she can put out the pretty possessions she saved from her old home and modestly entertain her friends. Without being under any obligation to anyone.

Last week she applied for a War Service Loan. There is a chance of her getting it, at a low rate of interest, if she can prove she is earning the basic wage. She is quite capable of earning the basic wage, but if she does she is ineligible for her widow's pension, and she is terrified to sacrifice that entirely. She has been sick. She might be sick again. Suppose she couldn't work full-time for the years necessary to repay the loan? As I said, she's a timid little thing, and at the moment half out of her wits with worry. She says she wakes up in the middle of the night and chases her own thoughts round an endless belt of frustration and fear and indecision.

I know that there are hundreds of cases, and probably thousands of cases, as poignant, or more poignant than this one. This one is poignant to me because I know her as a human being. She is very undemanding of life, really. Quiet. Conventional. A bit scared of authority. Distressed by the indignity of her situation, when she is quite prepared to help herself if only she were allowed to do so.

Of course this thing shouldn't have happened to her. Her husband shouldn't have died, because she needed him. But he did, and left her in a dilemma which she is not sly enough, or aggressive enough, or dishonest enough, to overcome. But what can you say of a system that forces people to be sly and aggressive and dishonest in order to live in only modest and basic comfort in a country that is growing more prosperous every day? A system that forbids people to help themselves? A system that casts the abandoned, the sick, the old, into the roles of helpless and humiliated suppliants, meekly accepting the niggardly pittance that our brand of paternalism doles out so grudgingly.

I think her soldier husband got a poor reward for his ten years' service.

A THOUGHT ON VIOLENCE

Practically every magazine, periodical or newspaper I pick up these days has another article about women. Their role in society. Their role in the family structure. Their role in the community. To work or not to work? To marry or not to marry? Conception or contraception? Submission or revolt? To band together or go it alone? Womanpower in action! Pow!

Every last part of us, from our minds to our innards, is under the scalpel for public dissection. Can it be—shush! tread softly—that we have become *in-ter-est-ing*? Not, perhaps, to be taken for granted after all?

It is true that commercial advertising still keeps us firmly in our places, Omo-ing our sheets and Handy-Andy-ing our floors, producing gourmet meals from tins and frozen packs and removing even the suspicion of aroma from such meals with a nifty spray can of spring flowers, polishing our furniture and cleaning our windows with the help of a cute wee gnome, and concentrating all our tiny minds on choosing the right brand of toilet tissue.

Unless of course we are young, when we move in leaping and bounding packs, having fun fun fun providing we munch the right chewies and drink the right pop, or in balletic slow motion if we are alone and about the business of mantrapping and happen to have washed our hair.

I wonder what all that patronising guff really has to do with what women think and feel. How they act. And I suspect . . . well, let's see, anyway.

Naturally one is at a disadvantage in being born a woman instead of a man. I don't think there is any doubt about that. Nobody in her right mind would choose it, if she had a choice, unless perhaps she could be born a woman who was also born to great beauty or great wealth or great power, and I'm not even sure about that. Anyway most of us aren't born Cleopatras or Elizabeth Taylors or Glorianas and have to put up with whatever we were allotted by capricious fortune and our unchosen ancestry.

One of the handicaps we were allotted was our unfortunate sex, which places us, even now, in a junior or lesser class, which is disagreeable. The onus of proof is always on us if we want to be accepted as whole human beings, and all this proving requires great and sustained effort, which we might have used for other purposes, like making money or having fun. And then, of course, we tend to marry into the ruling or oppressing class, which makes it difficult for us to be militant in revolt. Our fortunes are all too inextricably tied up with theirs.

Margot Hentoff, in the *New York Review of Books*, points out that for a depressed majority we are really rather cheerful, 'enjoying,' she says, 'a kind of culture of poverty in which lowered expectations allow us to be successful even when we have not really achieved anything. The wife of a president—so long as she does not fall down drunk in public—will invariably appear on a list of most admired women.'

Have a think about that one, and how aptly it applies here in Australia.

Margot Hentoff was reviewing three new books by women on women—*Up from the Pedestal*, edited by Eileen S. Kraditor, *Thinking about Women*, by Mary Ellman, and *Born Female*, by Caroline Bird with Sara Welles Briller. And it was this review that really started me off on one of my thinking-about-women bouts again, because Margot Hentoff seemed so very disheartened by thinking about women at all, let alone reading about them.

She seemed to feel that nothing had really changed, and that the notion of the existence of women's spheres in which it is possible to be both best-of-class and still inferior to half the population is a notion that has come down to us intact.

'Only the definition of woman's territory changes as conditions change. Activities tend to fall within her boundaries after having slipped from the highest status levels. One suspects that women doctors became emotionally acceptable at about the same time pure science leaped into prominence as the field for the best minds.'

True? How about all that astonished publicity when Professor Leonie Kramer was given a chair of literature at Sydney University, and Jean Battersby an official voice in the future of our culture. What was there to be astonished about? They are very capable human beings, both, and splendid at their jobs, and to be congratulated, I suppose, on getting them. But why the fuss? Because they are women. And then I remember, sadly, that I heard Geoffrey Dutton, who ought to know better, referring derisively, on a television programme, to *lady* novelists. Sinks the heart.

Yet as half the human population we ought to be able to assert ourselves a little more forcibly. Yes, I know, assertiveness is not feminine, and assertive women are likely to find themselves being avoided, even by other women. Assertive women make other people uncomfortable, and become, themselves, the subjects of much ridicule and bad jokes. Women should be—oh dear—soft. Soft, quiet, dignified, serene, thoughtful, peace-loving. And that's not the stuff revolutions are made of. Revolutions are hard and angry and noisy and undignified as all get out. Think of Mrs Pankhurst's mob of terrorists and how undignified they were, how shrill, how violent. How unwomanly. Of course they got things done. But it has never ceased to amaze me that those ladies were brave enough to shatter the soft, quiet, dignified image with actual bombs.

All women's organisations since are mild in comparison. Their objectives are excellent. The broadening of women's horizons, more active participation in public affairs, equality of opportunity, civil rights, international relations, saving sons from slaughter, feeding hungry children, stopping wars. But they are all going about it in a peaceful and dignified way. Nobody is actually pouring acid in letterboxes or blowing things up or heaving bricks, although I did read that there is a new women's liberation group in America called WITCH—Women's International Terrorist Conspiracy from Hell. Maybe there's hope there. (I am not actually advocating violence. Only having a little think about it.)

There is another way. A hard way. But it could prove effective. Lysistrata took it long ago in ancient Athens. And the way is to use our very weakness—our handicap as it were—as a weapon. Go on strike. Deny those superior males their bodily comforts until they even things out a bit. No. It wouldn't work. There would be too many scabs in that union.

And of course it occurs to me that all those articles I've been reading lately in magazines, periodicals and newspapers are in *women's* magazines, *women's* periodicals, and *women's* newspaper supplements. If we are becoming interesting I'm afraid it is only to ourselves.

And on that depressing thought this lady novelist will get back to her kitchen. All the same I'd hate to think those commercials have actually got it right.

IN RESPONSE TO LETTERS

After the response to the article I wrote about my widowed friend a couple of weeks ago we—my friend and I—have come to the conclusion that human beings can be pretty wonderful and officialdom isn't one.

Human beings sent sympathy, suggestions, personal stories that often paralleled hers, practical advice, offers ranging from money to the sharing of their own houses, the names and addresses of organisations that just might be of assistance to her, clues, lurks, plans, systems, honest outrage, and much gentleness and compassion.

Officialdom sent a set of statistics. To prove that the figures I quoted were inaccurate and that my friend can actually earn a whole $260 a year. Mercy! How's that for bounty! I would suggest that the official who wrote that curt cold statistical letter tries living on that sum himself, or—just for the hell of it—applies for a housing loan. And reads Kafka every evening for a while as a bit of illuminating homework. Sir, I was not writing about property components, means as assessed, and/or/but, income derived from but not including, in-reply-please-quote, or any of the other goblets of officialese with which you were so good as to regale me. I was writing about a human being in distress. A point you appear to have missed.

Other human beings did not, of course, miss the point, particularly the ones who've been in distress themselves. And among the human beings it gives me pleasure to include the Deputy Director of War Service Homes, whose letter was not couched in officialese but helpful words that we could both understand. And we thank him sincerely for his interest and trouble.

To the gentle lady of stubborn anonymity my friend wishes to send most grateful acknowledgments, for the enclosure which it was impossible to return, but mostly for the lovely kindliness of attitude, the story of the leg of lamb done up as a bunch of flowers, and for these words:

'I have learned to accept everything as gratefully as I can, but often at the beginning it was terribly hard, because I was completely unused to it. And sometimes the poorest people gave most, and this the hardest to take of all . . .'

Also to the Melbourne gentleman who insisted that he should remain nameless but offered to contribute $100 if I could find ninety-nine other readers who would do the same. My friend thanks you and so do I for such a practical expression of compassion, but asks me to decline on her behalf. Although her glasses got terribly fogged up reading your letter, sir. She thought it must be the humid day.

One of the letters I found of great interest was from a survivor of the Gallipoli campaign. A few months ago he, with other old soldiers, was awarded a Gallipoli Medallion, with a citation that read as follows:

In commemoration of the heroic deeds of the men of Anzac at Gallipoli in 1915 and in recognition of the great debt owed by all Australians. With the compliments of the Government of the Commonwealth of Australia.

'Surely it is time,' my correspondent writes, 'that officialdom and civic heads ceased to harp on the great debt to the ex-serviceman they undoubtedly will trot out again next Anzac Day but which they do not seem in any hurry to honour.'

He feels the great debt bit is a great laugh. He reminds me that many of them were boys of only seventeen and eighteen at Gallipoli and in France, that the Great Depression was upon them before they had really adjusted themselves to civilian life again, then another war, and by the time the country burgeoned into prosperity they were all old, and there was nothing for them but the pension, 'which denies us,' he writes, 'even the simple pleasures of a pot of beer now and again and fifty cents on the TAB.'

With refreshingly lively indignation this old and angry campaigner would make the federal treasurer the patron saint of pensioners. Perhaps to raise one belated blush on that plausible countenance?

It is evident that there are a very great many indignant and angry pensioners. Also, bless them, a great many sympathisers who are doing all they can to help.

Thank you very much to 'Carry On', and thank you to Legacy, from whom my friend has already received much help in the education and medical and dental care of her daughter. In fact she said that she does not know how she could have managed without Legacy's constant warm concern and wise counselling.

Thank you to the lady who telephoned me with all that helpful information about organisations I had never heard of, like the Australian Birthright Union. It is this sort of practical information that is so very valuable, and we will follow up all your clues diligently.

Thank you to my regular country correspondent who has offered to share her home and her dogs and cats. It is good of you, and greatly appreciated, but my little friend is an urban creature, scared of dogs, allergic to cats, and tied, for a few years yet anyway, to the fortunes of her daughter, who must pursue them in the city.

Thank you to the Association of Civilian Widows for sending me on a copy of the letter they intend to send to all federal members of parliament in time for the Budget Committee Session. 'Do you realise,' the letter says, 'that in this wonderful country of Australia there is a group of children who are being denied equal opportunity with other children to a full and satisfying education?' Well, I realise it now, and I hope that federal members will realise it too after reading your splendid letter and grant the educational allowance you so rightly ask for.

But what gets me really hopping mad is the fact that this petitioning and pleading and cajoling is necesary at all. How

238

on earth would it disrupt our 'buoyant' economy to do away with the Means Test altogether and let people get on with the business of helping themselves in dignity while they can and providing for their needs ungrudgingly when they can't? Not as a favour. As a basic right of citizenship.

Well, anyway, all you nice human beings, you have helped. Oh, maybe she hasn't got that little home unit yet, but you've helped just the same. My friend doesn't feel quite so alone now. Also she says she feels braver about taking some positive action.

So she has asked for her mean little pension to be suspended for six months, and she's going to go it alone and earn as much as she can and sock it away towards that place of her own. And now she knows there are so many sympathetic people barracking from the sidelines I'll bet she does it too. She isn't young, and she's not trained to any profession, but her spirit's up now, and her temper's up too, and her glasses might be a bit fogged with so much interest and kindness but she doesn't feel quite so desperately Class B.

Might the next step on the part of us interested barrackers be yet another concerted effort to petition (no, not petition—*demand*) the abolition of the Means Test?

239

THE MODERN ARTIST—
PRO OR CON?

There was a young American painter I knew once and his name was Sammy, and Sammy painted in a bare room above a lovely boatshed, very earnestly and with great concentration for many hours at a stretch and his back to the sea.

Sammy found the sea and the boats most distracting if he looked at them, because the object of his concentration was an enormous colour wheel, which he had constructed himself, and which he consulted frequently. Sammy painted gigantic optical illusions of great brilliance, quite maddening to the eye, and was a revolutionary.

The person to whom Sammy talked most, and with the greatest animation, was a painter too, and also an American. His name was Ted, and Ted painted enormous *Time* magazine covers and the labels of evaporated milk tins, soups, savouries and vegetables, and he was a revolutionary too.

They were somewhat delayed revolutionaries, having abandoned abstract painting some time after their more swinging, ruthless, or far-sighted contemporaries, but they were dedicated for all that, and knew without any faint niggle of doubt that they were on to a good thing.

All that was many years ago and far away, but I thought again of Sammy and Ted one evening lately when I attended yet another charity opening of yet another new gallery, which offered, along with the champers, a collection of paintings that were quite traditional—street scenes, landscapes, seascapes, the human form draped and undraped, and lots of gum trees. This was not only novel, but astonishing, and I found it quite instructive to stand in a corner with my glass of bubbly and watch the fashionable guests, charitably as well as culturally minded, arrive in pairs and groups and go through every social gallery-opening gambit that delayed the first cautious glance at what was hanging on the walls.

The effect was miraculous. The faces, still framing social smiles and responses, expressed suddenly the most naked relief. It was all right. These paintings put no strain on the understanding at all, required no special jargon of appreciation, demanded no strenuous feats of comprehension. It was evident from the relaxation of the smiles and the quickened activity of the champagne waiters that mental stays were being gratefully unlaced. They knew what they liked all right and what a relief it was to be able to like it unashamedly and in the name of charity and culture buy a nice scene for dining mantelpiece, feature wall, or the surgery waiting room.

Is there a big con trick going on in the world of art? Because one has seen those faces before at other gallery openings, where the walls were hung with works as like as damn it to Sammy's and Ted's (only remembering that Sammy and Ted, even as delayed revolutionaries, were still at their op and pop many years ago, so long does it take for revolutionary ripples to reach these shores). And the faces at these other gallery openings wore, not relief, but the bright imploring look of the frustrated, so anxious were they to convey aesthetic appreciation of what they did not understand, half suspected was a joke, and yet must admire if they were to be counted in with the discerning heads. Way out in front with the avant-garde.

However did the vanguard manoeuvre themselves into the happy position of holding the power of moral blackmail over the confused and conservative public?

I mean, there was a time when one of the things that distinguished the vanguard from the ruck was their patently fugitive air. They were fleeing like bats out of hell from what they considered to be staleness, mediocrity, pretension and hypocrisy, to find their fulfilment in their own internal concerns.

241

And in devoting themselves creatively to their own internal concerns what they did was to set up what Hilton Kramer in the *New York Review of Books* has called 'an alternative culture'. That the alternative culture was not acceptable to most of society is history. The avant-garde were jeered at and derided and even denounced as downright dangerous. They were an independent intransigent lot, and alienated from society in the way that students, protest marchers and bikies are these days.

But there's nothing fugitive about the present artistic vanguard. Publicly they cling to the old romantic myth of intransigence and independence, but surely they must do so tongue-in-cheek, knowing very well that way out actually means way in, with laurels and profits accruing.

I think the trick might lie in that we, the public, have been made all too painfully conscious of our lack of perception in the past. The old vanguard, the fugitives, the unacceptables, the artistic outcasts, have in the fullness of time not only been accepted but reverently elevated and proclaimed masters by those established institutions with the power, not only of prestige but money, to certify what is art and what is not art.

It's a very old story and the lesson is obvious. Yesterday's revolutionaries become today's establishment themselves, but everything goes so fast now and fashions change so quickly and we've been so shamefully and demonstrably wrong before that we are prepared to swallow anything on the assurance that we are displaying fine aesthetic sensibilities in so doing. Our critical faculties are disarmed before we even look. And when we look we may feel uneasily that what is lacking must lie within ourselves.

Besides, there is a whole new market for artistic wares. Lots of people have lots of money they never had before, including the young and the hip, hungry for new sensations, and the intellectually homeless, eager to be directed to the most fashionably decorated aesthetic pad.

Sammy and Ted used to talk profoundly about anti-art and the necessity of bridging the gap between art and life. Life in their terms being increasingly commercial and technological and

242

less able to allow thinking space and contemplative space for the appreciation of complex ideas and the experiencing of subtle nuances of feeling.

There is no longer time to stand and stare, they implied. Immediate impact is what we're after. Now! Pow! I've no doubt they were absolutely serious, and certainly the op and the pop boys struck a bonanza, but I wasn't convinced then and I'm not now. It still smacks of trickery.

It may be stimulating, momentarily, to have one's visual sensibilities crudely and violently assaulted, or fun to see the meretricious imagery of commercialism presented ironically in the terms of fine painting, and I know it is all terribly with-it. But is it art?

This vanguard is not really a vanguard at all. Obviously they have no quarrel whatever with society as it is constituted. What they evidence is an impatient ambition to identify themselves with it completely by trafficking in familiar and recognisable images that form the surface crud, and to cash in on these by doing the jeering and deriding themselves under the banner of the avant-garde. So turning the tables completely and providing themselves with a valid passport into the establishment, as well as the quick buck.

To be fashionable is to be establishment. And the op and pop and the cogwheel-and-bicycle-chain sculpture boys are certainly fashionable. But not—to me at least, and I suspect to a great many other people who are uninformed but responsive to the interior expressiveness of creative artists—satisfying.

Not even satisfying in the way that abstract painting is satisfying. Because at least the abstract artists are generous with rich visual sensations, sometimes exquisite sensations, and even though you're likely to find yourself adrift in them it can be quite a yummy feeling. Only, beautiful as the best of them are, they are finally more in the nature of decorations than anything else, and when you have said, 'Yes that is a beautiful visual experience and beautifully realised technically and I enjoy looking at it,' what do you say after that?

Because Matisse is a beautiful visual experience too, and so is Cezanne, and Van Gogh, and Gauguin, and Seurat, and Bonnard. And Modigliani and Klee and Kandinsky and Chagall and Picasso. And then they are so much more.

Who, fed on reproductions of the old avant-garde, has walked through some gallery and for the first time walked slap-bang into the real sunflowers bursting glory or the sombre pine trees or the river pulsing with light and not been bowled over and stupefied?

'As in love,' Matisse said, 'all depends on what the artist projects unconsciously on everything he sees.'

Well, what they see these days is what we all see, the comic strip, the plastics factory, the assembly line, the supermarket, and project upon this synthetic surface of modern living no whit of concern or interior expressiveness, but only (consciously or unconsciously I don't know) a thumb-at-nose derision and a very good sense of double entry bookkeeping. The mockers are mocked and the avant-garde ride the success wave with dizzy self-congratulation, blackmailing the credulous right left and centre. Impact! Now! Pow! It seems like the story of the Emperor's New Clothes.

Someone I know said, in mock puzzlement: 'The avant-garde? Aren't they the blokes who cut the ribbon on the Sydney Harbour Bridge?'

He might be right at that. He's a wake-up anyway, like the little boy at the Emperor's procession who cried out from the crowd in amazement: 'But he's got nothing on!'

ON STUDENT
DEMONSTRATIONS

He said, this old friend at a party the other night: 'Now, you've written a great deal in defence of students. So could you tell me what it is all about? Student action, student dissent, student rioting, student takeovers? Does what happens here stem directly from what's happening in America, or Germany, or France, or Japan?

'What are they after?' he said. And then he said: 'I'm beginning to think I'm too old to understand.'

Well, I'm beginning to think I'm too old to understand either. With the demo season upon us again and the arrests and the accusations and counter-accusations between students and police, I am surrounded with newspapers, pamphlets, periodicals and paperbacks, all carrying long explanations and expositions of student revolt, and the more I read the more muddled I become and the older I feel and the less able to do what I thought myself capable of doing once. And not so long ago either. That is, playing Janus looking in two directions at once, forward and back, middle age one way and youth the other, and me between somewhere, seeing clearly both ways.

Some months ago, at the request of a group of Melbourne secondary students, I read a selection of their underground newspapers—such a rash of them so suddenly that it seemed significant—and I said publicly that I thought their aims and ideas and ideals were eminently sensible and that their teachers, instead of hounding them and punishing them for such activities, should be standing up and cheering.

Now I have on my desk a similar selection of underground

news-sheets from Sydney schools—'The Spark', 'Super Rat', 'The Yellow Subterranean', 'Out of Apathy', 'Bleah'—all of which have mushroomed within the first week of the new school year and all of which express much the same aims and ideas and ideals as their Melbourne counterparts. And yes, I still think such aims and ideas and ideals eminently sensible and to be applauded.

More student participation in school government. More accent on individuality. Closer teacher–student relationship. Release—at least for seniors—from dreary and pointless assemblies. Freedom to form clubs without supervision—political or otherwise. The breaking down of the antiquated prefect system. No compulsory absentee notes for seniors (who are at school, presumably, from choice, not under coercion). Or compulsory sport. Or compulsory religious instruction. Freedom to question—politics, society, the exam system, conformity, war, peace, defence, inequalities, artificial insemination, bigotries. Anything and everything. Including why the automobile industry needs protection when it made such a whacking great profit last year and yet feels it necessary to put the prices of cars up and to resist safety legislation at all costs. I think it would be good and healthy for these matters to be debated out at secondary school level.

But where I get bushed now is at the tertiary level. Here is something I read this morning:

'In a sense we are lost, for we do drift about in rough and uncharted seas. We are fearful that if we do establish a steady course it may take us somewhere we do not want to go. We also know that the huge waves tossed up from the depths of conservative tradition and state authority may weaken, or even destroy us.

'Perhaps this is why we have only a dissenting ideology. We unhesitantly express what we are against, but are less sure of what we are for.'

All right, that's an American student speaking. Or rather, he was an American student. He is now an American teacher at the University of California, Dale L. Johnson, and has contributed a chapter to one of the paperbacks I've been searching in for enlightenment. (*The New Radicals*, a Pelican original, if you feel like searching too.)

He finds remarkable ideological similarities between the Cuban and campus revolutions, in that both Cuban and campus rebels are '*strong* dissenters, firm in their convictions and willing to speak out and act militantly in spite of the mighty coercive powers of the American state. Both are pragmatic, always putting first things first, with rarely an eye on ultimate ends.'

Is that what worries me? Makes me feel old? Of another generation? I can see that specific issues are important and worth fighting for—civil liberties, academic freedom, minority rights, conscription, and so on—but I suppose I was brought up in a generation that believed in ultimate goals and permanent directions, and however united students are momentarily on specific issues, what is going to come out of it if they are divided over basic questions, hesitant, and don't know where they're heading or even care?

If, as seems likely at the moment, the students of the world are going to take over the universities of the world altogether, what is the point of having universities? Or do they intend to teach themselves? Or what? Never having been a university student myself I don't know how that feels, but I imagine— particularly here in Australia—that there are many students who enter university as transients en route to careers elsewhere, and their business is to get their degrees without too much disruption. Are they going to be allowed to do that? I know too that there are others who enter university as into a livable home within the pressures and frustrations and dissatisfactions of the great admass society outside—a home where they might have a chance to own their own minds, to expand them, to grow and mature in a livable atmosphere. And I should think that if all they find within a university is more discipline, more controlled and meaningless work, they might react violently and want to change the whole university structure. But into what? Nobody has answered that one for me yet.

247

Or should we elders make an act of faith and believe without knowing why? Saying something like: 'We had our go and now it's their turn and their future and we should leave them alone to shape it their own way.'

To me their political and moral concerns are authentic and impressive. I just wish . . .

But never mind. Since I can't take a university course myself, which I imagine would be the best way to smell out what it's all about, I shall probably continue to muddle my already muddled head by reading all these pamphlets and periodicals and paperbacks.

And to my friend at the party who asked with such concern: 'What are they after?', the answer is simply:

I don't know. I wish one of them would tell me.

ON FLYING THE COOP

This subject has come under discussion so many times lately with so many different people that it might be worth exploring a bit.

Are you a parent with children of an age to fly the coop? Do you want them to fly the coop? Or, even if you don't really want them to, do you think it desirable that they should for their own sakes? Or do you deliberately pad the coop with such comforts and enticements as to keep them safe in it, dependent, and where you can keep your eye on them?

Most of my friends and acquaintances who are approximately in my age group and also parents are either coming up to this situation, or disturbingly in the middle of it, or irrevocably through to the other side of it and thinking, either sadly or adventurously, of looking for a smaller house or a unit (with one spare bedroom of course in case one of the chicks needs a temporary roost some time).

It's a queer business, coop-flying. You know that it is coming up one day, but the day is always unexpected, and shattering somehow. For nineteen or twenty years the pattern of your life has been dictated by the needs and desires and whims and temperaments and triumphs and tragedies of these creatures you so recklessly brought into the world. Laboriously, creatively, with hope and love and pain and sacrifice and much joy and some bitter disappointment, you have spent nineteen or twenty or twenty-one years building a complicated edifice called Family. Not perhaps an entirely satisfactory edifice, not perhaps entirely as perfect as planned, a rather surprising edifice really, but your own, and therefore the most interesting edifice in the world. And just when you might sit back and contemplate it and enjoy it with just and happy pride, its very cornerstones casually remove themselves and the whole crazy structure lurches and topples and falls about your ears. It was, after all, never more than temporary.

Some parents feel a kind of outrage at this point. But look, they say, we would never have mortgaged ourselves to this great place if we'd known you were going to leave it so soon. Why, it was only last year that we went to the expense of all those built-in cupboards for you (or bookshelves, or stereo, or desk, or whatever). And it's not as though you can't have your friends when you like, they say. Or come and go as you please, they say.

I sympathise with this attitude, mortgaged as I am up to the ears, and with all those expensive built-ins gracing those empty rooms upstairs. But I have found that this first flying of the coop is likely to be experimental in nature and more or less brief in duration. I mean, it is not yet time to start looking for a smaller place to live. Those big empty rooms will have lots of use yet.

Off the young go, certainly, taking with them everything they can scrounge in the way of old cooking and eating utensils, worn sheets, faded blankets, tatty towels, knobbly pillows, tinned food, rolls of toilet paper, cakes of soap, jars of sugar, anything they can prize off their own walls and make portable, and a choice selection of their parents' books slyly reefed from their parents' shelves. Dear God, you think, how are they going to manage? What are the cooking facilities like? Is there a laundry? An iron? A juice-squeezer? An alarm clock? A refrigerator? A bath, even?

None of these luxuries will matter in the least at first. They will set up camp in some decrepit old terrace house with others of their kind, pool the loot they brought from their parental homes, and sleep as soundly on lumpy kapok as ever they did on inner springs. They will cook nothing but cups of coffee, so the cooking facilities won't be important: they will nourish themselves adequately and happily on hamburgers, Chinese takeaway food, flagons of red wine, and nights of smoke-wreathed conversation. They will not need chairs, because they will sit on the floor.

They will not need built-ins, for they will hang all their clothes on the floor too, and pile their parents' precious books on old planks propped up with bricks. The state or colour of their walls won't matter, because they will paper them interestingly enough with blown-up posters, revolutionary slogans, political pamphlets and such like. As for baths and laundry, these are minor matters, because they can always come home for a visit when their best friends begin telling them, or when they get so whiffy it is evident even to themselves, whichever is the sooner. They will be delirious with freedom but probably, in this first period, will 'keep in touch' quite prudently, if only for the occasional orgies of hot water, mum-style washing and ironing, and a real baked dinner with three veg and lots of gravy.

Also they are not likely to go really far from the home coop, for the same reason. One young woman I know rather better than any other young woman, on her first flight out, moved only as far as the end of the street, and nipped back home practically every day to change her clothes, wash her smalls, shampoo her hair, pick up her mail, use the telephone, and write out recipes. The flat at the end of the street where she cooked weird meals and entertained weird friends in fabulous confusion was, in this case, nothing more or less than a cubbyhouse, and she and her girlfriend were playing cubbies as assiduously as they ever had at five years old. When they were tired of playing cubbies— it took two months or so—they both came home.

Usually it takes more like six months before the discomfort and inconvenience begin to tell. Not to mention the expense. For it is really instructive for them to learn that toilet rolls do not actually grow on lavatory walls nor coffee jars replace themselves without a money transaction. Even bread and cheese costs. And electricity, and gas, and those simple things that have always been there. Like light bulbs. When the bills start coming in they, in their turn, are startled and outraged, and probably reduced to candles as everything is cut off. But candles cost, too. You, the parents, may expect them home soon now.

And of course you are wildly happy. Because you've been really concerned lately how scruffy they've been looking on their rare appearances, and pale, and underfed, and nervous, and you've been certain they've not been eating enough or sleeping enough and suppose the flu epidemic does hit they won't have any resistance at all. Et cetera. How joyfully you shop and cook again, buying up all the little delicacies they've been missing, like peanut butter and Oxford marmalade, and making big, balanced and really nourishing meals. How willingly you rush backwards and forwards from the drycleaners with the revolting garments they've returned in (quite unrecognisable as the ones they departed in), and sing in the laundry, soaking all their washables in enzymes, bleach, detergent, or even disinfectant, preparatory to a wash that will take a week. How happy you are. Or are you?

Because in the last six months you've become accustomed to lighter domestic duties and lots more time to yourself. You've become accustomed to tidiness and quiet. You'd forgotten that litter always did exasperate you, and lights left burning all night, and soggy towels on the bathroom floor, and electronic music full blast, and doors banging, and the forgotten toaster burnt out, and dirty coffee cups on the rug, and spillings and droppings and crud and crumminess everywhere, and lids left off jars for the ants to get in, and nothing ever picked up or put away, and . . .

Never mind. Get as much happiness out of it as you can. Because after a certain recuperative period they'll be off again. Spasmodically. But for longer periods as they gain confidence in coping for themselves. And you should be glad really, because it will lessen the blow of that final day, the one yet in abeyance, when they find their mates at last, and begin to build themselves.

That sad genius Edward Lear put it prettily: 'Calico Jam/ the little Fish swam,/ over the syllabub sea . . .' Do you remember the ending? You'd better. 'But he never came back,/ he never came back,/ he never came back to me!'

THE SHAPE OF
STOCKADES TO COME

Next year, at Potomac, Maryland, in the United States of America, a new housing estate of 167 acres will begin construction, different from other housing estates in that it will be completely enclosed in wire mesh, with guard houses and checkpoints, and electronic devices in the shrubbery to detect anyone approaching.

The residents, who will pay in the vicinity of $180,000 for the privilege of living behind wire, will carry identification passes, their school-age children will be checked through morning and afternoon at guard points, and their guests will be checked too, by a confirming telephone call from guard to host. Obviously there will be no casual dropping-in.

How curious and sinister it is. I mean, back to the stockade already. I suppose that most of us have envisaged stockades as a future possibility, but *après le déluge* as it were, among rubble and shards. Not just now, not just yet, not in the mightiest civilisation on earth.

Although, of course, from one's reading of current events in that convulsed mess of corruption and dreams and dishonour and aspiration and fantastic achievement we call America, one might easily be led to believe that *le déluge* is already upon it and therefore palisades could be, at the very least, prudent. If you are a white Anglo-Saxon protestant, that is. Wasps, by the very nature of their waspishness, may feel the need to scurry into enclosures in order to sleep at nights.

Perhaps we will all live in stockades of one kind or another before long. If we don't already. For there are mental stockades as well as physical ones, there are stockades of environment and

253

prejudice and habit. There are intellectual stockades. There are individual stockades, and family stockades, as a walk down any Australian suburban street shows clearly: else why is every house fenced in, and the palings pointed?

I, being privileged to live in an old-fashioned, quiet, graceful suburb, where there are many trees and friendly people and little violence, and bus rides tend to be chatty and shopping pleasantly personal, know no better than a visitant from outer space what life might actually be like in the red brick belt or the industrial belt or the bohemian belt or the development belt or the stockbroker belt or the social belt. It is not that I lack curiosity or interest, or even opportunity if it comes to that, but I stay within my own pleasant stockade simply because it is so pleasant and suits me so well: an effort is required to move out.

It seems to me that cities are already so big, so complex, so splintered, so shifting in character that it is impossible to comprehend them except in fragments. Enclaves. You in your stockade and I in mine.

Then how much more difficult it is going to be when our cities grow into Megalopoli, as is confidently planned and predicted by the millennium, and five or six million people swarm in Greater Sydney and in Greater Melbourne, and the concrete crust creeps out and out over this old potent land, sealing it down, sealing it under, sealing it off, and the concrete towers rise in clusters of crenellations as far as a man could travel on a day's journey. If he could travel, that is. Because of course ordinary people won't be able to travel, needing passes and priorities even to get on to the crawling expressways, let alone get anywhere else.

Then I suppose we will all live in stockades of necessity. Concrete stockades. That we might arm our stockades is possible. Probable. We fear the unknown, and everything outside our own particular stockade will be unknown, except by rumour or soothing propaganda piped in to us by the Overlords, or Chief Wizards, or whatever They will be called then.

And of course every stockade, being cut off from every other stockade, is likely to develop differently. A couple of weeks ago

254

I was watching H. G. Wells' *Things to Come* on the box, and I thought there was a terrible reality to it. All right, so he was wrong in his predicted date for a moon landing, but the Chief in his sheepskins and barbaric splendour was all too plausible, more plausible perhaps than that dreamboat of my girlhood, Raymond Massey, in his futuristic sculptured gear and all the serenity of lofty ideals and abiding faith in the progression and elevation of the human race through beneficent science.

Raymond Massey was Aristotelian. 'A common life for a noble end.' A common life for a noble end is passionately to be desired, and passionately to be sought, but all the signs point to closer and tighter and more jealously guarded stockades, enclave within enclave within enclave, and outside the marauders, violent of intent and action, raiding and looting when and where they can.

As long as the Haves have they will guard what they have with ferocity and no quarter. And as long as the Have-nots have not they will pillage and destroy, also with ferocity and no quarter. And stockades will be necessary.

There was a time when every city was a stockade in itself, armed and guarded and the great gates closed at night. But cities were so little then, so little indeed that the cry of a single herald could be heard by every inhabitant. A common life was possible for citizens, at least in the sense of a common emotion of pride and allegiance.

It will be impossible, I think, to feel pride in, or allegiance to, Greater Sydney or Greater Melbourne. It is difficult already, although I know that strong partisanship is often stoutly declared. What the partisans are really declaring, I think, is allegiance to Toorak, or Paddington, or Carlton, or the Upper North Shore, or St Kilda, or Kings Cross, or a harbour view, or a commercial quarter. An enclave, outside which all else is foreign territory, all other ways foreign ways, suspicious ways, possibly even dangerous ways.

Unless we are ourselves part of the current movement of disruption and violence, which of course has its own logic, then it is also logical that we will retreat further and deeper into our enclaves, and protect them, at first with locks and bolts and burglar alarms, and later probably with stronger security measures. So many people have unwittingly made themselves prisoners of their own environments already. For the most desirable enclaves are, after all, places to get into, not out of.

Well, well. Curious and sinister it may be, but it is happening. Wasps behind wire at Potomac, Maryland. Scared wasps. With good reason. Thinking about them as I've been writing this, some words of Carl Sandburg came to me. He was describing a stockade too, this time a house, very rich and grand, with a high spiked fence all around it, and high spiked gates. Where nothing could get in, he said, 'except the wind and the rain. And death.'

CAGE ME AN OSTRICH

The St John affair, if it has done nothing else, has at least made one fact diamond bright and crystal clear. Bureaucracy means closed ranks. We, the public, are not supposed to know. It isn't good for us. It disturbs our confidence, which should be unquestioning.

Of course it is good for Them to know about us, by way of anonymous men in grey suits, dossiers, bugged telephones, cameras clicked at surprising moments, and whatever other devices They are currently using in the name of security. Funny, I almost wrote 'in the name of good order and military discipline'. It has the feel of that sometimes. Which is slightly scary.

I wonder at this moment, They knowing what They know, whether Their confidence is ever disturbed, and profoundly hope that it is. While gloomily suspecting that it isn't. The New South Wales lot have just voted themselves a nice fat increase in salaries, which looks like an act of supreme confidence. Some might even call it arrogance.

If it is arrogance, it is arrogance founded justifiably enough— from Their point of view, I mean—on this assumption that the greater proportion of Australian citizens don't want to know anyway. About anything. Except a bit of titillating gossip, stock market reports, sporting results, social events, weather forecasts, the state of the surf, and the price of real estate.

The greater proportion of Australian citizens seem to be living in a lovely dreamy golden noontime. And at noontime no shadows are cast. They are blameless sorts of people, I suppose, if being blameless is being completely disinterested. Their sins, generally, are not of commission. Only omission. And if you hear nothing, see nothing, say nothing and do nothing you might well believe that noon will go on forever.

Noon won't. And I can see some fairly long shadows creeping up. I wish I didn't. I wish I had the unquestioning confidence in Them that They blandly assume I have. Or arrogantly assume I have. Or flippantly assume I have. Which all adds up to the same thing. That They *patronisingly* assume I have.

Well then, I don't. Not at all. Not for a moment. And I don't like being patronised. I do believe that this country of Australia—which is my country as well as Their country—is in many ways one of the most backward on the face of the earth, which is all very well at noon, when you can tip your hat over your eyes and doze in the sun. But it might turn a bit chilly later in the afternoon.

For instance. What sort of a generation of adults is likely to come out of the cheeseparing, penny-pinching, mean, niggardly, last-ditch-authoritarian education system They think good enough for our children? It isn't good enough for our children. And out of it will come revolt. Revolt has started already, within the schools, by young people who are not in the least confident in Them or Their bland (arrogant?) assurances that everything will be improved in the near future. Revolt is carried on in the universities, and however puzzled I am at times about the ultimate objectives of the dissenting group, I do believe in their passionate concern in current affairs and current issues. Sometimes I think that the students are the only section of this dreamy dozing community to display any concern about anything, and, with Dr Coombs, would urge them to 'come out fighting'.

I wonder if They ever consider the fact that the students They so dismissively deride and fine and club and gaol and cavalierly send to kill and be killed are the next generation of voters?

I wonder if They ever consider how glaring is the disparity in the soothing censures—paternal admonishments, really—meted out to errant politicans and corrupt policemen, and the brutal punitive action taken against young men of moral conscience and courage? They rely, of course, upon our sleepiness in this lovely lazy noontime. Nobody notices. Nobody cares. But the shadows creep.

I wonder how They justify to Themselves Their splendid salary increases in the face of the poverty that is proved to exist in large sections of the community, or in the face of the demonstrable plight of the pensioners whose welfare should be Their loving and generous and grateful concern? Surely it is only decent that every increase in Their salaries should be accompanied automatically by a corresponding increase—per cent for per cent—in pensions? But pensioners are old or sick or weak or helpless or utterly dependent, and therefore of little account in Their eyes. Their negligence is shocking, but nobody notices. Nobody cares. Except, of course, the pensioners.

I wonder what sort of an inheritance will be left for the ones coming after us and after the wholesale desecration of sunny beaches, leafy valleys wild with flowers, noble rocks and ancient caves, tribal grounds so old as to be legend, shores and reefs and lovely coastlines, and all the natural places of great beauty and great grandeur that are being raped and despoiled by greedy men avid for immediate gain? Nobody notices. Nobody cares. Oh, but how the shadows creep.

I wonder what might happen if our friends of Nippon take it into their inscrutable heads one day to pull the bung out of our so buoyant economy. So solly. We don't want your bauxite. Or your coal. Or your minerals. Unless . . . Long shadow there. Very chilly shadow.

It's nice to doze at noon. Warm and drifting and comfortable. But perhaps we should make some provision for the inevitable afternoon. I've never heard of a boom time yet that was endless, or of rewards continuing to accrue for neglect and indifference. Things have a way of catching up. I do hear and understand that even the affluent are sometimes needy, in more ways than one.

Perhaps in our dozing we should keep an eye open. We should be more attentive to what They are letting us in for. Perhaps

259

we should even ask some questions. And demand answers. Rather primitive and nasty questions about sewerage and garbage and equal pay for equal work and medical schemes and education plans and rising prices and conservation and poverty and pensions and bribery and corruption and violation of civil liberties and banking and finance and who owns our country anyway and whatever happened about that story of Innisfail and what They might not be manufacturing there?

Because if we keep on sleeping, if we accept closed ranks and soothing smokescreens as being more agreeable and less of a bother, we might, one day soon, wake up and find ourselves cold. And disinherited.

SOME THOUGHTS ON
A LARGE FAMILY

Large families have gone out of fashion, you might say. By large I mean five children or more. I have a niece by marriage who has six, but that is rather unusual. Mostly it was our parents who were one of six or seven or eight, and our grandparents who were one of ten or twelve or fourteen. My late father-in-law was one of nineteen, but perhaps that was a number to be remarked on even then.

In those large families it was not usual for all the children to survive in good health, or even to survive at all, which is one of the reasons, I suppose, that we of the privileged countries tend these days to limit our families to the number we feel ourselves to be capable of caring for rather better than adequately.

But the underprivileged of the privileged countries, and the even more underprivileged of the underprivileged countries, are still more likely to go in for big families than not. Stubbornly and irresponsibly, some say in distaste and disapproval. Or in ignorance, say others, evangelically peddling the Pill. Whichever way it is, the big families are there, and of the big families it is not usual for all the children to survive in good health, or even to survive at all.

There are Nigerian children and Biafran children and Moroccan children and Korean children and Greek children and Italian children and Iranian children and Vietnamese children and Indian children and Algerian children and Yugoslavian children and West Indian children and Jamaican children and Lebanese children and Maltese children and Pakistani children and children of Uganda and Malawi and Swaziland and Lesotho and other such outlandish places where children are bred in quantities. There are children of Australia and England too. And of all these children many are undernourished and neglected, many are suffering from acute malnutrition, many are actually starving to death, many are diseased with various loathsome afflictions, and many are maimed, mutilated, burnt, bombed, and shattered mentally and physically to such an extent that they could scarcely be called children at all. Many, who might have been members of big families originally, don't have families at all any more, or homes apart from the streets and gutters, or food apart from what they can beg or steal.

In a sense they make up an enormous family in their common misfortune, a black, white, yellow, brindled, multi-racial, multilingual, scrofulous, tortured, wounded, disease-ridden, terror-maddened family. A very hungry family, living—if it can be called living—in a state of perpetual punishment for the crime of having been born.

Children ought not to be punished for being born, wherever they were born, whatever colour they were born, into whatever political atmosphere they were born, or whatever religion, social caste or financial state, or time of peace or war.

Children are tomorrow. All children.

This week is the annual Easter Appeal of the Save the Children Fund, an organisation that is one of the largest independent, international, voluntary bodies in the world. Their business is children, and they have adopted a family of 120 000 of the world's innocent and anguished in the belief that a good tomorrow is only possible if we start preparing for it today.

Since I am making a blatant appeal on their behalf I think it important to say here that the Save the Children Fund is not just a handout organisation. They operate in twenty-eight countries on the principle that—excepting in times of emergency relief, such as war, earthquake, flood, famine, epidemic and such holocausts and catastrophes—handouts are as outdated as 'the kind of charity which dropped a coin in the box for the poor and went uncaring on its way'.

262

It is an organisation that exists for one purpose and one only, to serve the welfare of needy children everywhere, but to serve them in such a way as to try to ensure that tomorrow's children will not be needy as well.

Through a professional team of more than a thousand field personnel, including doctors and nurses and welfare workers and administrators, they are equipped for twenty-four hour a day service, to go anywhere they are asked, at whatever time they are asked, wherever there are children in want.

They feed starving children and clothe naked children and heal sick and wounded children and soothe frightened children and tackle every immediate crisis immediately, but they do rather more than that in so far as their work is also educational. They teach mothers how to better safeguard their children against dirt and disease, they begin long-term community projects to raise standards, and in whatever country they work they train personnel to take over after them to keep the projects going. They help people to help their own people by helping their own people's children.

On my desk I have a selection of the Save the Children Fund's official magazine *The World's Children*, with case histories so terrible and harrowing that it makes you want to shake your fists in rage and impotence. Dozens of stories. And of course there are hundreds of stories. Thousands of stories.

But we are not quite impotent. Even if all we can do to help suffering children is to give money, money is needed for works of immediate mercy and long-term rehabilitation for children brutalised and degraded and corrupted and terrified and mutilated and hungry all over the world. It is such a very large family to look after, and it has been growing every year since 1919, when Miss Eglantyne Jebb, the founder of the fund, raised £1000 to send milk to the children of Vienna, and went on, gallant lady, to write a Declaration of the Rights of the Child and to have it adopted by the League of Nations. It was reaffirmed by the United Nations in 1946, only, more's the terrible pity of it, children still go on suffering.

263

It takes more than a Declaration of Rights. It takes money. And the fund's worldwide operations cost $10 000 every day.

Would you save a child? A Biafran or a Vietnamese or an earthquake victim somewhere? Even a coin will feed a child for a day. A banknote will feed a child for a week, or weeks, buy medicines and vitamins and clothes and medical care. If you feel the need for personal involvement in work that might be taking place thousands of miles away for children you will never see, you can sponsor a child personally for a year, or even a family. Personal sponsorship is personal involvement. If you feel that charity begins at home there is a lot of work for the Save the Children Fund right here in Australia. You might like to help with an Aboriginal preschool centre, for instance. Your money will be used in any way that you designate.

This year is the Jubilee Year of the Save the Children Fund. For fifty years now they have been caring for children. More and more children. Please help them to care for more yet.

As Bertolt Brecht said: 'A bit of tomorrow is asking for a today.'

ON TICK AND TOCK

I have a clock, very small, round, of chased gold (for gold read gilt) with beautiful numerals backed with black. It is not in any way valuable but it is a pretty thing and I like it very much and it makes me cross that my family disparage my clock only because it doesn't tell the time accurately.

I know it doesn't. Sometimes it is five minutes fast and sometimes it is fourteen minutes slow and very occasionally it is almost right and what I say is that it's close enough for my purposes. My purposes don't particularly depend upon seconds and if they did depend upon seconds I think I would abandon my purposes as not being worth it. Somewhere between galaxies and electrons there is an eloquence that begins with tick and ends with tock and that's the sort of time that suits me just fine. In fact I think that's the only sort of time I could possibly cope with.

Although, now I am considering the subject, what I might like even more than my little gold (gilt) clock is a sundial. I have one actually which I will get around to setting up and levelling in the garden one day when I feel like that. It's a very handsome sundial too, handmade, of brass, and on it is written: 'Some tell of storms and showers: I tell of sunny hours'. How very sensible that is. You might not be able to tell the time at all in dirty weather but maybe you'd be better off in bed anyway.

Some of those old sundial inscriptions are most instructive and conducive of deliberation. Like: 'I shall return: thou never'. Or: 'Hours are Time's shafts and one comes winged with death'. Or, so prettily and negligently: 'I count only the hours that are serene'.

And wouldn't that be nice? To count only the hours that are serene and to the devil with the rest of them. Let somebody else have that lot. Ah, but who? Dorian Gray managed it by way of a portrait, and then there was that Shangri-la lady of Hilton's, but time caught up with them too in the end, probably because their creators were so enmeshed in the time-trap themselves that their imaginations finally couldn't extend to a conception of timelessness.

Timelessness is unimaginable. But then time is too, apart from the tick-tock sort, I mean. And of course the older you get the more enigmatical it becomes and if you get out of the tick-tock area you are likely to get bushed.

Creatures of time we all are, but what sort of time, and time for what? Ecclesiastes maintained that there was a time for every purpose under heaven, Marvell saw deserts of vast eternity, and the computer operators at the Parkes radio telescope concern themselves with a million messages, or a billion messages, bounced back from heavenly happenings that took place thousands of millions of years ago.

When I was young and my heart beat faster and I lived at a furious rate there seemed to be immense quantities of time to play with and use and burn up and the days were long and the nights were long too and the right place most often coincided with the right time and even the right state of mind and body for whatever physical or intellectual need I was grasping. And I think it is very peculiar that as you grow older and your blood flows more slowly and you live more slowly the days get shorter and shorter and the years whizz past and time, as they say, flies. Something has obviously happened to your inner clock and the spring of it is unwinding.

It has always fascinated me that among men of genius there have always been those who knew in some mysterious way how much or how little time they had at their disposal. Those like Mozart, for instance, who developed his talent early and worked and lived in a frenzy and died young. Or those like Titian, who can afford to be more leisurely and save their best work for the long slow years, as if they know they have lots of time to spare. Or is it that the early starters die young just because of that early frenzy? It seems as though the hotter the faster is the general rule about life spans.

But that's genius and genius is extraordinary anyway. We ordinary mortals can probably expect an ordinary life span, a very ordinary amount of time to do our very ordinary business. And commonsense tells us that our ordinary business is real only when it is happening now, at the present moment. Reality is served up to us in thin slices of now. 'Unborn tomorrow, and dead yesterday, why fret about them if today be sweet?' One does fret, of course, against one's commonsense, which is so wedded to 'now' that if somebody says they have had a glimpse of the future, or looked back into the past, one's commonsense will denounce that somebody immediately as a charlatan. While still fretting. What happens between tick and tock anyway?

Between tick and tock time passes. But passes what? Has it passed us? Or do we flow along with it, and if it is flowing and we with it then surely it must have stationary banks, like past, present, and future, which would mean that everything is fixed and determined. And if everything is fixed and determined, then of what use is our vaunted free will? Or do we have any free will?

How can we use 'now' to throw a beam onto the future, or to illuminate the past? If our consciousness is only a torchlight moving along a back alley, what is the use of it? Did we invent time to explain change and succession, the irreversibility of events, the ageing process, the 'moving finger writes and, having writ, moves on' bit, or does it really exist as people like Priestley and that hard-headed military engineering type J. W. Dunne have believed, as another dimension, a fourth dimension in which we exist as irrevocably as we do in the other three?

And how about those 'deserts of vast eternity'? If they are there do we really want them? People get bored so easily in this life it continually surprises me that they should so passionately insist on another. Lasting forever. People are always 'filling in time' or 'passing time' or yawning between tick and tock. What are they going to do with eternity? Even, who are they going to be in eternity? Young selves, middle-aged selves, old selves? Will they even recognise themselves? Or their loved ones with whom they are reunited?

Funny business. I have never worn a watch in my life, because that has always seemed to me like wearing your death on your wrist. But I like my little gold clock, which is quite eccentric and has its own ideas about time past and passing and to come. Tick, it says. And tock, it says. And anything could happen in between.

Like I could finish this article. It's about time.

HALLELUJAH FOR A
GOOD PICK-UP!

They came in from the letterbox with a printed notice and whooping for joy. 'Hallelujah!' they cried. 'There's going to be a pick-up.'

It was not, of course, The Resurrection with a pick-up of seemly souls bound for everlasting bliss, but only what our municipality nicely refers to as 'Household Waste'. Meaning garbage.

We live in quite a benevolent and resident-mindful municipality, and earlier on there used to be a pick-up at least every two months of all the junk and crud that people accumulate and all the leftovers that just won't fit into the regulation-sized garbage bin no matter how many of you take turns in treading it down like a wine press. (We do it by numbers and to various treading-down songs. 'Step Inside Love' we find most encouraging.)

But for some reason or another that is known only to our benevolent municipal fathers their benevolence has not extended to pick-ups for at least six months. Seven, maybe. And I won't tell you how I date that particular pick-up. But no doubt our municipal fathers had other things on their minds, like rates and high-rise development and stray dogs and tree-lopping and street-sweeping and Their Image and whatever other little matters councillors squabble about in council and worry over in their beds at night.

What we'd been worrying about in our beds at night was whether benevolence in regard to household waste had ended altogether, and if it had ended how on earth were we going to dispose of our accumulation of the sordid evidence of two student parties, one welcome home, three birthdays, one Christmas, one New

Year, one Easter, and general hospitality dispensed in a six (or was it seven?) month span resulting in waste considerably in excess of anything that Hannibal's elephants—all of them, I mean, and before they got to the Alps—could have trampled down. Step Inside Love. I wonder if elephants do.

Let's face it. All those empties render gross, if not vile, a smart back deck that was designed for gracious living. How can one live graciously surrounded by cardboard cartons bulging and sagging with such squalid evidence of completely ungracious high jinks? Some would say 'boozing', but of course I don't, knowing the circumstances and how many guests pass through this house and my own hospitable instincts and the regulation size of the garbage bin. There are others, more sophisticated, or better equipped perhaps, who have what one young friend of mine calls 'a set of wheels', and they can load up and whizz off and dump it all on a municipal tip somewhere (like some shady leafy glen wild with flannel flowers: how do our municipal fathers choose where it is proper to dump garbage?) and pretend it never happened.

We don't have a set of wheels, excepting two very small ones belonging to a motor scooter and that's not much good for loading up and dumping purposes. Although stylish enough in its own right and useful for other purposes. But that's another story.

We got everything out on to the pavement before Hallelujah Day. In work gangs, hauling away two by two, and singing or whistling loudly to cover up a natural embarrassment at such public exposure of our domestic detritus. And since we had about a ton of old newspapers—there hadn't been a collection of paper for six months either—we arranged these artfully, in bundles, on top of the cartons to disguise their contents. And a more conspicuous bit of camouflage I have never seen in my life.

You believe that you don't care what your neighbours think but when it comes to the public exposure bit you find that you squirm with just such a degree of abashment that would be more proper to Aunt Julie or Maude, tucking the brandy bottle (for medicinal purposes only, dear) behind the sheets in the linen press.

270

Well, it is such a respectable street, after all. Nice. Lined with camphor laurels and desirable residences of the gentlemanly kind. My wicked wicked children, in a spirit of bravado that I could not muster, arranged to have themselves photographed sitting on top of that most formidable heap, under the camphor laurel tree and on the only unmown strip of grass in the whole street. With beer cans in their hands. Grinning.

'Oh, don't be such a square,' they said. 'Just wait till you see what the neighbours bring out.'

And what didn't the neighbours bring out! Boggles this mind at what orgies must have been going on—carrying on, rather—behind those discreet gentlemanly-residence-type doors and polished knockers. Funny, one was never aware. Although, come to think of it, there has been music—sort of on-and-off—and shrieks of girlish laughter and tootings of car horns and maybe it wasn't a dream after all that one night (waking?) I observed from my bedroom window a young man running up the street quite starko except for a net curtain and a German helmet. Dear me.

Anyway, emboldened by all this evidence of a suburban depravity that far exceeded our excesses, I added to our disgusting pile of household waste all the old clothes that had been shoved into the backs of closets and under the stairs on the chance that they would 'come in useful'. In the meantime the moths and the silverfish had found them more useful, and the mildew had claimed them, and, quite frankly, they stank.

But the neighbours added yet more. Old cane chairs and wicker whatnots, lengths of plumbers' piping, mouldy boots, garden taps, old-fashioned pink stays (the lace-up Scarlett O'Hara kind), busted bedroom lamps, astrolabes, chamber pots, umbrella stands, tired mattresses, feather boas, computer parts, cracked soup tureens, ceramic marvels, and such odds and ends and intriguing bits and pieces that kept us housekeeping ladies off the buses for days. We all walked up to the shops, prodding and examining as we went, and with such acquisitive instincts as would make me ashamed excepting I know that all the ladies felt the same

271

overwhelming urge to do a little picking-up for themselves.

It rained before the official pick-up. Torrents. The cardboard cartons sogged up and drifted apart in the corners. The picked-over old clothes, already moth-eaten and not worth anybody's notice, fell into the gutters and were rolled into damp and disgusting bundles, all messed up with the fallen leaves from the camphor laurels.

What do you do with one lamp base, an arty (nouveau I mean) mantel surround, a coil of wire, and a rather damaged print of 'The Stag at Bay'?

Easy. You put them out on the next pick-up. Let somebody else pick them over.

THE JOYS OF HOLIDAYS

Well, that was ever so nice. My holiday, I mean. But the most interesting thing about this holiday, anticipated, I must say, with a sort of childish gleefulness ('school's out! school's out!'), was that eventually I didn't go anywhere and I didn't do anything that was at all unusual.

Excepting, in the beginning, a few things I've been wanting to do for ages, like cleaning out my clothes closet and going in to town for a day's shopping and meeting friends for luncheon and asking friends for dinner and doing the marketing in a leisurely, choosy sort of way, and indulging in hours of conversation with people I like and arranging flowers and new curtains and pages of manuscript and notebooks and wallowing in reading. There is nothing more self-indulgent than reading a novel in the morning, particularly in your own familiar surroundings where you are normally 'getting on' with things.

I suppose a holiday is really a state of mind relieved of pressure. Most of us live under pressures of one kind or another, clocks and appointments and dates and times and contracts and obligations and the necessity to 'keep up', or 'get on', and of course we become so accustomed to our pressures that we go a little peculiar and light-headed when they are removed.

Anyway, I had chosen for my holiday reading the novels of Joyce Cary. (I like to do this—that is to take the entire corpus of work of a favourite writer and begin at the beginning and read through chronologically to the end. It is fascinating—at least to a writer—to see how the veriest germ of an idea or sketch of a character in an early book is gradually explored and developed in later ones and finally becomes a major theme.) So, I was reading *A Prisoner of Grace*—in the morning, too, sitting in the sun with

273

my feet up—and I came upon these words of Nina's:

'I felt an immense calm gaiety, as if, so to speak, I had just inherited such an immense wealth of delights that I did not need to be extravagant; I could afford simply to feel the comfort of being so rich without the trouble of spending.'

And I read those words with such a stinging sense of recognition. Because of course that's exactly the way I was feeling too. It was something to do with the way the morning light was skittering among the leaves of my young trees and the clump of papyrus at the bottom of the yard glittering like fresh-washed hair and the silly spoilt cats frolicking and pretending to be jungle beasts and little Wesley next door riding his tricycle round and round the clothes hoist (entirely for my admiration and attention) and I needn't bother with anything more elaborate than sandwiches for lunch and there was a dinner party in prospect with comfortable sorts of friends. And there were voices, comfortable sorts of voices too, being so familiar, and birds, and an aeroplane sky-writing on the vast expanse of tender autumn blue and I could take the time to crane my neck and watch it like a child, guessing what each letter was to be. Also I could hear the sound of the vacuum cleaner inside and know that my house was being cleaned and tidied and made seemly, and I know all these things are trivial in themselves but they added up to 'an immense wealth of delights' and I felt like laughing out of sheer pleasure. I was suddenly glad that I hadn't been able to go away for my holiday as I had planned and intended because the going away would have been alone and it seemed nicer not to be alone, particularly with a wedding anniversary coming up in a couple of days. More friendly and, again, comfortable.

That led me on to thinking of long-ago holidays we'd had together and the realisation that the last one was all of eighteen years ago. I suppose most married people with families find it difficult to get away together, unless there is a doting granny in the background or an obliging family friend with enough time and inclination to do stand-in duty with the children.

In England, when we took holidays, we used to board ours

out at an establishment in the country designed for that very purpose, and run, interestingly enough, by the English wife of Jomo 'Burning Spear' Kenyatta, a gentle lady whose son Peter was our kids' hero, not only on account of his thrilling parentage but because he took them exploring into dangerous chalk pits and encouraged them to climb the tallest trees and pinch goodies from the pantry and generally behave like the little savages they were. England used to abound with such places—one I remember with a shudder described itself as 'The Savoy for the Under Twelves'—and I have never quite recovered from my sense of guilt at having abandoned little children to such a soulless environment for the entirely frivolous reason that I wanted to go motoring around the Bordeaux area with my husband for the purpose of sloshing claret in famous chateaux.

But after we went to Greece we never had another holiday together again. We intended to. Every year. Venice, we would say. Or Istanbul. Or the Dalmatian Coast. Or the Lebanon. But of course there were no nice (or even nasty) boarding establishments for temporarily unwanted children (I sometimes think deep freeze might be the answer), no grannies, and as for family friends ... when it came to the point of trusting them with our young it was unfortunately evident that most of them were on the irresponsible side (if not downright ratty), and were in any case so involved in complicated love affairs, quarrels, feuds, works of genius, despair, drinking bouts, or what looked like (from parents' points of view I mean) debauchery of all kinds, that they would obviously not have had much time or patience left over to run a household that required a certain dull routine or to deal sympathetically and understandingly with three highly individual little monsters who would be bound to play up their temporary guardians on principle. Anyway, Venice wouldn't run away, or Istanbul, or the Lebanon, or the Dalmatian Coast either. We could go next year. And in the meantime the sun was shining, and we were swimming every day again, and the white yachts were coming in loaded with interesting summer visitors, and life had moved out of doors, and we always had a few extra children to care for because their parents were running away from each other (or sometimes even with each other: it happened occasionally). So we never did go.

And I suppose not going away together becomes such a habit that even since our children have far outgrown the 'being minded' stage it has never occurred to either of us that it might be possible to arrange our affairs, stock the larder, and just pack up and go.

So that is why my anniversary present was so surprising and delightful. Because I was given just such an invitation. And that is why I spent the rest of my holiday bashing the typewriter with such urgency that the keys kept bunching and sticking and the words coming out back to front.

'But I thought you were on holiday,' said a puzzled friend, discovering me at it. 'I am,' I said. 'Then what on earth are you working for?'

'So I can have a holiday.' There must be a zany logic in it somewhere. And perhaps I might even tell. When we get back.

ROYAL JELLY?

In the dank early morning hours of 6 February 1952, in our flat in the Bayswater Road, London, England, we rose from our warm beds, awakened the journalists who had camped the night on sofas and floor, breakfasted hurriedly but heartily (since it was going to be a long day), dressed ourselves and the children, and went to see the young Queen Elizabeth crowned.

My husband was dressed oddly for that bleak and dismal hour, in white tie and tails that were ill-fitting to say the least, he, apparently, having been the last man into Moss Bros to hire his coronation gear and finding nothing left but oddments—trousers that had been tailored originally for a man of the corpulence of Sidney Greenstreet, a tail coat turned in by a dwarf perhaps a century before, a vest designed for a very long stick-man, and a curious shirt-front, as stiff and bulging as a medieval knight's corselet. He was not consoled by his children's admiration, they likening him in his splendour to a gollywog, than which nothing could have been a greater compliment under the circumstances. The circumstances being that even after a frantic ransacking of every drawer in every room we could not find a pair of braces to hold up the voluminous laps and folds of his pants (the children having used said braces to hang a couple of rebel dolls by their necks out of the back nursery window, but not, of course, telling in that sizzling hour of the most terrifying profanity: they weren't silly).

After all, he had a row of chinking decorations on his breast, and he could hold up his pants with one hand. It was enough. And the only alternative to his festal costume, as I reminded him, would have been court dress, as laid down in the detailed order of dress for the day, and he might have felt even sillier in knee breeches and silk stockings and buckled shoon. He would have to make do as best he could. In any case it was not a question of whether he wanted to sit in Westminster Abbey for nine hours or so. He had been *ordered* to sit in Westminster Abbey, and the Lord knows what regal retribution might not fall upon his rebellious colonial head if he failed his loyal duty. What he said about his loyal duty was pointed and pungent, but not, I think, printable, even in the pages of this enlightened magazine.

How long ago and far away it seems now. That drive through the damp and soggy London early morning, dismal beyond telling, the colour of gruel, the texture of gruel, and the damp soggy banners hanging among the damp decorations, and the damp soggy gruel-coloured people who had camped all night on the gruel pavements beginning to bestir themselves and stretch and fold up their blankets and open packets of sandwiches, Scotch eggs, toad-in-the-hole, jellied eels and other national delicacies to fortify them for the long hours of waiting still ahead. In spite of the banners the streets did not have the appearance of a Triumphal Way. Coriolanus would not have thought it up to the mark. Still, the newspaper billboards on the pavements blazoned the tidings that Hillary and Tenzing had conquered Everest— 'done the old bitch'—and a young queen would indubitably be crowned this very day. There might be something in it, after all. Something auspicious, I half felt, something of a high singing noble order that would lift the hearts and spirits of these poor tired depressed and apathetic Englanders, defeated in victory, austerity-weary, but surely this day, for a few hours anyway, hopeful?

For us in the covered stand outside the Abbey it was a long and weary wait, but there was pomp and panoply enough, I suppose, at last, and drums and tuckets, and fleeting flashes of great brilliance, and hot tea from the thermos to keep us warm, and a clean arrangement of lavatories under the stand. (My husband's experiences, holding up his pants inside the Abbey, were of a different, more piquant—if more distressing—order, he having left my carefully arranged packet of sustenance in the way of food and drink in the car now parked in the Foreign Office, and having no nourishment whatever, while around and below him the high and mighty of the land swilled and guzzled with every appearance of enjoyment. Besides, in the Abbey the loyal subjects were summoned to the lavatories in rows, at the command of a Black Rod, or Gold Rod, or somebody equally splendid, and my husband's timing was out that day. Then again, he was seated next to Rebecca West, with whom he had quarrelled. In print too. If he had been an anti-monarchist before the coronation, that ancient ceremony passionately confirmed him in his republican tendencies.)

Outside, I do remember thinking at one time—slapping the bored and fretful children and discovering that my bottom was quite numb—that I might have done better to accept the invitation from my charlady to watch the ceremony on her telly. 'Lord love you, madam,' she had said, 'I wouldn't cross the street to see that lot.' Which was rather a curious statement from a very conservative woman of the old school, who had been in service from the age of twelve and had the highest reverence for the aristocracy.

Long ago, as I said, and far away. If there had been, that day, a hope for a renaissance of the spirit through the person of the young queen it was obviously not fulfilled, worthy of high office as she undoubedly is, and conscientiously diligent at her tedious duties. Somehow, in spite of all the splendour of the trappings, charisma is lacking.

The House of Windsor has not been notable for charisma. Respectable family people, mostly, with respectable tastes, average tastes, middle-of-the-road tastes. Nothing wild or scaring or original in the way of imagination. Really, under mantle and crown, just like Mr and Mrs Everybody. Only with a sterner sense of duty and propriety drilled into them and not so many opportunities to put their feet up.

Victoria, at least in retrospect, seems to have had some little additive in the way of mystique. Possibly India and the title of Empress. Even such a dowdy prudish small frump would have to take on a certain incandescence in the circumstances. And then, of course, she had the Empire, which was a reality then, a source of unquestioning pride and unquestioning belief to every stout-hearted Englishman, not to mention a limitless field of opportunity for younger sons in need of jobs and generals in need of glory. Besides, Victoria the Symbol of Empire lasted so very long, and a certain amount of charisma is bound to accrue just with the passage of all those years.

Edward her son did not inherit the charisma, but a certain glamour attached to him. His style was rakish and sporty. Even, perhaps, a little caddish. But definitely style. He lived largely if loosely, and set a high reckless tone, which was probably exciting. I think people like a bit of excitement to generate from their monarchs. After all, what is the point in being royal if you have to obey the ordinary dull conventions? Royalty should manage to be above and beyond convention if it's to maintain interest.

There hasn't been much to interest, really, since that jolly expansive king. I mean, apart from the brief and somehow terrible sad revolt of his grandson and namesake, Edward VIII, who, one feels, didn't want to be a king anyway. Because if he had wanted to be a king how differently he might have managed the business. In another age there would have been plot and counterplot, not to mention an armed uprising of loyalists gathering to the royal standard. The Archbishop of Canterbury would have been seized, Stanley Baldwin held under duress (if not poisoned), the little princesses locked up in the Tower as hostages, the lovely Lady Wallis protected night and day by the king's own guard, while the Duke of Gloucester (or Kent, or York) marched down from Scotland at the head of a rebel army to seize the throne by force. Or some such. Glory be! Endless speculation is possible.

But of course nothing bold or breathtaking happened at all, and nothing bold or breathtaking has happened since. The House of Windsor, shaken perhaps by such untoward events, closed ranks and settled firmly into the unimpeachable pattern of respectability it has maintained to this day. The late Queen Mary had indeed a queenly air, and some eccentricities of dress and manner that set her apart from the others. But then she was a foreigner anyway. When I was first in England there were some stories, apocryphal perhaps, but in popular currency, that endeared her to me, although probably not to the noble families she was in the habit of visiting occasionally, since it was said that she admired their finest pieces of furniture and china and silver and tapestry so pointedly and with such intent that there was no loyal and honourable course for them to follow but to make their royal guest a gift of the treasure she had so particularly admired. Or hide away all the best bits before she arrived. Well, if a queen can't do that, who can?

Has the monarchy run its appointed course? What purpose does it serve any longer? There is no Empire left to speak of to make a plinth imposing enough to support this glittering symbol of majesty, and it is an extremely expensive institution to maintain in a country positively floundering in economic swamps and quagmires and shrunk to mini-size in importance and influence. What point is there in creating another Prince of Wales? There are no Welsh Marches any more, no rallying point, nothing to be gained. There is, in fact, much disaffection, and I can't see that an investiture can do anything but stir it up a bit more, although Charles seems a likely lad enough and at least has the inestimable virtue—or appears to have—of displaying an interest in cultural matters of a more complex nature than *The Sound of Music*. Of course, speaking of that, the royal family are useful for film stars to meet at command performances. The film stars, wealthy as they are, might even club in to keep the grand occasions going.

Also, royalty might be worth the expense of keeping them on and keeping them up, as it were, for the sake of tourist revenue, which Britain needs and which the royal family and the royal paraphernalia do much to attract. There are still thousands of Christopher Robins in the world, adult Christopher Robins and mostly American, for whom England would scarcely be worth

281

visiting without the Changing of the Guard and the Horse Guards and the pageantry of Trooping the Colour. All that scarlet and jingle and jangle is very impressive as a spectacle. Or quaint. However you like to look at it. Interesting anyway. Picturesque. And well worth the trouble of coming over for the colour film to show back home. 'Did you know that if they faint they're court-martialled?' 'Not if they can prove they ate their proper breakfast. Cereal and all.' 'That's why they have bags of dry ice in their busbies.' 'They're not called busbies. Bearskins, man, bearskins. And they don't have dry ice in them, they have bowler hats.'

(My husband has just interrupted bitterly to say that he knows what peers have in their coronets. Chicken wings, he says, and breasts of grouse. And flasks of the best hooch. Funny how the memory of the coronation still rankles.)

Anyway, without a royal family all that pageantry would cease, and probably the tourist trade would drop off, which would be embarrassing just now.

Of course we in Australia accrue no advantages from any of that pomp and ritual. In fact some of us fail to see what advantage lies in having a monarch at all. We were never part of the Empire in the flag-planting sense, since the only purpose of our annexation was to provide a convenient dumping ground for undesirables. There are still the Birthday Honours and the New Year Honours, which may have some mystical significance for the businessmen, charity workers, and real estate agents who are preponderantly the recipients of such titles and decorations, but scarcely to anybody else. Court presentations are no longer the thing, so we do not even need a monarchy for the sake of the social advancement of our daughters. The fact of a monarchy gives us seven governors and a governor-general, thus, I suppose, providing jobs for persons too eminent or too fastidious to employ themselves further in the fields of commerce or politics, but hardly impinging on the lives of ordinary Australians in any way at all or imparting to them a proper sense of richness and tradition and heritage. We are honoured, every now and again, by a visit from the Queen of Australia, her husband, or a member of her family, when we may gawp if we choose or can wave a flag, or—if we are on an approved and vetted list—touch a royal hand.

Does it matter? Interest, predictably, has waned in such visits. It is not that we are rebellious or insurgent. Only disinterested and bored. There is not only no charisma. There doesn't seem to be any real meaning. Like my London charlady of long ago, most of us wouldn't be bothered to cross the street to see that lot. They might be very nice and worthy people, but what on earth have they got to do with us?

I wonder, at this time of Prince Charles' investiture, whether there will be ever again a King Charles of England. And oddly enough, even after what I've written here, I wouldn't put it past that likely lad to make it and those most peculiar English to thoroughly approve and endorse it, anachronistic as it might be.

For did not that flamboyant and discredited monárch, Farouk of Egypt, once prophesy:

'In fifty years there will be only five kings left in Europe. The King of Hearts. The King of Spades. The King of Clubs. The King of Diamonds. And the King of England.'

ON GOING TRENDY
AND KEEPING UP

There's been something of an inundation lately of sociological comment in learned books and smart mags on what is called the 'media society', the culture of admass, the age of gimmickry, the tense and transient time of the trendsetter.

I am not at all in the trendsetting line myself, unless I am setting a trend by keeping well clear of all the bother and effort and competition involved in being trendy, but I am quite interested in trendsetting from a spectator-sport viewpoint, and it seems to me that the game has speeded up considerably of late. What with commercial espionage and counterespionage, move and countermove, doing and outdoing, the business of trendsetting is bidding fair to beat the late James Bond for thrills and suspense.

There was, in my youth, a rather maddening song called 'Little Sir Echo', which might be a useful theme song for what I'm getting at. I mean, with the gimmick, as with the dirty story, there must be a single originator (who no doubt gets a credit card for two weeks at Miami Beach—or Surfers—as a bonus from his approving masters) but the originator is never known to anybody but his approving masters because his gimmick is at once swamped in a wave of trend.

Can you, for instance, imagine soap any longer? Plain ordinary soap for washing or bathing or laundry, good clean-smelling soap with no coloured chips or beads of anything or curious quasi-chemicals added or mysterious and magical properties virtually guaranteed to give instant seductibility or a marriage proposal (depending on your type) or, in the more mundane areas, that trouble-free and unimpeachable whiteness that used to come from

Mrs Beeton's book or below-stairs or inscrutable Chinese laundrymen?

Can you imagine spreading margarine with anything but a spoon? Unless, of course, we get to spreading it with a tyre lever or the back of a boot brush (come to think of it, do boot brushes exist any longer?). It's no use us saying that a knife used to do the job quite well: a new line of Australian honey is about to be marketed which is plugging a 'new plus—Spreadability'. Boggles this mind more boggly than ever.

Picture a garage attendant. Can you think of one who is neither a good-humoured soul mate or a Rutherford disguised in white overalls? (I can think of one because I was one once but—rather sadly too—I know that the sort of ramshackle girl I was wouldn't have a hope of keeping up with the trend.)

But I do think that—quite accidentally—I have stumbled on the secret of trendiness, and the secret lies with these latter-day Bonds of the advertising espionage and counterespionage world (all of whom are stealthily spying on each other to see what trend is coming up next). There have (quite fortuitously) 'fallen into my hands' as they say some secret documents which advertising agencies obviously put together to collate their espionage data on new developments and what are nicely called 'trends of interest'. And I must say that I do find some predictions and prophecies and promises in these documents more fascinating—in a hollow sort of way—than anything one is likely to cull from Mother Shipton's Almanac.

It is arresting to learn, for example, that a new line of vegetables-and-sauce mixes presages 'the end of the naked vegetable', so obviously the dealers in carrots and cabbages and good old Swede turnips will have to start in pretty briskly on plans to counter this sinister threat. The porcine world, too, will have to look to its toughest 007 when Kunkle Farm Products market their instant bacon (with instant sausages and hamburgers to follow) designed for fifteen-second preparation in a pop-up toaster. (Suppose you don't have a pop-up toaster?)

No twilit world of espionage, commercial or just everyday

murky, would be complete without exotic international flavours, so one wonders what oriental scrutability might be invoked to counter the imminent threat of Jan-U-Wine Pork Chop Suey dinners coming in cans. And one dare not think of the possibilities inherent in the appearance at last of the self-basting turkey.

Just having a riffle in these secret documents is calculated to pop one's eyes instead of the toaster at the thought of what is coming next in the way of trends. There are lollipops which are to be made without sugar, dry concentrated 'butter-flavoured buds' which presumably are to be made without butter (I bet he, or she, got two free weeks at Surfers for that one), something called 'Stripples' which looks like bacon and has a 'hickory-smoked meaty flavour' but actually will be made entirely of vegetable protein. (Why?) Hickory smoke seems to be terribly trendy, because there is also a new 'Barbecue Vittle' (sic) of unspecified derivation which is described as 'a barrel-shaped bite-sized snack flavoured with hickory smoke'. (Trendy hostesses, ring your nearest nursery gardeners and start planting your hickory copses right smart.)

Not all the secret information concerns food, of course. A Dutch firm is marketing a camera that has four lenses and takes four pictures at once (either identical—why four? phlegmatic lot, the Dutch—or different). There is paint in a square can which is boldly described as 'the first innovation in paint marketing in 100 years', talk of a laundry detergent made of potatoes and corn which will stop water pollution, an electric bicycle, high-frequency sound as a household cleanser, whisky in clear polyvinylchloride plastic instead of glass bottles (ah, but will it taste the same?), disposable blankets (sir, we get ours dirty but not *that* dirty) and a gadget that has freshly brewed hot coffee available the instant one opens one's eyes in the morning (like that one).

And in the secret fragrant garden of toiletries and health and beauty aids the undercover trend-spotters have been as indefatigable as one would expect undercover agents to be in a secret fragrant garden ('else what's a heaven for?'). I am intrigued by the thought of a 'new see-through lipstick and nail polish' even while conceding that I can't quite see the point. Although this won't matter, I suppose, if nobody can see the lipstick or the nail polish. (Mercy! To think of the Hedy Lamarr type of blacky-purple or puce we used to daub ourselves with. And those bloody claws. But we thought we were lovely, and so, more importantly, did our men. It is obvious now that we were, quite innocently, trendsetting.)

But the one that really gets me in, the one I can hardly wait for, is something called 'Flower Power' which, I am assured, is 'aimed at a wide range of women who only need 'a certain amount of daring'. Is that me? There are some who would say I've been quite daring enough already and watch yourself lady or there are some strong predictions about where you'll end up. Ah, but this is most inviting. It's something to do with spray-on colour and a stencil kit, and it's a do-it-yourself thing for easy application (that's what it says). And once I've done it, whatever it is (I only have to hold the stencil in place—but where, I wonder?— and 'spray on the product formulation'), I will have created 'the greatest and zaniest turned-on look since painted bodies'.

Oh oh oh! Roll on Flower Power! Roll on gimickry! Roll on trendsetters! I would, if I could, give you more weeks at Miami Beach, more weeks at Surfers. 'O brave new world that has such people in it!'

NORFOLK ISLAND (1)

Norfolk Island, roughly five miles by three miles in size, lies in the south Pacific Ocean at a latitude of 29 degrees south and a longitude of 168 degrees east. Apart from its two tiny and uninhabited satellite islands, its nearest neighbours are New Caledonia (420 miles), New Zealand (480 miles), Lord Howe Island (560 miles), and Australia (850 miles).

The island was discovered in 1774 by Captain James Cook, who claimed it for England and called it 'a paradise'. He saw in the lofty forests of pines, forests of lofty masts for the King's Navy. He saw in the fertile subtropical soil future acres of flax for the King's sails. But so exceedingly perverse is human nature that it persists in transforming even paradise into hell, and the paradise of Norfolk Island was destined to become a penal settlement of such inhuman brutality that some prisoners preferred the gallows to further torture and degradation. Such a stench arose from Norfolk in the Pacific that even authority seems to have been disturbed, because the penal settlement was abandoned in 1835 and the convicts transferred to mainland prisons or to Tasmania.

The noble administration buildings, the handsome houses of Quality Row, the military barracks, gracefully pillared Government House on the hill, the dam and the water mill, the salt house, the crank mill, the lime kiln, the blacksmiths' shop where prisoners had forged ploughshares as well as their own fetters, the hospital, the store, the beautifully austere cluster of small buildings at the jetty's edge, the cottages, the cultivated clearings, the roads, and the two great grim stone compounds that must have reeked of blood and madness, were left to the occupation of a different breed of incoming settlers, themselves quite as dramatic (historically speaking, that is) as the outgoing ones.

But in a different way.

More than sixty years after Fletcher Christian and some of his fellow mutineers had hidden themselves away on Pitcairn Island and scuttled the *Bounty* as too dangerous evidence of their exploit, their descendants, sired on gentle Polynesian dams and become something religious after the fervent conversion of the last living mutineer, John Adams, had already been discovered to an amazed and interested world, and, after such a long passage of time, had been discovered also—Rousseau's 'noble savage' being a fashionable idea at the time—to be exceedingly romantic. The sins of the fathers were not to be visited on such charming and simple children. In fact, Victorian England felt so indulgent towards this romantic (and by now exemplarily moral) community, that the Queen graciously offered them a new island, a bigger island, a better island, since they were getting to be rather cramped on tiny Pitcairn and such a moral and model community should be encouraged to be fruitful and multiply.

She gave them Norfolk.

On the fettered heels of the departing convicts the entire population of Pitcairn—194 of them—arrived on 9 June 1856 with royal approval, and took up the land, and settled. And apart from the few incorrigibly homesick who ungratefully refused to appreciate their betterment and returned to Pitcairn, here they are yet. Or rather, here their descendants are yet, Christians and Quintals and Adamses and McCoys and such, married in to Baileys and Buffets and Nobbses, inter-married back again, until nobody can really say for certain what the precise kin-tie is between person and person, although kin they all are, close or distant, and however they may bicker and litigate among themselves, one is aware of a tribal solidarity that is deep and unquestioning.

Norfolk Island may be (and actually is) administered by the Department of External Territories in Canberra, but to the descendants of the original Pitcairners it is now, always was, and always will be, their own private property, their very own private island, deeded to them in perpetuity by Queen Victoria herself. Stranger, walk with the politeness of a guest and curb your tongue and mind your manners. For all their generous hospitality and friendliness, for all their lovely gaiety, they carry themselves with all the authority and pride of inheritors, and all the obduracy of a nineteenth century community at the very moment of impact with the twentieth. It is, of course, this very sense of confrontation that makes the island so fascinating from a sociological point of view. At the moment it is shaped—metaphorically speaking, that is—like a question mark.

Working against their nineteenth century way of life is the very beauty of their island. Because it *is* beautiful. As an island connoisseur I do believe Norfolk to be one of the most beautiful—if not *the* most beautiful—islands I have ever seen. Its twenty miles of basalt and tufa cliffs (black and the tenderest rose pink) are like ramparts standing against the battering of the Pacific. Its multitude of hills are vertiginous but green and smooth as parkland. It has the charm of infinite variety. There are majestic mountain forests, and deep gullies leafy and lush with fern and reed, bamboo, wild hibiscus, and plants and flowers you have never seen before. Palm and pine mingle companionably about the steep red roofs and flagged verandahs of the island houses, randomly scattered on the hills and sheltered behind exotic tangles of poinsettia, bougainvillea, jasmine, ginger, hibiscus, banana trees, paw paws, avocado pears. There are dirt roads like English lanes, hedged with thickets of guava, red and yellow and sweet to eat. Cows graze on pastoral slopes, commons, road edges, cliff tops, the golf course, inside the old convict compounds, on the football field, anywhere and everywhere, with perfect bovine poise and equanimity, acting—I suppose—as municipal lawn-mowers and hedge-clippers. The place seems sweet and languorously heavy with time, but it smells tangy with pine needles and sea salt. The pines and the sea fight for visual dominance, vertical with horizontal, majesty with majesty, the serried ranks of the regnant tree with the serried ranks of the long blue breakers uncurling slow white banners. It is almost too much.

And if you add to this—as you must—possibly the most complete and the most interesting complex of historical buildings in the Commonwealth, a coral reef and a blue lagoon, tax-free land and duty-free shopping, the place has to become desirable, infinitely desirable, to retiring people wanting to settle somewhere cheap and beautiful and quiet, to speculators, to developers, to tax-dodgers and fiddlers, and to the ubiquitous tourist, ever-eager for the new and the strange (not to mention all those dirt-cheap watches and transistors and cameras and binoculars and Scottish knitteds and French perfumes and Mikimoto pearls and bottles of hooch and cartons of cigarettes).

In fact, I am so conscious of the potential danger to the island that I was tempted to refrain from writing anything about it at all, just in case any words of mine should damage or upset the present delicate social balance. It is fortunate, I suppose, that the inaccessibility of the place still works for the social balance. There is a ship only once in three weeks, unloaded with difficulty and danger, by longboats, because there is no real harbour. The airstrip is coral and as yet incapable of landing any aircraft more advanced than a DC-4, and only twice a week at that, weather permitting. And, importantly, the present administrator, Air Commodore Dalkin, is evidently a man deeply involved and deeply concerned in the future of the island and its inhabitants, in conservation, preservation, and restoration. The Australian Conservation Foundation have already published their report on the island. The National Trust is presently preparing their own.

And yet one feels that all these concerned and involved people are walking a tightrope. Tourists the island must have, because the agriculture is only for domestic use, freight-making export too uncertain a proposition. But how many tourists? What sort of tourists? I hope, for the sake of the island, not the sort of tourists who demand (and eventually get) casinos and nightclubs and plages and all the commercial razzamatazz that feeds on tourism. That lot can go to Surfers. But one has seen beautiful islands destroyed in their peace and simplicity before, never to regain it.

291

Still, last Sunday was Bounty Day, the anniversary of the arrival of the Pitcairners on Norfolk. They've held it in all its harmony since 1856. I hope they can hold it yet.

NORFOLK ISLAND (2)

Since our visit to Norfolk Island coincides with a tour of members of the Australian National Trust, and since we discover most happily that two of our best friends are of this party, we sneakily attach ourselves for guided excursions, inspections, cliff top barbecues, afternoon tea at Government House, or any part of the Trust programme that interests us particularly.

We have also discovered the nicest possible taxi-driver, who is informed and informative as well as amiable and has put himself at our disposal. 'Any hour of the day or night,' he promises largely. So we are mobile. And this is important, because although the island is really very small it is so hilly and the network of roads so intricate and winding that there is quite a distance between point and point. Others of the island guests rent Japanese or Italian mini-cars, which is the usual thing. Some young lovers hire scooters. But we have let our driving licences lapse years and years ago so this convenient arrangement is denied us. Next time I come to Norfolk Island (as of course I will: you can't do more than try to chew a bite of it in a couple of weeks) I intend to hire a horse to explore the marvellous bridle tracks and trails still inaccessible to motorised vehicles.

And hooray hooray for that too. There are quite enough roads already—fifty miles of them I am told—and we read with alarm in the Australian Conservation Foundation's report on the island that new roads bulldozed through the natural vegetation let in the weeds that will eventually choke and destroy the fascinating indigenous flora of these lovely leafy places; also we have already, and sorrowfully, seen the most magnificent banyan tree— originally covering, I suppose, half an acre—mangled and mutilated pitiably to make way for another road. There are already

1000 cars on Norfolk and I should think that quite enough.

We are staying in the area called Burnt Pine at the newest tourist hotel (or hotel-motel?). There are three other hotels on the island, lots of guesthouses, and tourist flats, but we are very happy with our choice. Our accommodation is comfortable, the water runs reliably hot, and the food is plentiful, if a bit monotonous in the way of ship's food or aeroplane food. Nonetheless we eat like pigs, and when in need of variety dine out at the very good restaurant a hundred yards up the road, where we stuff ourselves with avocados and French brown onion soup and peppered steaks and fresh green salads.

Burnt Pine is a ridge that has been given over to commercial ribbon development of horrendous ugliness. Aesthetically one would like to bulldoze the lot and start again with an architect and a master plan incorporating buildings as pleasing and unobtrusive as the Fletcher Christian Flats, which in this area are notable for their reticence—island timber, oiled, and shingled roofs, nice in the landscape. But the ladies are passionately in thrall to the duty-free shops (or bazaars, rather) and seem to spend fortunes saving money: how on earth are they going to pack the stuff? So I suppose Burnt Pine is a permanent institution. Anyway, for the moment commercialism is confined to this one ridge, and once out of it you can forget about it, because it can't be seen from anywhere else on the island.

We are mostly out of it. We have lost our hearts to Kingston, the original convict settlement, still the administration centre, and the very antithesis of contemporary Burnt Pine. How, one wonders, in the face of this beautiful and harmonious assembly of Georgian buildings, could the shambles of Burnt Pine have happened? Perhaps people can't see any more. There is even a modern (?) hotel down here, smack bang in elegant Quality Row, but one is given to understand that that's as far as commercialism will be allowed to encroach on this historic preserve. (Spit three times, cross your fingers, knock on wood, and pray that the Australian National Trust, at present—in the persons of Cedric Flower and John Morris—urgently exploring and classifying, has enough

294

influence to preserve what is left against the threat of the developers.)

Kingston is precise pale grey geometry drawn on green space in a relationship that is a marvel. And the sea beyond, boiling on the coral reef, and Phillip Island singing opal colours against a darkly turbulent sky. (Phillip Island has been ravaged by rabbits into complete erosion, but the gannets and the mutton birds and the terns nest there, although in declining numbers. More's the pity.)

Much of Kingston is intact, some of it is 'restored' (and I put that in quotes because I don't think the restoration is good enough) and much is in ruin. I am fascinated by the complete buildings, but I think I like the ruins best, perhaps because I can restore them myself in imagination. Ruins are somehow more eloquent than buildings even perfectly preserved. I know that is a romantic idea, but then I am a romantic and in Kingston I can indulge myself. And do. By daylight, scrambling through the shells of the houses of Quality Row, reassembling the most handsome rooms and courtyards from crumbling walls, fireplaces, bread ovens, scraps of coloured plaster, spiderwebs, and tangles of wild fig. Or prowling among the lazily grazing cows and horses in the convict compounds where some excavation has been done, revealing a bit of the ground plan of the radial complex of cells and dungeons and (maybe) part of the sewerage system.

Couldn't one of our university facilities of archaeology send a plane load of students over to Norfolk Island to dig up the rest? It is every bit as interesting and illuminating as Egyptian or Greek or Roman or Sumerian excavation sites. Possibly more so, being closer to us in time and emotion. The students would have a ball, and by exposing the original foundations might foil the rumoured plan of future bowling greens and tennis courts and (God save us all) floral clocks. And while they were at it they could have a go at the steep sandhill at the sea-edge of the cemetery, the oldest part of it, where the headstones march into the sand. What we found, scrabbling and scratching, was that the inscriptions actually buried in sand were as clear and

295

precise as the day they'd been cut, in contrast to the exposed stones which have been largely worn away, or are in process of being worn away. There's history under the sand. Maybe as poignant as this:

'Thou didst pardon Mary sighing
And the thief beside Thee dying
Thence I hope, on Thee relying.'

Here they lie, the lads from County Mayo and Tipperary and Dublin, Kilmurry in the County of Cork, the Parish of Connemara, from Belfast and Liverpool and London, aged twenty-two years, twenty-five years, twenty-nine years, twenty-three years. Executed. Executed. Executed. 'Stop Christian stop and meditate on this man's sad and awful fate . . .' And there beside them lie their gaolers, privates and corporals and captains and overseers too. 'Barbarously murdered', 'accidentally shot', 'drowned whilst crossing the bar', 'killed by a fall of rock', and they too were only twenty-two years old or twenty-five years old or twenty-eight years old, and far from home. They had wives too (convict women? they must have been), and little children. And the wives died young and their babies soon after. 'Buds.' 'Green lilies.' Lord, what a place. And then the Christians and the Quintals and the Adamses and the McCoys, the inheritors, lying in state and strict family groupings. And the high green hills above ridged like fine accordion-pleating, and the sweet blue water of the lagoon beyond. And 'the bar', of course, where so many were 'accidentally drowned'. *Feng-shui*. Wind and water. A propitious place, finally, calculated to soothe the most angry or violent or troubled spirit.

Oh well, it's all one now, whether they came here by way of Gallows Gate or in all the dignity of full military ceremonial or domestically, as it were, with families lamenting.

And Kingston's one, too, so pale and austere and precisely drawn on green space. Haunting. And talking of space I realise, to my horror, that mine has run out. Before I've even fairly begun too. Before I've even got to the Kingston-by-moonlight bit, which I intended for a set piece. Oh dear. I suppose it only goes to show how hooked a romantic can get by a few old buildings, a scatter of gravestones, a whiff of history, and enough time, for once, to dawdle over these things. I won't apologise. It's quite something to be hooked on Norfolk Island.

NORFOLK ISLAND (3)

A young man who bears a famous Norfolk Island name is flogging Gallows Gate, where condemned convicts used to pass out to their hangings. The transaction is a joke, of course. A joke? Of course? I am not at all sure. But I do see what a temptation it is to tease the National Trust.

Besides, the young man in question, a lineal descendant of Fletcher Christian, is reputed to be the scamp of the family, capable of anything. He is slight, wirily strong, and looks (perhaps he is?) a bit piratical. His grin is in the nature of a dare, his pride is fine-honed and edgy. He wears a little arrogant bit of a beard and flaunts himself in working gear, well muddied from the potato patch he's been sowing.

'Well, I might be able to let you have it then,' he says, his voice lilting a little with pleasure (nice accents they have on Norfolk Island: West Country? North Country? I can't place it quite). 'The price is forty thousand dollars. It's a bargain. I've got the receipt for it somewhere or other. My grandfather bought it for paving stones for his pig pen and never bothered to take it away. So it's come down to me, you might say, as an inheritance. Of course, if you don't want it . . . ?' He laughs on a high note of excitement. 'There's a Texan millionaire who's interested. As Benjamin Franklin said . . .' Benjamin Franklin seems to be his doppelgänger, nudging and prompting him to further devilry.

Gravely we appoint ourselves his agents in the matter of Gallows Gate. We might just bump into an even richer millionaire back on the mainland. And while we're at it, how about the Arches, that enigmatical ruin of handsomely tuck-pointed stone that has been loosely identified as former stables. Surely a millionaire would like that re-erected on his ranch?

The nonsense that isn't quite nonsense goes on, elaborately, with a great deal of laughter. Immoderate laughter, it seems to be, but then I have the queerest feeling that everybody is laughing at something else entirely, something quite private.

We have, of course, become involved with the descendants of the *Bounty* mutineers. Impossible not to. Finally, people are so much more interesting than things—buildings and scenery and logbooks and manifests and invoices and leg irons and old nails, or even the horribly accurate replica of a cat-o'-nine-tails, of which a lady says, lingeringly: 'They were beaten until the blood ran.'

'Wouldn't you think,' says her companion, 'that it would have made them more docile?'

'Oh, but look at our criminals of today,' says the first. 'Psychiatrists maintain . . .' and expands on the theme.

'Of course. That's it precisely. It is something lacking in *them*. The criminal mind.'

Oh. Oh. Oh. Pat Flaherty of County Mayo, Pat Glenny of Limerick, Walter Berry of Tipperary, Thomas Ford of London, William McCulloch, John Butler, Thomas Berry, Michael Anderson, James Saye, why weren't you—so young as you were—more docile? Why were you driven to mutiny and the gallows? Through that grim gate whose sale is presently being negotiated. In jest, naturally. Jests are just as natural as earnestness, and sharper when they are a mixture of both. I like this sort of thing.

We had a barbecue picnic today, out on Steeles Point. Tagging on to the National Trust again. (We had better join and make it legitimate.) A group of the island ladies turn this on with pretty artistry. Steak and chops and sausages, charcoal grilled. Fresh battered fish. Crisp salads. Fruit pies with cream. And you sit on a log on a cliff top stuffing yourself with all these goodies and watching the angled white terns wheeling in pairs around the jagged dark pines all hung with pale chiffon frills of moss, and the air is boundless and beautiful and smells of the pines and the sea. What is it about islands? I mean, I know I am addicted to them, but I'm not sure why. Perhaps D. H. Lawrence explained it in his strange story *The Man Who Loved Islands*.

'. . . Once isolate yourself on a little island in a sea of space and the moment begins to heave and expand in great circles, the solid earth is gone, and your slippery, naked dark soul finds herself out in the timeless world . . . The souls of all the dead are alive again, and pulsating actively around you. You are out in the other infinity.'

Maybe it's something like that. I'm all for that moment heaving and expanding for all it's worth. No piker, I, about rushing to meet it.

The moment transfers itself to the jetty at Kingston and there is the awaited ship standing off half a mile out and the lighters going out through the bar and coming in through the bar on a wild grey sea, loaded with cargo—crates and bales of food and drink and furniture, and merchandise for those enticing duty-free shops. And cars too. More bright minis, like Matchbox toys in the fat-bellied longboats, and swung up like toys by crane to the jetty, in rope nets. I do love the trades of the sea. And we are lucky to see this because a ship comes only once in three weeks, and the 'weather permitting' clause applies here too. In fact this ship drifts dangerously close to the reef and has to take shelter around the headland. It is all very dramatic and thrilling and the tourists go mad with their cameras. We don't have a camera so must record it in our heads, the sea colour and the sky colour and the mottled marbling of clouds and breakers and the briny smell of it and the angry sound of the sea on the reef and one blue-jerseyed figure at the sweep of a lighter, laughing as he rides the bar on the crest of a foiled wave and swoops in to the jetty. What a nice bit of silent swagger. We are freezing but in thrall. Don't need cameras. What does it remind you of? Greece? Cornwall? Devon? Brittany? You are sifting and comparing in your writer's head all the time. And of course it isn't like anything but Norfolk Island.

On our way back to Burnt Pine and dinner we pick up a young girl in bare feet and blue jeans, carrying a bridle. Her cropped black hair is like tousled fur, her skin is dusky pink with wind and cold. She has very white and crooked teeth which catch on her full lower lip when she smiles, which she does politely but shyly, apologetic about her muddy feet. She has twelve horses and wants to start a riding stables. She is a charming young creature. A bit Bronte-ish, we think, still indulging ourselves in a jag of literary allusions. That's the way the place gets you.

She's even more Bronte-ish when we see her next, at a splendid party that has developed in another hotel on the other side of the island. The hotels take it in turns to have what is called 'open night', meaning music and dancing and entertainment and general jollity, and we have been swept here willy-nilly by the host of our own hotel, who is completely generous about competition from his rivals, and by our dinner guests, who are interesting in that they are mutineer descendants both and cousins of both first and second degree, but representing, as it were, the serious and the flip side of the family coin. As in the matter of Gallows Gate. Or do they? When is a joke not a joke? You can't quite tell with islanders. There are mainlanders at our table too, people who came here for a holiday years ago and fell in love with Norfolk and settled, and are deeply concerned in the future of the island. And there is commercialism, also concerned, but perhaps in a different way. And there are tourists, having a ball. Like us. And there is the Bronte girl now in a white ruffled Bronte blouse and miniskirt, twisting happily on the dance floor. And she is involved in the island's future too. And as the party loosens up and the dancing grows wilder and the laughter reduces us to helpless chokings and snortings one is, in one's head, and so very impertinently, casting and plotting a novel in which all these people play out their roles. The temptation is irresistible. But since it is only mental cavorting it probably doesn't matter, and won't affect the future of Gallows Gate one way or another.

I have a feeling that time will provide the appropriate tag-line to that joke. If it's a joke. And I also have a feeling that I have written as much as I dare about these curious outer limits to our continent. Until I have a chance to go back.

THE KELLY SAGA
BEGINS AGAIN

'I think now,' he said, 'that I would treat it more on the brevity of his life, the transitory nature of his life. This being his real destiny. And the mask—although in some way it must be there— is more the covering for this other shell that took this very brief life through this particular existence in this particular place.

'And I would do it much more like a figure in a Chinese poem. Like the unfolding of a screen. Like a Sung landscape. And the figures smaller, more minute, playing out their parts against this dreaming landscape. Because it's clear that the dreaming landscape goes on, after the figures have lived in it. This ineffable thing, like the scent of wattle. Indestructible. All that's indestructible about us is that we are witnesses to the events and lives of the people who pass through the dream.

'I'd like to think,' he said, 'that Kelly was full of courage in that he tried to match his destiny to what he knew would conquer him and annihilate him, and if we don't respect other things about him we respect that. He met it face on.'

Thus Sidney Nolan, arch-mythographer of Ned Kelly, musing under the lacy leaves of a giant old peppercorn tree on the prospect of two desolate chimneys rising from rubble, an iron wheel rim, an ancient buggy seat sitting in the paddock grass as incongruous and haughty as a Rousseau sofa, the remains of a forge, and a scattering of rusted nuts and bolts. There were a couple of magpies melodious in the pepper tree and a chirpy little yellow bird hopping cheekily along the ruined wall of a former outbuilding, uncaring that this was all that was left of the house where the Kelly family had lived through events of such a dramatic and romantic order as to become Australian legend.

'That chimney is in one of the paintings I painted of Constable Fitzpatrick and Kate Kelly,' he said, 'and you can imagine it then with the clock up on the sill, and the fire going, and a pot of stew on the fire, and the whole feeling of life as it went on . . .'

That was a couple of years ago, and Sidney Nolan was starring in a film of his own, a television documentary made on his return to Australia at the time of his retrospective exhibition, and one section of the film was concerned with his re-exploration of the Kelly country, which had inspired him, more than twenty years before, to begin the series of paintings that, more than any other, brought him international recognition. (Incidentally it is interesting to speculate on why the ABC has never seen fit to release that film. A lot of time and work and passion and poetry and high excitement went into it, and I know it to have been finished long since.)

But about the Kelly country. Even a couple of years ago people kept mum in those parts. They were suspicious, unforthcoming. Tracking down the remains of the Kelly house was a task requiring tenacity and the most delicate diplomacy. Nobody knew anything, or if they did they weren't telling. And when the poignant ruin was located at last there was a notice on the post-and-wire fence which said: 'Private Property. Keep Out'.

It was even difficult to find the grave of the last Kelly brother, Jim, who was not involved in the 'Kelly Outbreak' because he happened to be in gaol at the time, and lived on in Greta until 1946, when he died at the age of eighty-seven. In Greta cemetery his grave was only an unmarked weed-grown mound—scarcely a mound even—with some melancholy grass blowing on it that grey day and one wildflower, a four-o'clock, stubbornly asserting the right to live and bloom. This touched Mr Nolan deeply. It was, after all, such a very forlorn resting place.

I wonder if Jim Kelly will rate a headstone now that the Kelly saga is going to be sung on a wide world screen. And whether the people of the Kelly country will drop their defensive attitude and begin to take a pride in their own mythology. Or even to make a profit from it. After all, Ned has become so respectable a figure that only an actor of unimpeachable morality is considered worthy to portray him, which is a pretty turn of the wheel. Only a few years ago I was visiting in Euroa at a time when feelings were running pretty high on the subject of a proposed Kelly festival or pageant, and while commercial interests were all for it on the grounds that it would attract tourists to the town there were many citizens of moral rectitude who were working actively to spike the jolly festival as an unseemly glorification of a common criminal. It was all very like David Martin's novel *The Hero of Too* (which I still think would make a splendid film itself) and I must say I enjoyed the plotting and counterplotting very much indeed and wished I could stay for the real fun.

I have noted that commercial interests are likely to get in for the profits again with all those tourists and visitors and film people pouring into the Kelly country and needing food and drink and beds and comforts of one sort and another, and I don't see why they should pull all the plums out of the pudding. After all, the real people of the Kelly country have been living down and hushing up the exploits of Ned and Dan for so long it seems only fair they should come in for a slice too. If ever a local boy has made good their Ned has. And now, instead of prevaricating and hedging, they can signpost the way to the Kelly house as boldly as they may, conduct guided tours, sell souvenirs if they like (like the rusted buggy bolt I use as a paperweight), run up Kelly dolls for the kiddies, or even, if they are really enterprising, forge suits of armour and Kelly masks for sale as pot-plant holders or umbrella stands. I should think, too, that the Kelly house could be restored to its original state without too much expense—dirt floors, hessian bag partitions, bark roof and all—and utilised as a tea room, with waitresses in authentic Kate Kelly gear.

It's all very far from Mr Nolan's musings, of course, but I don't think he will be at all surprised. 'There's no umpire,' he said, 'to decide that the subject for a myth should be respectable. Myths arise in obscure places, in unknown or anonymous circumstances, but people pour passion into it, storytelling, and it gets round like a pebble, and ultimately it comes to represent something basic in the community, and it's called a myth.' And looking at a wattle tree in bloom he said, 'Even though the heroes and the policemen are dead something exists here, and it's spring now and all you wish is that the young people who were once gay and loving and living could be here again in this dreaming landscape.'

Well, well. And so they will. Or representations of them. But, you know, try as I may, I cannot quite see Mick Jagger as a minute figure in a Sung landscape. Although, when you come to think of it, our Ned was a bit of a rolling stone himself.

ANYONE FOR
FISH AND CHIPS?

In the Sydney harbour suburb where I live there has been some controversy lately about an application for a liquor licence from a beach restaurant which intends to specialise in seafoods.

The comments of residents living within a quarter-mile radius of the proposed restaurant, as reported in our local newspaper, are interesting. Of course one can't be sure that it is a completely unbiased report, or a really representative cross-section of the community, but just taking it as it reads you begin to realise why our foreshores (and this goes for Melbourne too) are for the most part innocent of any place to eat and drink more civilised than plastic-lined milk bars and pie shops.

The residents in opposition (and one, of course, is the mother of teenage daughters) are 'apprehensive' that the granting of a liquor licence to a beach restaurant would attract 'rowdy elements', 'rough elements', 'drunken louts', 'hooligan types', who are, they admit, 'with us always' and 'get drunk and cause a nuisance by throwing sand, pushing and shoving, fighting and using indecent language'.

Now it is a very curious thing that in four or five years of occasional lunching and dining out in restaurants with liquor licences, both in Sydney and Melbourne, I have never once noticed that such restaurants attract 'hooligan types' or 'drunken louts'. The restaurants I've been in have been rather quiet, discreet places, catering—or at least appearing to cater—for rather quiet, discreet people who seemed to know what knife and fork to use and the purpose of a table napkin and didn't look at all likely to push or shove or fight or use indecent language (unless they were doing so in discreet whispers, which would be their business and not mine).

On the other hand I've seen rare young specimens propping themselves up around milk bars and pie stalls and looking willing for any sort of caper. Looking bored, actually—poor sad little sillies—and I suspect that boredom might be the real cause of most of the capering. But it never would have occurred to me that these aimless packs of hair-and-Levis might be potential customers at a lunching-and-dining-and-wining seafood restaurant.

Seafood is scarcely cheap, not if it is served elegantly, I mean, with all the razzamatazz of appropriate sauces and napery and cunning lighting and deft waiters and long, comprehensive wine lists. The likely lads in the disposal store gear will probably get their seafood from the nearest fish and chip shop, just as they've always done, and their liquor in cans from the nearest pub. And go on throwing sand and pushing and shoving and fighting and using indecent language and chucking their empties over residents' front fences after they've had their fun. But it won't be anything to do with a nice civilised restaurant, because in nice civilised restaurants people, on the whole, behave themselves.

And wouldn't you say that we desperately need some nice civilised restaurants around our foreshores? With all those stupendous seascapes to look at, and the water traffic bustling or idling, and the lovely briny smell of it all, and the sweet crumpling swoosh of waves on sand, and the dance and dapple by day and the jewellery of lights by night—with all that it seems a deprivation that when we lunch or dine out we are forced to do so in dark cellars, like furtive conspirators, peering across the candles and fumbling for our specs to even hazard a guess at the menu.

It's not that I'm against cellars, having had much pleasure in many, but I'm dead against the cellar complex which pertains here and decrees that eating and drinking, although necessary and even permissible, is tantamount to indecent exposure if you do it in full view of the world.

I think that eating by the water (all right, and drinking by

307

the water, too) is a pleasure of a high and particular order. Of course, there are some lucky people who have their own beach views or water views, but most of us don't, even though most of us feel that all that water is actually communal property, and we ought properly to be able to live on it and around it and by it in as familiar a way as if it was our own backyard.

So all this fuss about one restaurant has saddened me rather. Because it isn't one restaurant we need, but many. With licences and without, and of all sorts of price ranges. And coffee courtyards and beer gardens and informal places as well as special-event places.

Any other country in the world with a stretch of water, even if it is only a pretty turgid-looking river, utilises it for public enjoyment. And eating and drinking are really rather enjoyable. I suspect, too, that the more agreeable and civilised you make the atmosphere for eating and drinking, the more agreeable and civilised will be the clientele.

Some of my pleasantest memories of meals are meals by the water. Lunching at Bray in the summer with the punts sliding by on the Thames and spilling over with pretty girls and tasselled cushions and picnic hampers, and the bad-tempered swans waddling up the lawn to the luncheon table to demand pickings. And a Marseilles waterfront like a stage set, peopled by costumed bit players obviously acting their heads off, and smelling of acrid French cigarettes and hot bread and the delicious dinner being prepared for us.

Oh, and all the meals, breakfasts and luncheons and dinners, along the coasts of France and Italy, and by the rivers of Europe, the Rhine and the Rhone and the Loire and the Gironde and the Mosel, and some of these meals were of the bread-and-cheese sort and some were extravagant with truffles and cream and bottles of famous vintage, but they are memorable not so much for the food one ate and the drink one drank as for the sense of ease and contentment one always has by the water. A sort of large brimming peacefulness, which I am certain must be good for the digestion, not to mention one's attitude towards one's fellow men.

I suppose I've been spoiled by living in the Mediterranean for too long, where you take your meals by the water as a matter of course and in the most public fashion and order wine with your food with never a guilty thought that you might be helping to attract 'rowdy elements' or 'hooligan types' or contributing towards a deterioration of the language into indecency.

I must say I miss all that very much, in spite of the many excellent cellars there are around these days and the excellent food and wine that are served in them. Oh well, next time I'm asked out to a meal in the way of business or pleasure, I suppose I could suggest we have a picnic on the foreshores instead. Or would that outrage propriety? If I made it a meat pie and a milkshake I might just get away with it.

ON *CLEAN STRAW*
FOR NOTHING

Somebody—Frank Benier I think it was—once called him 'a benevolent steamroller'.

The writer George Johnston, that is, with whom I have lived now for something more than twenty-three years. No woman lives with a man for that long out of sheer masochism so there is obviously a great deal to him apart from the steamroller, or flattening out bit, although I do believe that to be a true observation. Or true in so far as he is inclined to be a conversational bully—being better informed about more things than most, liking to dominate, and having a most devastating turn of wit (it occurs to me that he is the only person I know who can make a compliment into an accusation). He is also a steamroller in his purposes.

His purposes are, of course, various. But one of them is to write novels. To say what he knows. What he knows uniquely, because everybody's experience is made up of unique particulars, and nobody can say for anybody else. I know this to be so because I have shared a great deal of his experience, and I know too that we both remember the experience quite differently. It affected us quite differently. We write about it quite differently. I suspect it is the difference between optimism and pessimism, but I am not entirely sure. All people have both in varying mixtures. Nobody is absolutely a Yea Sayer and nobody is absolutely a Nay Sayer. I tend to Yea and George Johnston tends to Nay, but then I am a good deal younger than he is, had a much happier beginning and launching into life, and haven't been so sick for so many years.

His purpose was not always to say what he knows. In his leaping time—trench coat, beret, dressing-gown from de Pinna, pigskin luggage, passport fabulously stamped with nearly every country in the world—he was inclined to hide what he knew, suspected, was troubled by, behind a glitteringly competent dazzle of professional observation. He could give you, in words, the look and the smell and the taste and the sound of an experience (usually an exotic experience, because he collected exotic experiences the way some people collect luggage labels: like travelling in Tibet and living with the Chinese communists and visiting the last of the great ivory-painters in Isphahan), but he couldn't or wouldn't tell you how it felt.

Perhaps he was afraid of how things felt. Certainly he shied away from any written expression of his own emotional reactions to things and settled instead for what he thought his reactions should have been if he had been in the skin of an elderly professor of archaeology or however he was disguising himself for that particular novel (it was most often elderly and tremendously erudite, but sometimes also heroic-male-writ-large—which I suppose was understandable enough coming from a very sensitive un-physical sort of man who had never had any education excepting for what he had scratched and scrabbled for himself: rather marvellously too: the range of his knowledge still staggers me).

Some words of Gerard Manley Hopkins come to me here. 'Sickness broke him.' But I'm not sure whether sickness broke him, or, in a cruel sort of way, made him. He raged against it for years, despaired, became bitter and hating and not easy to live with. He was, of course, affronted and outraged by the corruption working in his lungs. And there were times when he was affronted and outraged by anybody who didn't have corruption working in his lungs. (Or so it seemed then: it was the impression he gave.) Why did it have to pick on him? Him of all people who had never been sick in his life. I do not like to think much on those years because we almost foundered, but I do like to think on those years because in those years he began to write in a different way. To me, a truer way. Perhaps he thought he had nothing to lose any more. Perhaps he thought if people didn't like what he was and what he thought and what he felt they could bloody well lump him. The necessity to charm, to please, to entertain, to be approved (Golden Boy they used to call him), dropped out of his make-up like so much unwanted baggage, and as he fined down alarmingly in weight (for a man six feet tall a weight of seven stone is alarming) he also fined down in character, persona, or whatever you call it. And of course this, in a way, was alarming too—for a wife, that is, who found she was married to somebody else entirely.

Closer to the Sun was the first novel he wrote in that time, apart from the Professor Challis series of thrillers written under the pseudonym Shane Martin (the names of our daughter and elder son) which were bread and butter and which he wrote at white-heat at the rate of a couple of months for each one as insurance policies for me and the kids.

Closer to the Sun was different. I don't think it was a good novel, but it was a very important one to me because it was halfway honest—that is, honest for half its length, when obviously uncertainty engulfed him and he retreated into story-line and the old trick of dazzling observation. And it was an important novel because it was an exploratory sort of one, feeling out the ground for the one that was to come so many years later—like now, or actually next month when Collins publish it—called *Clean Straw for Nothing*.

I've been living with *Clean Straw for Nothing* for all those years since *Closer to the Sun*. There have been novels in between, of course, because that's the man's business. After *Closer to the Sun* there was *The Far Road*, which I still think is one of the best things he's ever written and in which I have a personal pride because I nagged him into writing a novel about two men, a jeep, and 100,000 corpses. I believe it sold all of eighty-two copies in Australia, but that doesn't really matter now (although it did at the time, naturally). What matters is that he set down, as truly as he could, an experience that had shattered him. Fictionalised,

312

but not the less true for that. Maybe even more true for that. Distilled. The very essence of the thing in all its dreadfulness. I loved that novel. I stood up and cheered for it. Perhaps my cheering mozzed it, because it was a complete failure commercially, and because the poor man had all of us lot dependent upon him he went back to what I call 'faction-fiction' and wrote a novel—quite a good novel, in fact—called *The Far Face of the Moon*. Very exotic again, set in Burma in the time of the last war and all about pilots flying The Hump and its heroine was a nymphomaniac and its hero was impotent and where he dredged that lot up God alone knows (since he has no truck with psychiatrists, mistrusting that profession profoundly).

And his publishers didn't like that novel a scrap. In fact, he was told in so many words that as a writer he couldn't afford even one more near-miss. That's an awful thing to be told when you're fifty and sick almost to death and you have all this wretched family whose very breaths depend upon your breath and you can't breathe much anyway.

But what he did, instead of tearing up the manuscript or tearing his hair or slashing his wrists or shooting his publishers or indulging in any similar despairing dramatic action (and I cannot say how I admire him for this), was to withdraw *The Far Face of the Moon*, quite quietly and reasonably, and write *My Brother Jack* instead. Which proved to be wise, not only because it has been what they call 'successful' in the trade and was the lever which moved us all back to Australia and him into the proper medical care which has undoubtedly lengthened his life by some years, but also because *My Brother Jack* committed him totally to exploring his own experiences. There would be no more aged professors of archaeology or bitter exiled Englishmen of vast erudition or rambunctious sponge divers. There would be George Johnston being, quite unapologetically, George Johnston.

This pleased me because—even when I was hating him, and I was hating him quite frequently for a period—I always did believe George Johnston to be more interesting than the characters he made up. I know that everybody, particularly every creative body, makes himself up to a certain extent, and to that degree the narrator of *My Brother Jack*—that David Meredith who begins tentatively in *Closer to the Sun* and is expanded and developed and really begins to sing in *The Far Road*—is a fictional person. But it was obvious in the very writing of *My Brother Jack* that this person David Meredith wasn't going to be dismissed with the last page and the words 'The End'. He had a great deal more to say and to do and to suffer and to witness and to record, so in a mad way (or a writer's way, which is mad anyhow) all the time *My Brother Jack* was being written *Clean Straw for Nothing* was just as certainly evolving, although it would be five years and more before it was formed and finished, and six years and more before publication.

That is a long time between books for such a prolific and (formerly) facile writer. Of course *The Australians* came in between, and some film scripts, and a couple of longish hospital bouts, and a bit of savage surgery, but I suspect that the real difficulty about writing *Clean Straw for Nothing* was (a) finding a form sufficiently tight and still sufficiently flexible to compress such an enormous mass of material—twenty-five years of growing and suffering and learning and changing—I mean, if you're raging to say your say before it's too late you still have to find how to say it within a compass that is acceptable ('don't do it in the street and frighten the horses'), and (b) the unfortunate fact that for the first time in all our years together I was totally incapable of giving him the sort of help he needs with work in progress. He needs a constant presence, an ear, a sounding-board, an audience. Some writers are like that and it has been my peculiar pleasure to perform this function for him. In fact, while *My Brother Jack* was being written I sat on the step by his desk every day for seven months so that I would be there when I was wanted for discussion or suggestion or maybe only to listen.

But with *Clean Straw* I've had a complete emotional block, and not all my deep and genuine sympathy at the sight of him struggling and fighting with what was obviously proving to be recalcitrant (sometimes I thought intractable) could force me into the old familiar step-sitting role. Nor all my professionalism could lure me into listening dispassionately. I do believe that novelists must be free to write what they like, in any way they like to write it (and after all who but myself had urged and nagged him into it?), but the stuff of which *Clean Straw for Nothing* is made is largely experience in which I, too, have shared and—as I said earlier—have felt differently because I am a different person.

I was concerned that it was so hard for him, and grieved that I could not help. He had dreadful fits of depression and days of such incapacity that even half a page seemed an effort that drained him. And this from a man who could, once, churn out 5000 words a day without turning a hair and 'never blot a line of it'. Of course most of the novel—as with the text of *The Australians*—was written in hospital and he was pretty heavily drugged all the time so in a way it seems miraculous that he finished it at all. I suppose it's that inexorable steamroller quality he has. And the fact that he'd been given a Commonwealth Literary Fellowship and felt morally obliged to produce the goods.

But what was troubling too was that when the novel was finished at last he wouldn't—or couldn't—give it up. For weeks he tinkered and polished and fiddled and re-wrote until, watching him, I felt that the wisest thing to do was to ring his publisher and get rid of the damn thing. For better or worse. Which I did. I think he was relieved by this action, but nervous too, more nervous than I have ever seen him. That waiting time is always jittery for a writer, but usually you have some idea of what sort of a job you've done, and this time he evidently had none at all. He only knew that he had committed himself absolutely, as a professional and as a person too, and it had been the hardest piece of writing he'd ever done in a long writing life.

Fortunately he didn't have to wait all that long. He heard from London in ten days and they liked it. There have been a lot of readings since, and all favourable. That helps. But the waiting

315

goes on. Because now there will be the critics, and throwing your guts to the critics is, I suppose, just asking them to treat your guts like so much offal.

Most people ask what the title *Clean Straw for Nothing* means.

It comes from a sign in Gin Lane in the time of Hogarth, and the sign says: 'Drunk for a Penny, Dead Drunk for Tuppence, Clean Straw for Nothing.'

Clean straw for *nothing*? Whatever anybody says, I will read that book myself one day. When I'm brave enough. Or when I feel I've really earned my own small bundle of clean straw.

END-NOTES

Abbreviations:

IA: *Images in Aspic*
WCC: *The World of Charmian Clift*
TILL: *Trouble in Lotus Land,* Essays 1964–1967

A Rift in My Lute

This essay provides a kind of summary of Charmian Clift's life. In January 1928 she was four years old and living with her family in a small rented cottage on the Princes Highway at North Kiama. By 1938 the Clifts had moved a couple of hundred metres up the hill and across the road to a cottage that backed onto the wild Bombo Beach. In 1948 Charmian Clift and George Johnston and their baby son were living in a flat in Bondi. By 1958 the couple had three children and had bought a house on the Greek island of Hydra. In 1968 the family home was in Raglan Street, Mosman.

Concerning the Hippopotamus

After Harold Holt's death in December 1967 the Country Party leader John McEwen was commissioned as interim prime minister. It was then up to the Liberal Party to elect a new party leader and prime minister. The candidates were John Grey Gorton, Paul Hasluck, Leslie Bury and Billy Sneddon.

Sir William Yeo was the president of the New South Wales RSL.

*

Charmian Clift's father, Sydney Clift, was born in New Town, Huntingdon, in 1887; he migrated to Australia in about 1909. (cf. 'The Pleasure of Leisure'.) Syd's parents, Will and Emma (*née* Sharman), came to Australia when Charmian was about two, and bought a house in the 'good' part of Kiama.

In 1951 Clift and Johnston and their two children moved to London, where Johnston had been put in charge of the London office of Associated Newspaper Services.

The Voices of Greece

On 21 April 1967, while the Greek parliament was in recess pending elections, a military coup transferred power to a group of army officers, known familiarly as the Colonels. This military junta immediately established strict censorship and began arresting large numbers of politicians, academics, civil servants, unsympathetic army personnel and ordinary citizens. In December that year, trial by jury was abolished. At the same time Colonel Papadopoulos and Brigadier Patakos took over as prime minister and deputy prime minister respectively.

While any criticism of the regime was stifled within Greece, outspoken opposition was organised from abroad; in retaliation, the Junta deprived many prominent expatriates (such as Melina Mercouri) of their nationality. One of the most striking acts of resistance was that of the conservative newspaper proprietor Eleni Vlachos (Helen Vlachou), who stopped publication of her two major dailies and her weekly periodical.

In Australia, public protest meetings were organised by the Committee for the Restoration of Democracy in Greece (cf. 'Long Live Democracy!'), of which Charmian Clift was an honorary vice-president. When Nikolas Nikolaides, a prominent opponent of the Junta, was invited here to speak, he was refused a visa by the Minister for Immigration, Billy Snedden.

Though Clift notes here that she has hesitated to write anything about the Greek situation, she had already referred to it in December 1967. (cf. 'What'll the Boys in the Back Room Have?' *TILL.*)

318

Tomorrow Is Another Day

Alf Garnett (played by Warren Mitchell) was the outspoken and bigoted anti-hero of the British television series 'Till Death Us Do Part', which was shown here with certain episodes omitted.

Don't Fence Me In

In one of her earliest essays, 'On Painting Bricks White' (*IA*), Charmian Clift declared that 'Australian suburban architecture is without doubt or question the ugliest in the world', and in 'The Creeping Towers' (*TILL*) she compared the suburban sprawl to 'a great cancerous growth', noting that 'we seem to like to be fenced in'. Though Clift was always keen to point out ways in which the appearance of the city could be improved, she was equally quick to applaud any move in the right direction. (cf. 'Omens of Promise', *IA*; 'Pilgrimage to a Possibility', *WCC*.)

The Hungry Ones

'The global problem of the Haves and Have-nots' was one of Charmian Clift's recurrent concerns. (cf. 'Towards the Millennium', *WCC*; 'Towards What Millennium?' *TILL*.)

Guru to You Too

The Hindu monk, Maharishi Mehesh Yogi, was the leader of the movement known as Transcendental Meditation. In January 1968 the Beatles and actress Mia Farrow stayed at the Maharishi's centre in India.

Some of George Johnston's tales of his meetings with eastern mystics are recounted in his Asian travel book, *Journey Through Tomorrow*, Cheshire, Melbourne, 1947.

319

More on the Lonely Ones

Though Clift in the opening sentence of this essay refers to a divorced bachelor friend of whom she had written 'a couple of weeks ago', the first essay, 'Bachelor Boys' (cf. *WCC*), was published on 7 September 1967 and this follow-up piece did not appear until 9 April 1968. After submitting a piece, Clift would occasionally ask her editor to hold it over, as she had something more urgent to say. This is probably what happened with the timing of this essay, for 'Bachelor Boys' was followed by a piece advertising the Girls' Training School fête, and then by one about a new production of Hedda Gabler.

On Plugging Poetry

'We all know about Yevtushenko' . . . When the Russian poet Yevgeny Yevtushenko toured Australia in early 1966, large and enthusiastic audiences flocked to his public readings.

The Things I Cannot Change

One of Charmian Clift's hobbyhorses was the inadequacy of public or private funding for the Australian film industry and the fledgling television industry, for she maintained that 'it is up to us to define ourselves' through our own filmic representation. (cf. 'Images in Aspic', *IA*.) While shoestring budgets hampered all Australian film projects, yet another problem faced by documentary-makers was 'the childish cover-up nonsense about out great way of life'. Thus when, in 1965, the ABC documentary *Living on the Fringe* presented stark images of urban poverty, there was an outcry lest it have an adverse affect on immigration. (cf. 'Pssst! Your Dichotomy is Showing', *TILL*.)

A Matter of Conscience

In mid May 1968 the federal government introduced a new National Service Bill which obliged employers, teachers, church leaders and other citizens to report any young man whom they suspected of not registering; failure to do so could result in a penalty of $400. On 17 May the *Sydney Morning Herald* editorial attacked this 'obligation of pimping'.

On 22 May 1968 Private Simon Townsend, a registered conscientious objector who had been conscripted into the army, was sentenced by court martial to twenty-eight days' detention at Ingleburn military camp for disobeying an order.

On Little Noddy, Christopher Robin, Gargantua, Don Quixote, and All That Lot

Charmian Clift's anecdote about discovering reading on the woodblock provides a fascinating insight into the way the writer would work and rework her store of childhood memories, for the incident is recounted again in 'The Magic Carpet of Learning'. In an earlier essay, 'On Being a Private Ham' (*TILL*), Clift had evoked the hot tin and the wood-chips and the smell of the stock along the paling fence in her account of her discovery of the joy of poetry.

The somewhat idiosyncratic reading programme that Syd Clift enforced on his children is also discussed in 'Read Any Good Books Lately?' (*TILL*).

Here There Be Crocodiles

In early July 1968 a 6500 ton Russian trawler, the *Van Gogh*, arrived in the Gulf with a crew of 103 and began working right on the twelve-mile territorial limit. A week later the issue became front page news when the *Van Gogh* steamed at Australian prawn trawlers, scattering them away from the 'boil'. After the Russian ambassador had rejected official complaints, the prime minister sent a navy patrol boat and a

321

RAAF bomber into the Gulf to protect the rights of local boats. Meanwhile, the local member warned that 'there will be shooting going on before long', and indeed an Australian fisherman fired two shots at the *Van Gogh*. The issue was eventually resolved when the *Van Gogh* rescued five shipwrecked Australians.

More accounts of Charmian Clift's time in the Gulf country in late 1967 can be found in 'The Gulf' (*WCC*) and 'Karumba Observed' (*TILL*).

Charmian Clift's dream of escaping to the Gulf country has a strange echo in the last paragraph of George Johnston's unfinished novel, *A Cartload of Clay*. As David Meredith, alone after the death of Cressida Morley, sits yarning with the Ocker, the Ocker explains that he too is alone now: his 'old girl' had 'pissed off with another bloke. Last I heard of them they was livin' in a caravan up around the Gulf somewhere. Karumba, I think. Prawnin'.'

On Black and White Balls

Charmian Clift also wrote of her friendship with Faith Bandler in 'Now You See Them, Now You Don't' (*TILL*). In her earlier piece about Miss Young, 'Requiem for a Spinster' (*WCC*), Clift noted that they had bought their house from the old music teacher when she had no longer been able to manage the big place.

Miss Young appears in a fictionalised form as Miss Aubrey in *A Cartload of Clay*, where she is described as moving from the Merediths' house after the death of her lifelong friend and companion. In the novel the old music teacher doesn't die, but remains as a kind of frail and benign spirit of the street; it is through a remark made by Miss Aubrey— 'I have greatly missed your wife, Mr Meredith'—that the reader first learns of Cressida Morley's death. The cat Sabrina also exists in *Cartload*, but is described as formerly belonging to a middle-aged couple who had separated 'in violence and scandal and gone from the district'. With this, as with the conversation with the Ocker, we see how George Johnston skilfully transmuted real details into the pattern of separation and loss that he sought to evoke.

On The Right of Dissent

Clift had used the same title for her piece on LBJ's visit (cf. *TILL*). 'Mr Askin's little blunder' was the premier's famous injunction to 'Run over the bastards'—the bastards in question being demonstrators.

In July 1968 Eric Willis, the New South Wales Chief Secretary, banned the last short play in *America Hurrah*, declaring that 'only hippies and the lunatic fringe would object'.

A Tale of Two Cities

As well as working over certain elements of personal experience, Charmian Clift would rework her own images over a period of many years. Thus the description in this essay of 'the little terrace houses swinging over [the hills] like absurd frilly shoulder straps' is a development of a simile used in one of the writer's first published stories, 'The Awakening', which appeared in the *Australasian Post* on 11 April 1946. It begins: 'Hannah plodded wearily along the simmering bitumen road that swung like a strap over the shoulder of the hill.'

On Not Seeing America Hurrah

At the end of the banned short play *Motel*, four-letter words were spray-painted onto a wall. A free performance of the play was given as a protest against the banning.

In Praise of the GP

The first heart transplant had been performed in South Africa in December 1967. By September 1968 some Australian hospitals were preparing to undertake the operation, amidst controversy over both moral and physical side-effects. The first Australian transplant was eventually performed in October.

In *Peel Me a Lotus* Charmian Clift writes at greater length about the birth of her third child on Hydra.

Lamentable Brothers

Charmian Clift was always willing to advertise a good cause—particularly if that cause concerned children and hunger. Thus on two occasions in 1967 she wrote a piece on the Save the Children Fund (cf. Let's Save Some Children', and 'On a Second Chance', both *TILL*), and she promoted the Fund and the Freedom from Hunger Campaign again in 'I Shall Not Want' and 'Some Thoughts on a Large Family'.

The Pleasure of Leisure

Clift also discussed the possible use (or misuse) of extra leisure time in 'On Time to Kill' (*TILL*).

The Twilight Zone

For weeks before the US presidential elections on 5 November 1968, the Australian press profiled the candidates and reported the popularity polls.

Clift's dig at Spiro Agnew is a reference to his support for the Greek Junta.

A Pride of Lions?

Clift had explored this theme—and had used the concluding Dorothy Parker quote—in 'Men' (*TILL*).

This piece appeared in December 1968 in the first issue of *Pol* magazine, edited by Richard Walsh. Billed as 'a new monthly magazine for modern Australian women', this first *Pol* also had articles by Ray Taylor, Julie Rigg and Craig McGregor.

Charmian Clift had an essay in the first ten issues of the magazine. Her other *Pol* pieces were:

January 1969: 'The Restless Old' (published in *WCC* as 'The Rule of the Olds').

February 1969: 'February' (published in *WCC* as 'This Way to Megalopolis').

March 1969: 'The Modern Artist—Pro or Con?'

April 1969: 'Charmian Clift's Greek Easter' (published in *TILL* as 'The Loftiest Form of Springtime').

May 1969: 'Charmian Clift Goes Memory Gathering' (published in *WCC* as 'Getting Away From it All').

June 1969: 'Royal Jelly?'

July 1969: 'Winter Solstice' (published *WCC*).

August 1969: 'My Husband George'.

September 1969: 'Wine Country'.

A Graceful Gift

Charmian Clift had earlier referred to Pat and Cedric Flower's alphabet book in 'We Three Kings of Orients Aren't' (*TILL*). Cedric Flower had provided evocative black and white line drawings for the original edition of Clift's travel book *Mermaid Singing* (Michael Joseph, London, 1958) and for the first edition of *Images in Aspic* (Horwitz, Sydney, 1965).

Death by Misadventure

Though the typescript of this essay is in Charmian Clift's papers (in the National Library of Australia), I have not found it in published form; as I am unsure about the dating of it, I have placed it between the published essays for 1968 and 1969.

As I noted in the introduction to *Trouble in Lotus Land* there is, with the possible exception of this piece and 'On Lucky Dips' (*TILL*), no reason to suspect that an article submitted by Clift was ever rejected. When I recently showed this essay to Clift's editors, Margaret Vaile and John Douglas Pringle, neither could remember ever having seen it before; both also freely admitted that they wouldn't have liked to publish it. It is quite possible that Charmian Clift, after writing it, decided that it might be rejected and didn't bother sending it in. It is clear, however, that Clift herself didn't disavow the piece, for in the top right-hand corner of the typescript she wrote 'No 7'. (Quite a few of Clift's essays bear page numbers or order numbers of this kind.) Before her death Clift was selecting pieces of her work for an anthology; she obviously intended to include the essay on abortion.

On Getting Your Name in the Paper

After William White's application to the civil courts for exemption as a conscientious objector were rejected, he refused to obey his call-up notice; a court-martial sentenced him to twenty-one days in a military prison. His case coincided with the 1966 federal election and received wide press coverage. Unlike White and Townsend, John Zarb was imprisoned in a civil jail, for failing to register for National Service.

Last of the Old?

'It is seventeen years ago today that the drums and tuckets sounded for a new young Queen' . . . By 'today' Clift meant the day of publication— 6 February 1969. But cf. note to 'Royal Jelly?'

A Thought on Violence

Though Charmian Clift once noted 'I am not a crusading feminist' (cf. 'On Trouble in Lotus Land', *TILL*), her essays often railed against the inferior position that women were forced into in Australian society. (cf. 'Second Class Citizens', *IA*; 'Men', *TILL*; 'What Price Rubies?', *TILL*; 'Action or Activities?', *TILL*.) In reading this piece, it should be remembered that topics such as working wives, pre-marital sex, and the pill were still controversial in 1969, and that New Wave feminism had not yet made its mark here in any organised way.

Dr Jean Battersby was Executive Officer of the Australian Council for the Arts.

The Modern Artist—Pro or Con?

This essay appeared in the March 1969 issue of *Pol*.

The topic of trends in modern art is also discussed in 'Art Fashions and Discipline', *TILL*.

The Shape of Stockades to Come

Clift had also used the Carl Sandburg poem, with which she ends this essay, at the conclusion of 'Don't Fence Me In', written a year earlier. While the first essay expresses the writer's distaste for the appearance of fences, by the time of the second piece she is more concerned with their moral aspect.

Cage Me an Ostrich

In the House of Representatives on Wednesday 19 March 1969 Mr A.W. James, a Labor MP, questioned Prime Minister John Gorton's conduct in relation to an alleged incident at Chequers nightclub concerning the singer Liza Minelli. The debate was gagged. The next day, 'in one of the tensest scenes in Australian parliamentary history' (according to the *Sydney Morning Herald*), Gorton denied the charges. A motion that the Privileges Committee examine the allegations was lost.

Later that day the Liberal MP for Warringah, Mr Edward St John, described in the House 'an incident in which he said Mr Gorton, accompanied by his press secretary and a nineteen-year-old girl, had gone from a formal dinner to the US Embassy at 2.30 a.m. and had stayed until about 5.30 a.m.'. For the next week, St John's allegations, Gorton's denials, and the nineteen-year-old girl's confirmations of the incident were splashed over the front pages of the newspapers. The fact that this was an election year made the issue particularly dangerous for the Liberal Party.

While the Embassy story was hardly a secret, Clift's objection was to the way the Liberal Party immediately closed ranks and effectively stifled the debate by ostracising St John. While Gorton himself told a party meeting 'There will be no debate', members barred St John from the party room. Meanwhile pressure was put on the Electorate Council for Warringah not to endorse St John in the next election. Finally, on Friday 28 March, St John announced that he had decided to surrender his endorsement.

As I noted in the introduction to *Trouble in Lotus Land*, this piece provoked a 'furious' reaction from the *Sydney Morning Herald*'s editor, John Douglas Pringle, who at the time was under considerable pressure from the paper's new managing director. When I showed the essay to him in 1990, he agreed that he 'would have been very annoyed with it because it would have infuriated a great many people—a great many of our readers'. He added that he felt it was a bad article, that 'this sort of Them and Us business is really too crude for words'. The important thing of course is not Pringle's disapproval, but the fact that the piece was published.

Some Thoughts on a Large Family

'My late father-in-law was one of nineteen' . . . According to Garry Kinnane's biography of George Johnston, Clift's father-in-law, John Johnston, was the youngest of four children, one of whom died in infancy. (As Clift freely admitted, all her own family were 'terrible liars and inventors and embroiderers'. cf. 'Things That Go Boomp in the Night', *IA*.)

Hallelujah for a Good Pick-up!

One of the sources of Charmian Clift's appeal to her readers was the way she dealt with the commonplace frustrations of urban living—such as the garbage disposal problem. She had earlier discussed this in 'On Waste Not Want Not' and 'O Brave New World!' (*TILL*).

The Joys of Holidays

For the three weeks prior to this piece there was a note in the Women's Section of the *Sydney Morning Herald* that 'Charmian Clift is on vacation'. In her absence, Mrs W. C. Wentworth, Dr Jean Battersby and Mrs Gwen Plumb were invited to write a column.

'A wedding anniversary coming up in a few days' . . . As this essay was written in May and Charmian Clift and George Johnston had been married in August (1947), this must actually have been an anniversary of their meeting at the *Argus* in May 1946.

Royal Jelly?

This essay appeared in the May 1969 issue of *Pol.*

Here, as in 'Last of the Old?', Charmian Clift gives 6 February 1952 as the date of the Coronation. In fact, the Coronation was on 2 June 1953. Clift has obviously subconsciously transposed 6/2/52—the date of George VI's death and Elizabeth's *accession*—and 2/6/53.

Though politically a republican, Clift was (as she noted in 'On England, My England') 'Cavalier enough' to rejoice in the pageantry of the event. Besides, she loved telling the story of George at the Abbey minus his braces. (cf. also 'On Choosing a National Costume', *TILL.*)

The Kelly Saga Begins Again

While Charmian Clift had a general passion for bushrangers, she had a particular love for Ned Kelly and the Kelly country.

The Sidney Nolan documentary, 'This Dreaming, Spinning Thing', for which George Johnston wrote the script, was filmed during August–September 1967. Clift accompanied the crew to the Centre and Glenrowan; her job was to get Nolan to talk.

When Mick Jagger was cast for the lead in the *Ned Kelly* feature film there was controversy about his morals as well as his nationality. This piece was written just before Jagger's arrival in Australia.

Anyone for Fish and Chips?

In November 1964, in her second essay to be published, Clift had made a similar plea for more outdoor eating and drinking places. (cf. 'Social Drinking', *IA*.)

On Clean Straw for Nothing

This piece, written in June 1969, was published posthumously in the August issue of *Pol*. Titled 'My Husband George', it was accompanied by a photo of George Johnston with an out-of-focus Charmian Clift decidedly in the background. As Clift's typescript was untitled, I have taken the liberty of renaming the piece.

Clift's account of the writing of both *My Brother Jack* and *Clean Straw for Nothing*, including her encouragement to Johnston to send the *Clean Straw* typescript off, is confirmed by an interview Johnston gave after his wife's death. (cf. Kay Keavney, 'From George, With Sadness', *The Australian Women's Weekly*, 3 September 1969.)

The remaining *Pol* essay, 'Wine Country', has not been included, partly because it uses the same material as 'The Last Magic' (*IA*), but also because its publication here would provide a bit of an anticlimax to Charmian Clift's account of her relationship with George Johnston and *Clean Straw for Nothing*.

Apart from this last *Pol* essay, and an essay on childhood Christmases published in *Walkabout* December 1966, it does seem that the collection of Charmian Clift's essays is now complete. However, it is possible that further research will unearth a few more 'pieces' from her enormous four-and-a-half-year output.

APPENDIX

Chronological Listing of Essays
Published in the Sydney Morning Herald

The following is a list of Charmian Clift's essays as they appeared in the *Sydney Morning Herald*.

The title given to an essay by the *Sydney Morning Herald* often differed from Clift's title. I have used. her chosen titles, as they appear on her typescripts and in *The World of Charmian Clift*. In cases where the original is either not extant or not titled, I have given the *Sydney Morning Herald* title, followed by an asterisk. The letters *WCC* beneath a title indicate that the essay can be found in *The World of Charmian Clift*.

Readers will notice that there are occasionally more or less than seven days between publication dates. If the day following a Thursday was not a shopping day (e.g. Good Friday), the Women's Section was moved back to the Tuesday.

ALSO BY CHARMIAN CLIFT

TROUBLE IN LOTUS LAND

In late 1964 Charmian Clift was asked to write a weekly column for the *Sydney Morning Herald* Women's Section. Her brief was to give readers 'real writing' and controversial opinions. Of the 240 or so essays that she contributed over the next four and a half years, 107 were collected in the anthologies *Images in Aspic* and *The World of Charmian Clift*.

Edited and introduced by Nadia Wheatley, *Trouble in Lotus Land* is the companion volume to those anthologies and brings together for the first time in book form the remaining essays from 1964 to 1967. Although the quality of these pieces is as outstanding as always, this volume includes Clift's more topical and contentious observations while also opening a window on the turbulent passions of the 1960s.

Trouble in Lotus Land is both informative and a delight to read, and presents some of the lost work of one of Australia's finest and most popular prose writers.

THE WORLD OF CHARMIAN CLIFT
CHARMIAN CLIFT

Between 1947 and 1964 Charmian Clift won critical acclaim as a novelist and travel writer, with books such as *The Sponge Divers* (written in collaboration with her husband George Johnston), *Mermaid Singing* and *Peel Me A Lotus*. In 1964 her writing took a different turn — she started writing a weekly newspaper column, and her gift of observation, along with her qualities of compassion, honesty and wit, quickly established a wide and devoted following.

Introduced by Rodney Hall, *The World of Charmian Clift* brings together seventy-one of Charmian Clift's outstanding essays, most of which were selected by her before her tragic death in 1969. The majority come from her last two years of writing for the Melbourne *Herald* and the *Sydney Morning Herald*, where her weekly audience numbered a million or more readers.